PRINCIPLES, VALUES, VIRTUES:

Universal Truth Lives Among Us

 **Published by the Institute of Human Performance**

ISBN: 978-0-9748674-9-6

First published by the Institute of Human Performance, 2025.

Typeset by g sammons [*design group*] inc.

Printed and bound by Amazon Publishing.

Principles, Values, and Virtues are essential elements of the human experience. We've created a website where you can explore a wide range of educational materials and commentary on these topics. To learn more, please visit:

www.principlesvaluesvirtues.com

IHP, known as the 'Mecca of Functional Training', has become a global destination for fitness professionals, athletes, and anyone seeking to enhance their performance. IHP also offers a comprehensive online platform featuring certifications, educational videos, books, and professional fitness equipment-including our renowned JC "Pro Line" Resistance Band collection. Become part of the IHP movement by visiting:

www.ihpfit.com

To my parents, Arnaldo and Celerina, who gave me Principles;

to my children—Rio, Caila, Dante, and Mia—
who taught me as much as I taught them;

to my sister Belkis, my family, and lifelong friends from Callahan Plaza,
FAU, and IHP, who shaped my sense of family, culture and brotherhood;

and to my wife Giedre, my 'living movie',
whose love and mystery continue to make me a better man.

CREDITS

Visual Design, Formatting, and Production: Greg Sammons

I extend my heartfelt thanks to Greg Sammons for his involvement in this project and his contributions to my life. Greg handled all of the typesetting, graphics, design, formatting, and a ton of editing. This book simply would not exist in its current form without him. He is also my 3 AM friend, my training partner, and one of my biggest supporters.

Spanish Translation and Editing: Sandino Figueroa

Much gratitude and appreciation go to my friend Sandino. Sandino has been my Latin brother for the last six years, translating all of our educational materials and helping me bring the Perfect Trainer App to life. His arrival from Ecuador has been one of the greatest things to happen to IHP and to me personally. IHP gained a great soldier—and I gained a great friend.

ASSISTANT EDITORS AND SUPPORTING PROJECTS

IHP Staff

The IHP staff is the heartbeat of our church, IHP. I want to thank them for their dedication and integrity. Every day they bring their best and make every aspect of our professional home a culture of excellence. Each of them contributed to editing this book and providing valuable feedback.

Adam Brush	Sandino Figueroa	Rio Santana
Bowen Colon	Jillian Fisher	William Terry
Chase Delanoy	Josh Ryckman	Gandhi Valcena

EDITING AND CONCEPTUAL CONTRIBUTION

Max Alperovich	Monique Machado	Alberto Rodriguez
Annie Aponte	Stephanie Machado	Caila Santana
Mark Bagg	Marke Meade	Giedre Santana
Barry Pavel	David Morse	Mia Santana
Belkis Gebensleben	Eric Olson	Rio Santana
Scott Goodpaster	Michelle Olson	Scott Smith
David Gottschalk	Barry Pavel	Andrew Wells
Dr. Sue Grave	Ruben Payan	All whom I missed...
Jeff Harpster	Bill Rintz	

JUAN CARLOS SANTANA

PRINCIPLES, VALUES, VIRTUES:

Universal Truth Lives Among Us

iHP
INSTITUTE OF HUMAN PERFORMANCE

A Message from JC

Yesterday, conservative activist Charlie Kirk was assassinated. Last month, an innocent Ukrainian girl returning from work on the subway was stabbed in the neck three times and died. Just weeks earlier, children praying in church were gunned down. Sadly, we could go on ad nauseam.

No matter where you stand politically, nobody can justify or explain away these senseless killings. If you have any conscience, spirit, or good-will, you can't help but be left bewildered, angry, afraid, or confused. I can tell you last night was a very heavy night at the Santana household. Like most of you, I asked myself: Why is this happening? What does it mean? How do I keep moving forward? What direction do I take?

This book came at the right time in my life. The years, the scars, and the perspective I now carry allow me to put into words not just why events like this shake us—but also how we can move forward despite them. Writing this book forced me to reflect deeply on my own experiences, their impact on my evolution, and the meaning behind them.

For me, hardship has never been abstract. My life has taken me through fighting bullies at five years old, exile from Cuba at seven, becoming a martial artist to never be a victim, grinding through thirty years of sports competition, bankruptcy, divorce, financial recessions, the chaos of COVID, personal ailments and surgeries, and the heartbreak of losing loved ones. At the same time, I've been blessed with the grind of education, the joy of writing 19 books, and the responsibility of raising four children, and starting businesses with investors relying on my reputation.

And through it all, the Institute of Human Performance was my anchor.

IHP was never just a gym. It became a living laboratory—a church of sorts—where I could observe human nature in action. Within its walls, I saw how culture forms, how people respond to challenges, and how a framework of principles and values shapes not only fitness and business, but also the way we face life itself. IHP gave me proof that principles, when lived, create cultures that are stronger, happier, and more resilient than circumstances. This book is my attempt to share that framework. It's not abstract philosophy—it's the product of both personal struggle and professional practice, tested over decades in life, business, and the crucible of IHP.

I don't promise to fix the world's problems or hand you a ready-made meaning of life. What I do offer is this: you are not alone. Everyone is tested, and there is a way to meet those tests without bitterness, resentment, or victimhood. Tragedies—whether personal or societal—may be random, but all force us to evolve. Life's challenges can be seen as training for the soul.

Perhaps the Creator knew He made us prone to comfort, and that unless forced, we would never voluntarily embrace intense and grueling experiences for the sake of growth. Just like exercise, unless we endure the challenge of hard training, we don't get stronger.

The meaning of these experiences, whether individual or societal, is to develop more evolved human beings—and through that, a more evolved society. The stronger each of us becomes, the stronger we all become. A rising tide lifts all ships.

The common thread through every challenge is this: actions and decisions in the presence of fear. Whether facing bullies, leaving a homeland, risking everything on a business, or living through societal injustice and violence, the challenge is the same. You learn to move forward despite fear and uncertainty.

The best path forward will always be paved by universal principles— the very ones in this book. They are self-evident truths: easy to understand, not always easy to live by, but unfailing in their ability to guide. Looking back, I see that the values my parents taught me and the virtues they modeled carried me through my darkest days. And I also see that many of my hardest challenges came when I strayed from those principles.

This book is my way of organizing those lessons into a system that makes sense of life—its beauty, its wonder, and its mysteries. When you feel shaken by personal loss or by the tragedies that surround us in society, I hope these pages give you a way to move forward— and become part of the tide that lifts all ships.

MENTAL PRIMER: TIMELESS VS. NOW

TIMELESS
- **Principles:** Universal, self-evident truths that remain constant across time, place, and culture.
  - o *Example:* Honesty fosters trust in every relationship, no matter the context.
  - o *Key Idea:* No matter your nationality, ethnicity, or religion, honesty builds trust and strengthens relationships.
- **Style:** Personal expression that transcends trends and time, reflecting your core identity.
  - o *Example:* A person who is always neat and well-groomed, consistently presenting themselves with care and intention.
  - o *Key Idea:* Regardless of changing fashion trends, you can never go wrong with a clean, polished, and thoughtfully presented appearance—that's style.
- **Facts:** Objective realities that are measurable and independent of opinion or interpretation.
  - o *Example:* Gravity applies universally, regardless of beliefs.
  - o *Key Idea:* Facts serve as a stable foundation for rational thinking and sound decision-making.

NOW
- **Opinions:** Personal perspectives shaped by emotions, biases, or circum-stances.
  - o *Example:* "I prefer this method because it feels right for me."
  - o *Key Idea:* Opinions are subjective, adaptable, and often fleeting.
- **Fashion:** Trends shaped by collective preferences, cultural moments, or societal influences.
  - o *Example:* Popular slang or clothing styles that fade over time.
  - o *Key Idea:* Fashion reflects the transient mood of the moment, not enduring truth.

- **Feelings:** Emotional states influenced by internal and external conditions.
  - o Example: Feeling anxious about a new challenge but succeeding despite it.
  - o Key Idea: Feelings are valid and meaningful but unreliable for long-term decisions.

DISTINCTIONS
Principles vs. Opinions
- **Principles:** Built to last, forming the foundation of effective action.
  - o Apply universally across industries, cultures, and generations
  - o Remain constant because they are rooted in truth
  - o *Example:* "Effort yields growth" is a principle in fitness, business, and relationships.
- **Opinions:** Personal judgments shaped by perspective and emotion
  - o Subject to change with new information or experiences
  - o Limited to specific individuals or circumstances
  - o *Example:* "This exercise is the best" reflects personal preference or bias.

Facts vs. Feelings
- **Facts:** Objective, measurable truths remain constant regardless of perception
  - o Provide a rational foundation for decisions
  - o *Example:* "Calories in versus calories out" governs energy balance.
- **Feelings:** Subjective emotional states that vary based on mood or context.
  - o Powerful but not always reliable for action
  - o *Example:* Feeling tired doesn't negate the fact that consistency delivers results.

Style vs. Fashion
- **Style:** Timeless and personal, reflecting individuality and authenticity.
  - o Rooted in who you are, remaining relevant over time
  - o *Example:* A coach's unique and lasting way of inspiring a team.
- **Fashion:** Short-lived trends shaped by culture and collective preferences.
  - o Frequently changes, often losing significance quickly
  - o *Example:* buzzwords in business that fade as trends shift.

TABLE OF CONTENTS

*"The greatness of a man is not measured
by the fortunes he creates for himself,
but by the emotions he creates in others."*
~ JCS

01

MY JOURNEY THROUGH PRINCIPLES, VALUES AND VIRTUES (PV²)

Introduction

In this chapter, I share the experiences that shaped my understanding and relationship with principles, values, and virtues—from my early years in Cuba to becoming a leader in the fitness and human performance industry. Looking back, I realize that the tools I needed were instilled in me during childhood. Each chapter of my life revealed new ways to apply those tools of character across countless scenarios and over many years. I came to understand the timeless power of principles—how they shape your values and, when honored over time, forge the virtues of a good man. A man who does good, or at least does better, no matter how hard the road, how unjust life may seem, or how undeserved the injustice might be. Principles, values, and virtues lay the foundation to stay steadfast and unshaken on the path less traveled—the path of a Principled life.

From Cuba with Love: A Journey Toward Freedom

My story begins in Cuba, a country where life's challenges were clear even as a child. Growing up, I experienced firsthand the resilience and resourcefulness needed to survive in a society with limited freedoms and opportunities. My family applied for exile when I was five. Let me tell you how that goes in a communist country. You're labeled a deserter. All your assets are frozen. You're fired from your government job and expected to support your family with no income and no legal way to earn one. If you try to make money on the side—which is the only option when everything is frozen—you risk arrest or worse. Every neighborhood has informants (the local committees), so you never know who's listening.

I still remember the fear I felt every day when my father left the house to try to provide for us. I never knew if he would come back. My father knew restaurants, so he made desserts and sold them on the black market—the only way to feed us once the government froze everything. For two years, the whole house became a kitchen. Militia inspections were routine. If they'd found the freshly baked trays cooling beneath the beds, that wasn't a fine—that was prison. By the grace of God, they never looked under the beds, and they never asked why the entire house smelled like candy.

Our exit papers finally came, and at seven years old, I left Cuba with my family. I remember the pure joy I felt—I was moving to the United States, the land of milk and honey! To a child, it felt like stepping out of a cage into open air. No more oppression, no more fear—only the freedom to work for a better life, to dream, and to build a future without invisible chains around our necks.

In the United States, I found myself in a world full of possibilities. My family instilled in me a strong work ethic, encouraging me to work hard, respect others, and make the most of every opportunity. I threw myself into American culture, playing sports and forming friendships. In many ways, it was a classic story of the American Dream. I felt fortunate to live in a country where anything was possible with enough determination and work. Early on, I understood the value of dedication, adaptability, and Resilience—qualities that would become essential to my journey.

From a young age, I witnessed the principles that guide a family out of oppression and toward freedom. I was instilled with the traditional values of a strong father who protected and provided, and a strong, educated mother who shaped and cared for the family. My father epitomized Responsibility, Sacrifice, Perseverance, and Facing Fear. My mother exemplified Humility, Self-Reflection, Self-Awareness, and Consistency. Together, they showed me how values lived out over time forge lasting virtues. That was my introduction to the world.

I realize now that the reason I felt—and still feel—so strongly about freedom is because freedom is the environment in which PV² and its relational expressions live. I didn't understand this when I came from Cuba, but I fell in love with the feeling of freedom. Looking back on my life, it's now very clear to me. It does not matter if you see freedom as a Principle from a philosophical perspective or as a foundational context that enables relational expressions to manifest. Without freedom, PV² collapses:

- Responsibility becomes control (forced obedience, not chosen ownership).
- Accountability becomes blame (punishment, not growth or ownership).
- Integrity becomes compliance (doing what you're told, not what's right).

Freedom is the foundation of laws and ethics, underpinning democracy and human rights. It is the open space where PV² can take root and flourish—an amusement park where principles, values, and virtues play out in real time. When lived out, our resulting virtues counter malevolence (destructive forces) with benevolence (constructive forces). And as individuals embody PV² and express it in daily life, their communities feel the ripple effect: less malevolence (division, deceit, selfishness) and more benevolence (unity, truth, sacrifice). That's how society heals and moves forward—one person's relational expressions becoming another person's lived experience.

Lesson Box: Lessons from Cuba

- **Resilience Requires Resourcefulness:** Adversity forces us to find creative solutions. Watching my father survive by selling desserts taught me how to think outside the box.
- **Freedom Is Multifaceted:** As a Principle, it's a universal truth about the right to self-determination. As a value, it's what you choose to cherish and protect. As a virtue, it's how you live responsibly, respectfully, and courageously.
- **Fear Tests Character:** The fear I experienced during inspections taught me that character is forged under pressure. Principles and virtues like courage and integrity are most evident when tested.
- **Strong Foundations Start at Home:** The values instilled by my parents provided the tools to navigate life's toughest challenges.

Martial Arts: Strength, Fear, and Courage

As a young teenager, I was drawn to combat sports, beginning my journey into martial arts around age 12. Martial arts became a cornerstone of my youth, shaping not only my body but also my character. Early in training, I learned the proverb: "It's better to be a warrior in a garden than a gardener in war." I couldn't articulate it then, but its essence struck me at the core and shaped my personality.

Jordan Peterson often emphasizes becoming strong, dangerous, and formidable—having the capacity for great violence and destruction. That capacity provides security for those under your protection and deters those who would do harm. It aligns with Principles like "Peace through strength,' and "The best defense is a strong offense." But strength and capability don't become Virtues until they're harnessed, controlled, and directed toward good. Virtue isn't found in destruction—it's found in measured restraint. The greater your capacity for destruction, the greater the control required. And the greater the control, the greater the Virtue.

Lesson Box: True Strength and Virtue

- **Strength Becomes Virtue:** When controlled and directed toward good, strength transforms into moral power.
- **Power in Restraint:** Refraining from destruction shows more character than wielding it.
- **Balance Physical and Moral Strength:** True mastery lies in harmonizing physical capability with ethical responsibility.

In my early teens, I was deeply influenced by Bruce Lee's philosophy. He emphasized the real-world application of fighting techniques and strategies, not just tradition for tradition's sake. Bruce believed in stepping outside of dogma, staying open to new ideas, and integrating martial arts once considered mutually exclusive. He created Jeet Kune Do—"a style without a style." His mantra, "It's not daily increase, but daily decrease—hack away at the unessential," became mine. I applied it everywhere: in training, in learning skills, even in shaping my personality. That mindset pushed me to innovate training systems, methods, and protocols the fitness industry had never seen. At the time, I didn't realize how much Bruce's philosophy was shaping me, but now I know: it was foundational. I remain forever grateful for his legacy.

Around the same time, another giant entered my life from a very different angle—Masutatsu Oyama, founder of Kyokushin Karate. Where Bruce was supple, quick, and precise, Mas was a wrecking ball. His thick build and body-hardening training turned his limbs into weapons. He broke objects that shouldn't be breakable by human hands. Legend even says he fought bulls, maiming or killing some with strikes from his bare hands.

Mas taught me rigor and body-hardening. At 14, I was leading older guys—some who could already drive—to the beaches of Crandon Park (Key Biscayne, Florida) for 4–6 hour training sessions. We ran and walked miles in waist-deep water, drove our fingers into wet sand until they were raw, smashed our shins and forearms into trees, absorbed kicks and punches to the body, and cranked out thousands of reps of calisthenic exercises. Through this discipline I learned Sacrifice, Perseverance, Courage, and delayed gratification. Mas showed me that martial arts were never just about physical strength—they were about forging character through Principles lived daily.

Lesson Box: Lessons from My Mentors

- **Bruce Lee's Teachings:** Innovate, adapt, and hack away at the unessential to master efficiency in all areas.
- **Mas Oyama's Influence:** Emphasized grit, relentless practice, and the value of physical and mental hardening.
- **Holistic Growth:** Both mentors showed the importance of balancing physical mastery with character development.

By 16, I was a walking nightmare wrapped in quiet Humility. I knew my body was a weapon, but I carried myself like Caine—the wandering monk from the *Kung Fu* TV series. Caine was deadly yet compassionate, powerful yet peaceful, using violence only when absolutely necessary. He embodied lethality, discipline, and compassion. That balance captivated me. It became my north star: develop the capacity to be a nightmare, yet choose to live with grace and purpose. That has been my work in progress ever since—admittedly, with many falls from grace.

Lesson Box: Strength, Control, and Purpose

- **True Strength Is Measured by Control:** Strength without virtue leads to chaos; restraint shows true mastery.
- **Mentorship as a Catalyst for Growth:** Bruce Lee's creativity and Mas Oyama's resilience provided a foundation for my personal evolution.
- **Quiet Confidence Reflects Power:** Humility is the hallmark of those who possess great strength.

The Role of Fear in Growth and Strength

My martial arts career taught me one of the most profound lessons of my life—the real relationship between courage and fear. For years, I thought courage was the absence of fear. I wanted to be courageous because I hated the feelings that came with fear: feeling inferior, being oppressed, being less than. The few times I was bullied by bigger kids, I despised it and swore it would never happen again. That's when I dove headfirst into physical training and martial arts. I thought if I became a badass, fear would vanish—at least the fear I knew from playground bullies. I was dead wrong. The fear of bullies is child's play compared to the fear your own demons can create. Before every match, every fight, every confrontation, I was terrified. Sometimes even in training with other killers who weren't about to take it easy. I would think: "How can I fight when I can't even breathe" "My legs feel like cement." "I'm so nervous I can't move." Yet, I never backed down. I engaged. And the second contact was made, it was on—my training would take over with precision.

In my teens and early 20s, this cycle repeated itself. Fear showed up before every fight, every challenge, and it led me to question myself. How could someone courageous feel this much fear? More than once, I wondered if I had built my body into a machine of destruction just to hide a coward buried inside me.

For most of my athletic career, I didn't fully understand what I was feeling or how to handle it. It wasn't until my 60s that I finally understood what I had been experiencing all along—what I'd been managing, and what I now teach athletes, professionals, and teams: fear doesn't go away, but it can be confronted, managed, and used.

Lesson Box: Understanding Fear and Growth

- **Fear Isn't Weakness:** Feeling fear doesn't make you a coward; it's part of being human.
- **Action Conquers Fear:** The antidote to fear is engagement—facing it head-on transforms it into strength.
- **Growth Through Discomfort:** Fear often signals the boundaries of your comfort zone. Step into it to grow.

Courage: Be with Fear

But before we glorify Fear, let's recognize that it's a double-edged sword. When used properly, it can transform you into a heightened version of yourself. However, when misunderstood, it can paralyze you. Fear often feeds on the unknown—the future—and morphs into the 'what if' syndrome. While it's useful to plan and consider alternatives, Fear can corrupt those processes, forcing you to imagine and act on the worst and most unlikely outcomes. **FEAR** can even turn into **False Evidence Appearing Real** if you let it run wild. At that point, Fear doesn't empower you—it creates self-limiting beliefs, turning you into a victim of the very force meant to help you rise above victimhood.

To manage and utilize Fear, you must accept that it will always be present during moments of crisis or conflict—even if you are well-trained. Training provides confidence in your ability to handle challenges, reducing the intensity of Fear—but it doesn't eliminate it. Outcomes are never 100% guaranteed, and that small 'what if' will always linger. And that's okay. Fear is manageable, and it can push you to become a superhero in your own right. Without Fear, you'd be fearless—and that's not ideal. Fearlessness ignores danger, leaving you vulnerable to it. Courage isn't the absence of Fear; it's acting with righteous indignation in the very presence of Fear.

Lesson Box: Harnessing Fear for Strength

- **Fear as a Tool:** Fear is your body's way of preparing for high performance—use it to your advantage.
- **Fear Can Empower or Paralyze:** Properly managed, fear enhances your abilities; left unchecked, it can cripple your progress.
- **Courage Is Action in Fear's Presence:** Real courage isn't about feeling fearless; it's about acting despite the fear.

Managing Fear

Managing Fear doesn't mean making it disappear. Managing Fear starts long before it ever shows up. Proactive preparation that builds strength and competence is the best way to manage it. As the saying goes, "An ounce of prevention is worth a pound of cure." Competence, developed through disciplined preparation, increases confidence and reduces the self-limiting beliefs that fuel Fear. It also allows you to focus on execution in the moment of truth, even with Fear's lingering presence. The virtue isn't in erasing Fear but in managing it and executing competently despite it. That's the essence of Courage—acting in the face of Fear.

The entire process of martial arts, from respecting the art to respecting myself, taught me the importance of showing up. And by 'show up', I don't just mean physically—I mean psychologically and spiritually. That lesson echoed one of the most common techniques used in psychological therapy to overcome phobias: repeated exposure. Repeated exposure tackles Fear by facing it in small, manageable increments, each with a slight increase in intensity. Little by little, you realize most Fear is unjustified—often just an illusion.

For me, the repeated exposure to grueling, painful workouts forced me to confront and overcome what I thought were my limits—both physical and mental. In competitions, the more I stepped onto the mat, the better I became at handling pre-competition jitters. I experienced the satisfaction of victory and the humbling sting of defeat.

When I was younger, losing felt crushing—sometimes leaving me crying for hours. But over time, I not only learned to handle Fear better, I learned to see losses differently. The mental fortitude I developed through combat sports became a defining part of who I am. I became competent through hard work, guided by Discipline and Resilience. Competence gave me the ability to stay calm under pressure and face adversity head-on. Martial arts taught me to see losses as lessons while respecting both my opponents and myself.

This respect wasn't just about winning or losing—it was about honoring the process, acknowledging hard work, and growing from every experience. The Discipline, Humility, and Resilience I developed during those years laid the foundation for everything I would later accomplish in fitness, business, and life. More importantly, they defined how I saw my flaws and how I came back from low points due to my indiscretions.

Lesson Box: Overcoming Fear Through Practice

- **Repeated Exposure:** Gradual exposure to fear builds resilience and reduces its grip on your actions.
- **Losses Are Lessons:** Failure isn't final—it's an opportunity to refine your approach and grow.
- **Show up Fully:** Psychological, physical, and emotional presence is critical in overcoming fear and succeeding.

Lessons in Growth: From Local Trainer to Global Performance Coach

My career in fitness began in an unexpected way. After years of bouncing between engineering, owning a bar, and touring with a band, I became a father at 32. The birth of my first child, my son Rio, changed everything. His arrival didn't just make me a dad—it forced me to confront myself. I knew it was time to take Responsibility for my life and build a career that could provide stability for both of us. Unsure of what path to take, I asked the most important question of my life: What was I doing when I was at my happiest? By 'happy', I didn't mean casual fun—I meant the deep fulfillment that comes from purpose. Purpose surrounded by like-minded people who respect you because you're competent and an asset to the community. The answer was clear: the best part of my life had always been fitness—training as an athlete and helping others become strong and formidable. So at 32, with Rio as my motivation, I went back to school. I earned a master's in exercise science, began doctoral work, and started my career as a personal trainer.

It didn't take long to know I had made the right decision. Training gave me a front-row seat to transformation—not just in strength, but in Resilience and confidence. I became passionate about helping people unlock their potential, immersing myself in coaching, anatomy, biomechanics, and human performance. Rio came when I needed him the most. Perhaps, in more ways than I'll ever fully understand, he even saved my life.

Lesson Box: Turning Points into Growth

- **Responsibility Drives Purpose:** Life's major turning points often come disguised as challenges. Embracing them leads to growth.
- **Reflection Guides Decisions:** Asking what truly fulfills you is critical to making meaningful changes.
- **Late Starts Still Lead to Success:** It's never too late to start over and pursue your purpose with determination.

From Bankruptcy to Breakthrough

I evolved quickly in the fitness industry, applying the integration and creativity I learned from Bruce Lee while embracing the Discipline and Resilience I learned from Masutatsu Oyama. Over time, my dedication to learning and commitment to excellence began to attract attention. Much like Bruce Lee, I developed my own training system.

My approach to fitness stood apart from traditional methods. I combined the raw strength of conventional bodybuilding with functional movements that mimicked real-life actions. This system, which I later called *Hybrid Training,* was built upon the Principles I learned during my early years in martial arts. Hybrid Training became my version of Bruce Lee's Jeet Kune Do.

Over time, I began to categorize and coach these Principles universally—applying them across sports, occupations, and everyday life. I truly believe that my method of coaching, which used physical training to teach deeper universal Principles, is what allowed me to stand out as a leading figure in fitness.

The 1990s saw my journey transform dramatically—from bankruptcy in 1992 to reaching the top of the fitness world by 1999. For the first time, I felt truly happy, mentally and spiritually in the right place. I was driven, disciplined, and most importantly, living with a purpose bigger than myself. That Purpose fueled me with the energy to maintain a grueling pace for nearly two decades. By the late 1990s, I had become one of the top presenters in fitness, launched my own training studio, and published six books and ten videos—all within five years of graduating with my master's degree.

Lesson Box: Turning Experiences Into Innovations

- **Adaptability and Integration Spur Innovation:** Drawing from varied influences and adapting strategies from mentors like Bruce Lee and Mas Oyama led to the creation of Hybrid Training.
- **Purpose Fuels Energy:** A life rooted in meaningful work provides the drive to overcome challenges and achieve greatness. Your purpose is your WHY, and if your why is big enough—you can overcome any how.
- **Hard Times Lead to Reinvention:** Bankruptcy became my starting point for breakthroughs, especially when paired with discipline and resilience.

Building a Legacy: The Institute of Human Performance (IHP)

In 2001, I founded the Institute of Human Performance (IHP) in Boca Raton, Florida. My vision was clear: create a place where fitness professionals and athletes could learn, train, and grow. Over the years, IHP earned a global reputation as the Mecca of Functional Training, drawing trainers, athletes, and professionals from around the world eager to experience our systems and philosophy.

I never slowed down—writing books, touring as a presenter, building certifications, and launching a university internship program. By 2010, IHP and our methods were featured in leading fitness publications. IHP was voted the Best Core Gym in the Country and ranked among the top ten facilities by Men's Health, Men's Fitness, and Men's Journal. Even mainstream outlets like Glamour, SELF, and Women's Fitness recognized IHP as one of the nation's top gyms, spotlighting the resistance bands I designed and the training protocols we pioneered.

Lesson Box: Building a Vision and Earning Recognition

- **Vision Creates Legacy:** Starting with a clear purpose lays the groundwork for impactful institutions like IHP.
- **Innovation Sets Standards:** Tools like resistance bands and functional training protocols changed the fitness landscape.
- **Consistency Drives Recognition:** Sustained effort over years results in widespread acknowledgment and influence.

Principles in Adversity: Growth Through Challenges

What were the lessons of the 1990–2010 period? For two decades, I lived by Principles, which took me from single and bankrupt to a thriving business, a family of five, and a lead position in my industry. I was happy, and I realized I got there the old-fashioned way—by living a principled life full of challenges and lessons. I invested my most valuable resource, time, into my family and IHP. I showed up, and life delivered.

The recession of 2008 hit hard, and its effects lingered until 2011. In response, I stopped touring in the U.S. and threw myself into a decade-long international grind from 2010 to 2020. I traveled twenty to thirty times per year, so often I stopped even getting jet-lagged—even on trips to Argentina, China, or Singapore. I was the first American in fitness to truly go international. While it brought in money, my narrow focus on the road left me fatigued and confused. Without realizing it, I was drifting into a dark place, losing the clarity that had made me successful.

From 2010 to 2018, I lost touch with IHP. I staffed it heavily so I wouldn't have to lead day-to-day, and though I provided at the highest level for my four children and wife, inside I was spent. I was at their events, but I wasn't present. My family needed leadership, my team needed guidance, and I was trying to substitute both with cash. But you can't buy presence. You can't buy leadership.

That period beat the hell out of me. My marriage ended. Another relationship came and went. IHP was struggling. Everyone suffered. Finally, I cried, I prayed, and I took the first steps back. Through Humility I took Responsibility. I rededicated myself to living my Principles. In a matter of weeks, the turnaround began. I met a beautiful woman who reminded me love is always there if you're open to it. Rio hit his stride as a man and became IHP's manager. The staff responded to stronger leadership. The business responded, too. Living and role-modeling Principles is contagious. It inspires. It transforms. Imagine that?

Lesson Box: Learning from the 2008 Recession

- **Prioritize Relationships:** Financial success cannot replace the time and leadership your family and team need.
- **Self-Awareness Prevents Burnout:** Understand when your actions are misaligned with your principles and values.
- **Balance Is Critical:** Over-focus on one aspect of life, like work, often leads to neglect in other vital areas.

Resilience and Rebuilding in the Face of Crisis

By 2020, it seemed like a comeback was finally on the horizon—then COVID hit. In January, my multiple six-figure international business disintegrated overnight. Faced with the choice of closing IHP or betting everything on survival, Rio and I doubled down and took out a $300,000 SBA loan. By December 2024, we had paid down enormous credit card debt, learned how to truly operate a business, and built a strong brand and social media presence. In 2022, I married the woman who brought new light into my life, Giedre Santana.

Along the way, I faced other challenges—from losing loved ones to battling my own body. In July 2021, I lost my hero—my dad. Jordan Peterson talks about aiming to be "the strongest man at your father's funeral." Mission accomplished. I delivered his eulogy in both English and Spanish—with respect, pride, and compassion.

Physically, my body has been through hell: prostate issues, kidney stone hospitalizations, multiple joint surgeries (hip and knee replacements), and infections—including a near-death brush with sepsis in 2023. What's funny is, only now, as I recount my life for this book, do I actually see all I've been through. I guess I tackled life the same way I tackle big projects: so focused on the process that I rarely stopped to notice the pitfalls or the milestones. For me, it's always been simple—right foot, left foot, repeat.

I've lived an exciting and beautiful life, but I now realize it hasn't been easy. Challenges were constant, yet every one carried lessons. The good times came from adhering to Principles. The comebacks demanded PV². The lessons of 2007–2024 were crystal clear: only Principles can bring you back from the brink—and they are not for sale. Money can mask problems, but it cannot replace presence, Character, Discipline, or hard work. Money won't fix the cracks in your life—it only hides them until they grow deeper. Principles pay debts money never can.

Lesson Box: Lessons from 2007–2024

- **Principles Are Your Anchor:** In times of crisis, returning to your core principles guides recovery and growth.
- **Invest in Relationships:** Toxic dynamics must be addressed and resolved to make room for healthier connections.
- **Rebuild with Resilience:** Crisis often presents an opportunity to rebuild with clarity and purpose.

A Life Rooted in Principles

My journey has been one of learning, adaptation, and commitment to something greater than myself. This book is my 19th, and everything I've achieved—from IHP's success to my global training systems—stems from the same core Principles: Humility, Responsibility, Sacrifice, Facing Fear, and Perseverance.

In the chapters that follow, I will explore how Principles, Values, and Virtues have shaped the foundation of my training style, my business, my family, and my life. My hope is that this ethos inspires you to pursue your own path with Resilience, purpose, and unwavering Integrity—because the same tools that carried me can carry anyone willing to do the work.

Lesson Box: Reflections on Principles

- **Principles Are Timeless:** They don't expire. They stay true and guide you through every season of life.
- **Resilience Through Adversity:** When life gets hard, return to your principles. That's how you build character and grow.
- **Purpose Drives Integrity:** Chase your **WHY** and live your values. That strengthens your integrity—and in turn, it inspires the people around you.

"An old tree sheds many leaves
while keeping its roots;
a wise person changes many opinions
while keeping their principles."

~ JCS

02

UNDERSTANDING PRINCIPLES, VALUES AND VIRTUES (PV²)

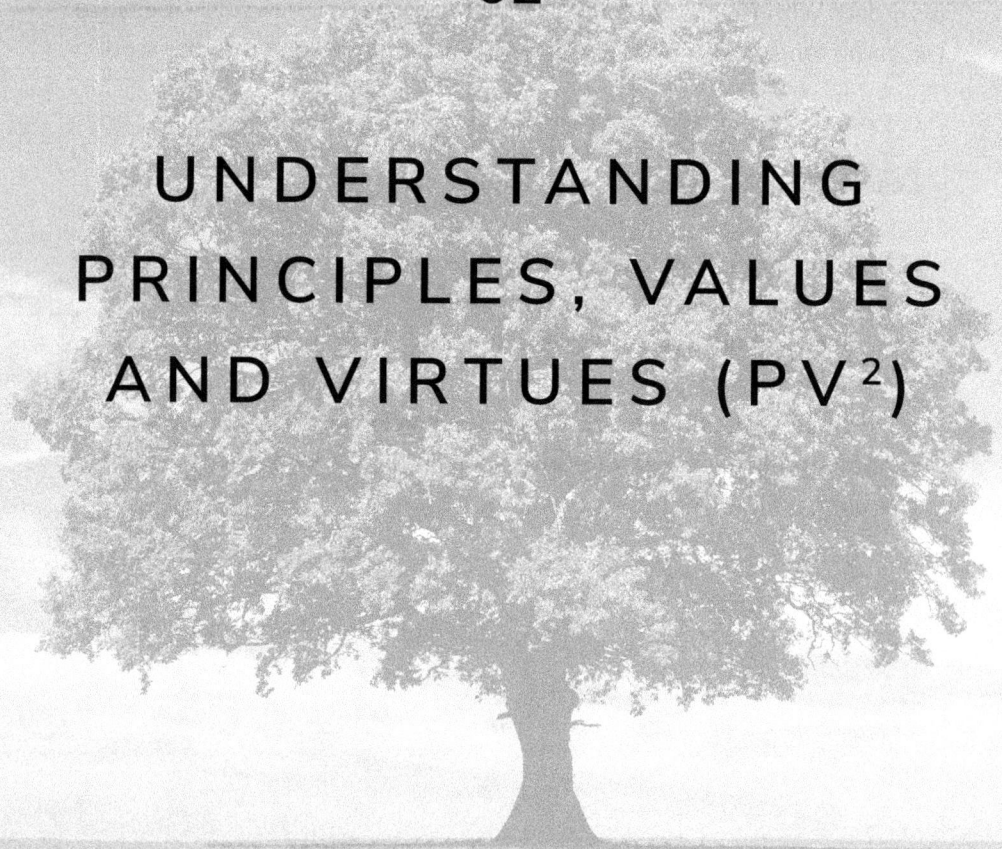

Tutorial Primer

Purpose: familiarize readers with terms, abbreviations, and how to approach and utilize the book's content

Goal: enhance readers' ability to use the system developed through the book.

Before You Begin

This book is about **Principles, Values, and Virtues (PV²)**. It defines each term and how they relate to one another. It also provides a 10-step program known as the **Principle-Based Breakthrough (PB²)** system that delineates the order in which we use these Principles and their corresponding Values and Virtues to live a Principle-driven life and troubleshoot critical moments. Because this is a 10-step program—and each step has a Principle, a Value, and a Virtue—we sometimes refer to PB² as a '10 × 3 format'.

Understand that PB² is *my* system, not *the* system. The idea was to develop a system that would be effective and give the reader tools to shape their own Principle-driven life—and if, in the process, they develop their own system, then all the better.

Basic Terms and Acronyms

- **PV²** = **Principles, Values**, and **Virtues.**
- **PB²** = **Principle-Based Breakthrough System**—the structure of 10 Principles, 10 Values, and 10 Virtues used in this book.
- **10 × 3** = 10 steps deep, each with a **Principle, Value**, and **Virtue** (3) wide.
- **Relational expressions** = the outputs or results of living the **PB²** system. They describe the observable states, dynamics, and relationships that naturally emerge when someone embodies their **PV²**.

Why this Book? Foundations Matter.

Building a Principle-driven life is no different than building a solid house. A house can be aesthetically beautiful, even made of the best materials, but without a solid foundation and well-built structure, the house will not withstand the challenges Mother Nature can unleash. Likewise, one can take care of all the external aesthetic features of a cool life—even be blessed with genetics and talent—but without living by unshakable Principles, one's fake 'house of cards' will surely fall when life's challenges come knocking. How many times have you heard, "What a waste of talent?" That's potential and resources lost in the storm of life, not being guided (driven) by the PB² Principles.

Rarely Taught

This book was originally slated to be a 'coaching' book for personal trainers and coaches. However, as I started writing, I realized I was work-ing with constructs society has termed Principles, Values, and Virtues. Then I realized that it was not even clear to me what the difference was between a Principle, a Value, and a Virtue—much less how other terms were associated with them.

Have you ever taken a class, read a book, or come across any material that explained the difference and organized them into executable action? I have not, and most of the people I asked did not either. I also did a review of the self-help literature out there—especially from my favorite authors—and I could not find any work that defined each category and put them together into an executable algorithm. That's what gave this book wings.

PV² Definitions—Principles, Values, and Virtues

Principles are universal and self-evident truths or natural laws. They apply to everyone, everywhere, all the time. Much like gravity, you don't have to believe in Principles for them to affect you—they simply exist, exerting their influence regardless of your awareness or acknowledgment. Principles are non-negotiable. You can't bargain with them or twist them to fit your preferences or narrative. Instead, you align with them—or risk the consequences of ignoring them.

Values are often what you preach. They are the personal or cultural priorities that guide how we live and make decisions; values are basically our opinions . Think of values as a compass that points you in the direction you feel is most important. Unlike Principles, which are universal and self-evident, values are your beliefs and opinions shaped by your experiences, culture, and choices. When values align with universal Principles, they gain power that can inspire and drive meaningful action.

Virtues are what you practice—thus, the "practice what you preach" axiom. Virtues are qualities expressed in consistent actions. While values guide your priorities, virtues are the tangible habits and behaviors that reflect those priorities in the real world. Virtues require deliberate cultivation. You don't wake up one day and become brave, honest, or compassionate. Instead, you develop these traits, which we call **relational expressions,** constantly practicing Integrity, Execution, Bravery, Tenacity, and Resilience.

PB² = Principle-Based Breakthrough System

The PB² system aligns 10 important Principles I selected. There were many to choose from—and you may prefer others—and that's fine. I chose these for my PB² because I found them to function as action *triggers* that drive behavior. I sequenced them to guide a progressive problem-solving flowchart that is logical, actionable, and easy to follow. It is meant to get a person from point A to point B in their life. Whether point A is the lowest point of a drug addiction, or running a small business you want to scale, the road to point B can follow the same flowchart of sequential Principles—the PB².

Chapter 10 includes a summary table of the PB² system and explains how the PB² 10 × 3 system is divided into three stages of execution.

The PB² 10 × 3 System
Using the PB²

Don't get hung up on words or definitions. Depending on context, culture, and personal preferences, PV² are often used interchangeably in everyday speech. What matters isn't grammatical accuracy—it's the utility of the model.

Also, understand the order can change depending on the situation. For example, you might fall into a crisis that requires immediate Execution and enormous Courage before you even have a moment to think. After the crisis is over, the experience starts to sink in while you reflect. All of a sudden, Humility and Self-Reflection appear. As long as you have this PB² , you will always have a GPS that can steer you to your desired destination. Whether you identify and act on a Principle, a Value or a Virtue does not matter; that you act and are able to understand you actions is all that matters.

I Don't See Some Popular Words in this System

As you go through the PB² framework, you might notice that some important-sounding traits don't appear on the official chart. You may be asking yourself: "Where's respect?" "Where's patience?" "What about kindness?" Those are great observations—and the right questions to ask.

The reason you don't see those items listed as PV² within the PB² system is because I don't consider them main drivers; they're byproducts—relational expressions. These are what you get when you live by Principles. They reflect how your behavior shows up in the real world and what others experience when you live by PV² through the PB² system.

Respect Is the Result—Not the Driver

Respect isn't something you chase. It's something you develop and earn by living these PV². For a simple example, when you adopt:

- **Responsibility** and display **Integrity.** Own your mistakes.
- **Self-Reflection** and act with **Clarity.** Do what you say you'll do.
- **Strategizing** and **Execute** with purpose. Displaying competence.
- **Facing Fear** and demonstrate **Bravery.** Symbolize Courage.
- **Perseverance** and exhibit **Resilience.** Showcase undying grit.

How can you not respect others—or be respected by all? Live a Principle-driven life long enough, and you'll walk into any room and be surrounded by respect—the respect you give and the respect you get. Not because you demanded it—but because you lived the Principles that command it.

Patience Is Fuel for the Process

You'll need patience to:

- Reflect on your actions without freaking out.
- Stay consistent when progress is slow.
- Persevere when life punches you in the face.

Patience isn't passive—it's the inner calm that lets you work the PB² system when everything around you is loud and chaotic. It keeps Resilience from turning into rage, and Consistency from turning into burnout.

Don't Look for Everything on the Checklist

PB² isn't some magic grocery list where every good trait has its own box; *it's a framework that produces outcomes.* You'll start seeing:

- Empathy when you've been humbled by your own process
- Respect when you persevere through adversity
- Kindness because you act with Integrity and Selflessness
- Patience because you believe in Sacrifice and Consistency

These traits may not appear on the PB² chart, but you won't make it through the system without them. They're the fruits of living a Principle-driven life. Work the system—and they'll come find you. So when someone says, "Where's respect in the PB² system?" just smile and say, "It's already in there—if you're doing it right."

Making Your PB² Yours

THIS IS IMPORTANT: The PB² framework I'm teaching is the official model I built. But once you understand it, you're free to *build your own PB².*

- You may prefer different words that resonate with you.
- You may decide your PB² only needs eight steps instead of 10.
- You may put Self-Awareness before Humility, or flip the order depending on where you are in life.
- In a crisis, you may need to act with Courage first—and only later reflect, gain awareness, and find humility.

That's not breaking the system—it's applying it. PB² is the map I'm giving you. But the road...? That's yours.

PB² in Three Stages

There are 10 Principles divided into 3 stages for ease of application (i.e., 10 × 3 system). The first stage is about taking responsibility and coming up with a way out. The second stage is about executing the plan. Stage three is about sticking with the plan and Finishing Big.

Stage 1—Principles 1–4: Own the Problem and Find the Way Out

- **Humility**—Admit it.
- **Responsibility**—Own it.
- **Self-Reflection**—What caused it?
- **Self-Awareness**—What will fix it?

Stage 2—Principles 5–7: Create and Execute the Plan

- **Strategizing**—The plan to fix it
- **Sacrifice**—Be willing to pay the price.
- **Facing Fear**—Just do it (even in the presence of fear).

Stage 3—Principles 8–10: Stay the Course and Finish Big

- **Consistency**—Stay with it.
- **Perseverance**—Push through obstacles.
- **Finish Big**—Integrate your learning.

When you live by this system, you will be on your way to constant evolution. Remember, our goal is not perfection; that is unrealistic—and I dare to say an 'anticlimactic' end. Instead of perfection, we are looking for corrections. This is the secret to constant growth and evolution.

Introduction

Take anyone you really admire and respect—not just for what they've accomplished, but for how they accomplished it. Don't just look at the material abundance they've acquired—look at how many lives they've impacted and how people see them. What qualities do they possess? Do they live by a code? Do their actions match their words?

The people you admire most share common characteristics and are guided by simple, universal truths. They hold themselves to a standard, and they live it. What sets them apart is how they live, what they stand for, and how they turn their beliefs into action.

In this chapter, I want to establish a few key definitions that will guide our journey. But let's be clear—exact definitions matter less than the clarity of intent behind them. Words can shift meaning depending on context, and rigid definitions can distract from the bigger picture. What's important is that we share a common understanding so we can build a meaningful and actionable framework for life.

You'll recognize many of the words in this book—principles, values, virtues, ideas, beliefs, and emotions. They're familiar, yet most people struggle to define them clearly or understand how they interact. These distinctions shape decisions, relationships, and growth. When we give these concepts deeper meaning and structure, they become more than abstract ideas—they become the foundation for a life of stability, integrity, and purpose. That foundation becomes even more powerful when applied through the PB²—a Principle-Based Breakthrough System that puts PV² into real-world motion.

Defining Principles: Timeless Truths for a Meaningful Now

As defined in the *Tutorial Primer*, a principle is a universal, enduring truth—a natural law that applies across all cultures, time periods, and circumstances. Principles are simple yet profound, such as "honesty builds trust" or "actions have consequences." Unlike values, which can shift based on society, upbringing, or trends, principles remain unchanged. They govern outcomes with consistency and impartiality.

Think of principles like gravity—they exist whether we acknowledge them or not. You don't have to believe in gravity for it to pull you down. Ignore it, and you suffer the consequences. Principles work the same way. The law of cause and effect is a perfect example: every action produces an outcome, whether you accept it or not. Here's how principles play out across life:

- **In fitness:** The General Adaptation Syndrome shows how the body responds to stress. Push it with the right dose, and it adapts and grows. Ignore it, and you either plateau or break down with injury.
- **In business:** Long-term success lives or dies on the principle of value creation. If what you offer solves a real problem and delivers more benefit than cost, you build momentum. If not, the market buries you.
- **In relationships:** Trust is the principle that holds every bond together. Violate it, and the relationship weakens or collapses. Honor it, and the connection grows deeper with time.

Lesson Box: Why Principles Matter

- Principles are universal and unchanging, providing stability in a world of constant change.
- Ignoring principles leads to predictable, often negative, outcomes.
- Recognizing and applying principles creates resilience and long-term success.
- Principles form the foundation of PV^2—Values and Virtues flow from them.

Principles vs. Values: Universal Truth vs. Personal Preference

Before we dive into values, we need to draw the line between principles and values. Principles are universal—they don't bend. Values are in essence your 'adopted' or 'personal' principles—but they can shift. Principles are like the laws of nature; values are how each of us interprets and reacts to those laws. Values are rooted in beliefs, experiences, and culture. That's why they can look different across people and places. That's where, "Well, that's my opinion" comes from.

- A teenager might value freedom above all else, while a parent might value responsibility to family. Both are valid, but both are personal.
- A principle like "an ounce of prevention is worth a pound of cure" holds true in every arena—from training, to business, to emergency response.

Here's the key: alignment. When values line up with principles, they create strength and direction. When they drift, chaos follows.

Take leadership. If a leader is driven by the value of popularity, they'll chase applause. But if chasing the applause breaks the principle of integrity, trust erodes and the whole thing collapses. On the other hand, when values are anchored to principles, decisions gain clarity, teams gain confidence, and purpose takes root.

Lesson Box: The Alignment of Principles and Values

- Principles are the foundation of PV²—universal truths that don't shift with time or opinion.
- Values are personal and adaptable beliefs or opinions.
- Alignment between principles and values creates clarity and purpose.

Virtues: The Behavior that Brings PV² to Life

Principles anchor us. Values guide us. Virtues bring both to life. They're the behaviors that align belief with action. Put simply: values reflect what you preach; virtues reflect what you practice. Virtues don't appear overnight—they're built through practice, reflection, and consistent effort.

Integrity—aligning words and actions with truth, even when it costs you.

As a business owner, I had the option to classify my trainers as independent contractors (ICs). Many gym owners do this to dodge taxes and employee benefits—it would have saved IHP about $2.5 million over 25 years. Tempting, right? But here's the truth: ICs are supposed to set their own rates, run their own business, and work for multiple clients. If a trainer depends on your gym for their livelihood, have to wear a uniform, have to follow your training philosophy, and must attend meetings, they're most likely not an IC—they're an employee. It's not the classification you claim that creates an IC, it's the working relationship that determines how the IRS will classify them. Plain and simple.

I was advised countless times to take the cheaper route. I refused. Why? Because integrity isn't about what's easy—it's about what's right, even when no one is watching. Anything built on a lie eventually becomes a lie. That's why I chose to classify my staff as employees and pay the full taxes and benefits. That decision cost more financially, but it gave IHP a foundation of integrity—like a newborn being born into a home with values. I wanted IHP to stand for something real:

- Professionalism
- Accountability
- Excellence in service

When you commit to integrity, you create something that lasts. Twenty-five years later—look at what we built!

Bravery—acting on Courage in the face of fear.

One of my defining coaching moments happened in a stairwell at the Florida Regional Wrestling Championships. One of my wrestlers, Alex Jones, was expected to reach the finals. Instead, he was pinned in the quarterfinals—the first time in his career. Crushed, he disappeared. His next match—against a rival who had beaten him three times—was announced. That match would decide if he made it to the state championships. I found Alex crying in the stairwell. I told him: "Alex, the decision you make today will shape the man you become. I love you and will support you no matter what. But it's time to do what's necessary, not what's convenient."

I walked away. Moments later, the doors to the stair well burst open and Alex came out, headgear on, ready to go. He didn't just wrestle—he dominated. He beat the rival who had haunted him for years. That day wasn't just about winning a match—it was about Alex stepping into manhood. Bravery is forged in moments like these.

Selflessness—putting others above ego or convenience.

I'm significantly older than my wife. She's educated, intelligent, and strong—we share equal say in everything. But our backgrounds shape how we see roles in the home: her European upbringing, my Cuban roots.

My father used to say: "I'm the man of this house. I have the first and last word—but there's a lot of discussion in between." The truth? His "final word" was almost always, "whatever she said," as he pointed to my mother. It's often the same in my house.

I love debate. I treat it like intellectual sparring—testing ideas, sharpening arguments. But in relationships, debate isn't about winning. Over time, I realized that pressing harder, even when I was "right," only created distance. That's when I learned: when you dominate a debate, you win. When you dominate your significant other, nobody wins.

Selflessness means setting aside your ego—the need to be right— in favor of the relationship. Now, instead of overwhelming with relentless logic, I give space for reflection and understanding. Sometimes, time does the work better than words. Because when you stand on solid Principles, you don't need instant validation. The truth will surface, and understanding will come in time.

Lesson Box: Virtues bring Values to life

- Virtues are values in action.
- Cultivating virtues requires deliberate practice and reflection.
- Selflessness allows time to foster understanding.
- Do you want to right or do you want to be understood?
- Give it time.

Conclusion

One of my favorite bands, Earth, Wind & Fire, is named after three fundamental elements of the universe. In the same way, Principles, Values, and Virtues are the three elements of a meaningful life.

- **Principles** are self-evident truths—the universal foundation.
- **Values** are the beliefs that guide our behavior.
- **Virtues** are the actions that prove we're living what we claim.

When these three are aligned, life has clarity, strength, and resilience. We act with integrity, live with purpose, and build legacies that last. But when they're misaligned—or ignored—the result is confusion, inconsistency, and drift. So ask yourself:

- Are my values aligned with universal principles?
- Am I practicing the virtues I claim to value?
- How can I bring my PV² into tighter alignment?

The world is drowning in opinions but starving for truth. Too often, preferences replace principles, trends replace values, and convenience replaces virtues. That's why the next chapter matters. We're going to see what happens when societies walk away from principles—when comfort replaces sacrifice, when indulgence replaces discipline, and when honor gets traded for image. Because at the end of the day, what you live is what you believe. And if you don't define your principles, the world will define them for you.

"We are the sum of our actions,
not our thoughts."

~ JCS

03

AM I WHO I AM, OR CAN I REALLY CHANGE?

Personality Traits vs. Character Traits

One of the biggest roadblocks to growth is a simple phrase: **"That's just the way I am."**

You'll hear it all the time: "I've always been like this." "I was born this way." "This is just my personality." People throw this out when they feel cornered—when change is needed or expected—and they want to shut the conversation down. But that's not a fact. It's a defense. A shield to avoid the uncomfortable work of growth.

But here's the truth—if you genuinely believe change isn't possible, then this book, and any other self-help book, is already dead in the water. The entire PB² system depends on the idea that character is trainable, and that behavior in responsible people evolves.

The confusion usually starts with the difference between personality traits and character traits. Most people blur the line between the two. **Personality traits** are how you're wired. They're your default mode—how you tend to show up to the world, in both good times and bad. It's how you process situations, and how you relate to others.

Introverted. Talkative. Moody. Anxious. Optimistic. Reactive.

These traits are shaped by your genetics and early experiences. They influence your tendencies—but they don't define your values, and they don't determine your character.

Character traits are different; they're about choice. They reflect how you act, what you stand for, and what you build your life on: honesty, Courage, loyalty, Discipline. These don't come built in. They're developed through action and repetition. You don't inherit Discipline—you build it. You don't "have" Courage—you choose it when fear shows up.

So here's the real question: **Can personality traits change too?**

Yes. Personality traits are highly malleable. You may never fully rewrite your wiring, but you can absolutely retrain how it shows up. You can be introverted and still learn to speak in public—I'm living proof. You can feel anxiety and still lead with Clarity. You can be emotional and still act with Discipline. You can feel fear and still choose Courage when it matters. That's the difference between being ruled by your personality—and evolving into a better version of you.

Psychology used to teach that personality was mostly fixed after early adulthood. That's changed. We now know the "Big Five" personality traits—*Openness, Conscientiousness, Extroversion, Agreeableness*, and *Neuroticism*—can shift. Therapy, deliberate practice, or life-altering experiences move the needle. Structured environments like military service, parenthood, long-term training, therapy, or principled leadership reshape personality. People become more stable, more focused, more assertive—because repetition conditions them to. This is why experience matters—if you choose to learn and adapt. That's how your personality evolves. But if you choose the victim mindset—"I can't change, I was born this way"—then yes, you're stuck. Not by design. By choice.

It's important to distinguish between completely changing your core wiring and simply growing up. Are you the same person at 8, 17, 28, 40, or 55? Of course not. Everything about you shifts over time. That alone proves personality isn't hardwired—it's trainable.

If a personality trait is consistently wrecking your career, your relationships, or your peace of mind, clinging to "that's just who I am" guarantees you'll stay stuck. Everyone is capable of learning new behaviors, adopting new patterns, and showing up differently. You can call it personality change or personality evolution, whatever floats your boat - but it is change nonetheless. And here's the key: you're not just capable of change—as a responsible adult, you're obligated to change over time - it's called maturity. Change doesn't come from wishing for it. It comes from valuing it enough to engage in consistent, deliberate practice.

Your ego can't be bigger than your evolution.

The bottom line?
Personality isn't set in stone—
it bends under pressure, repetition, and responsibility.

When someone tells me, "You want me to change who I am—I can't do that," especially if their life is in chaos, my response is simple: I'm not asking you to change. I'm asking you to evolve.

That's what this book is about—evolution. Real growth, built one Principle at a time. You don't need a new personality. You need the courage and discipline to do the work evolution demands. You don't need to escape who you are—you need to embrace who you can become, with enough work and the right kind of love.

Principles Shape Values. Values Shape Virtues. Virtues Shape Life.

And the best part? That cycle is repeatable by anyone willing to do the work.

Recommended Reading (Scientific Support for Change)

- **Roberts, Walton & Viechtbauer (2006):** Found consistent shifts in personality across life—especially more conscientiousness and emotional stability with age and responsibility.
- **Hudson & Fraley (2015):** Showed people who deliberately worked on personality change over 16 weeks produced measurable results.
- **Damian, Spengler & Roberts (2017):** Linked changes in traits— especially conscientiousness—to long-term career success.
- **Magidson et al. (2014):** Demonstrated personality can shift through behavioral strategies (like reducing neuroticism with targeted training).

*"Sing a song long enough
and your life becomes the song."*
~ JCS

04

SOCIETY'S MORAL DECLINE: EROSION OF PRINCIPLES, VALUES AND VIRTUES

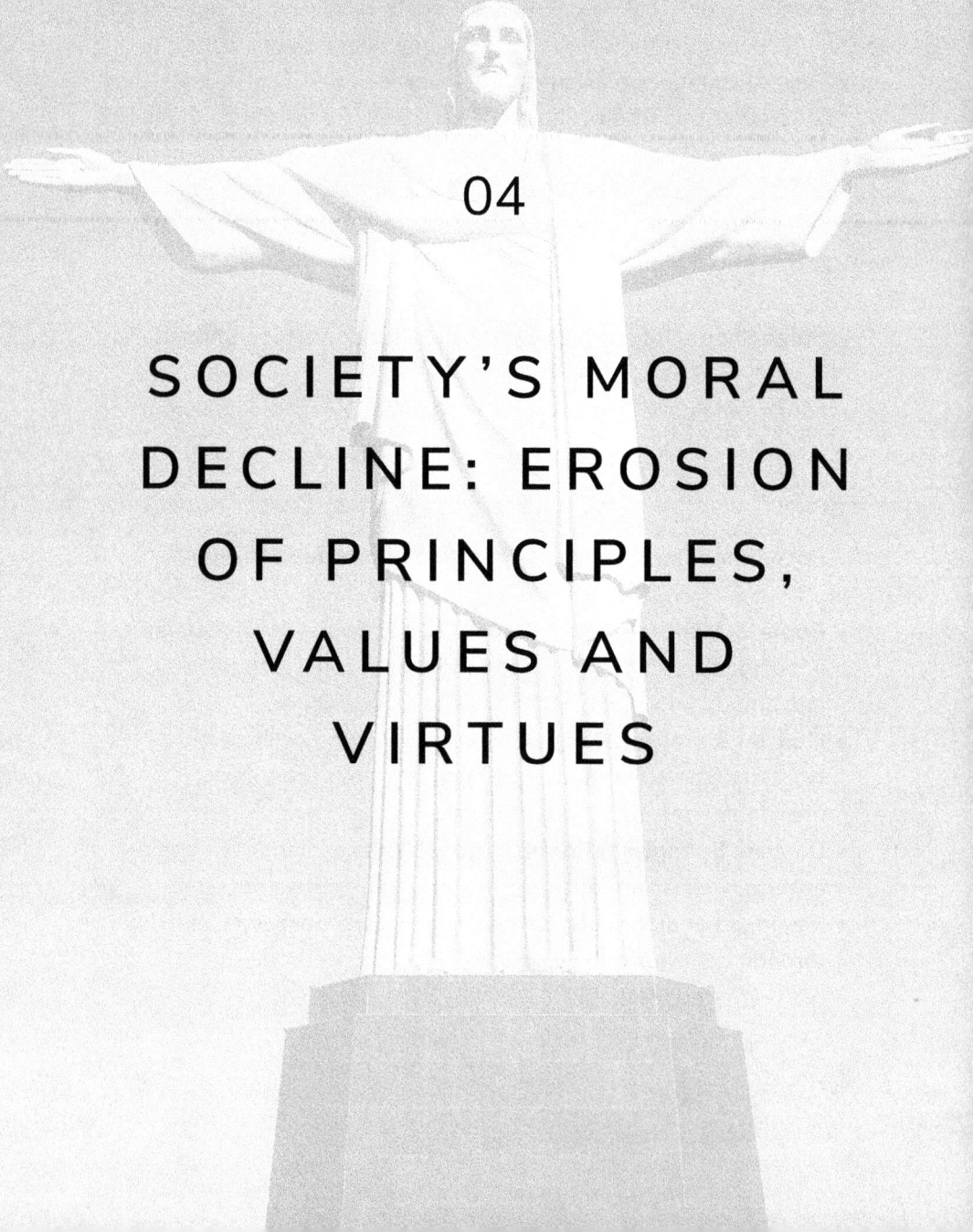

Don't 'Rome' Me

You know the old saying, "When in Rome, do as the Romans do?" Well, we're in Rome—and we can't do as the Romans did.

The worst and most dangerous enemy is always the one within— the one you aren't defending against. No better example exists than the fall of the Roman Empire. Rome wasn't conquered by an outside force. It collapsed from within, brought down by excess, indulgence, and moral decay. What began as a disciplined warrior society—founded on duty, sacrifice, and responsibility—slowly rotted into hedonism, corruption, and self-indulgence. Gladiator games, lavish feasts, and political betrayal dulled the people's focus while their principles eroded.

The first step in the collapse of any civilization is the loss of its principles. When principles are lost, values decay. When values decay, virtues disappear. A nation built by men of principle—warriors, visionaries, and builders—collapsed into a society of spectators and self-indulgence.

Sound Familiar?

Today, our distractions are different—but the decay is the same. TikTok has replaced purpose. Entitlement has replaced accomplishment. Convenience has replaced work ethic. We have more wealth, more access, more comfort—and yet, we're crumbling under the weight of our own indulgence.

Lesson Box: The Fall of Civilizations

- No civilization falls solely due to external threats.
- Collapse happens from within, when principles are abandoned.
- Discipline and sacrifice build greatness; indulgence and convenience destroy it.
- If we don't defend self-evident principles, we will repeat history.

The Numbing of Society

It's hard to deny that when morals decay, we get exactly what we see today—instability, weakness, apathy, and a society disconnected from itself. Never in history have we had more abundance, comfort, and freedom— yet people feel spiritually empty and emotionally trapped. And this emptiness doesn't sit quietly. It screams through senseless acts of violence and the skyrocketing use of antidepressants, painkillers, and every other drug people can get their hands on. The numbers tell the story:

Antidepressants

Used to manage emotional and psychological pain, antidepressants are now a normalized escape from existential discomfort.

- **U.S.:** Adult usage rose from 10.6% (2009–10) to 13.8% (2017–18), according to the CDC.
- **Women: The largest increase, climbing from 13.8% to 18.6% in the same period** (CDC/NCHS Data Brief No. 377, 2020).
- **England:** Prescriptions surged by 34.8% over six years, hitting 83.4 million in 2021/22 (UK Pharmaceutical Journal).
- **Scotland:** By December 2024, nearly 1 in 4 adults were on antide-pressants—up from 630,000 in 2010 (The Times, UK).

Painkillers & Opioids

These drugs may start by masking physical pain—but now, they're often numbing emotional and spiritual voids.

- **U.S.:** There were approximately 81,000 opioid-related overdose deaths in 2023, according to *The Atlantic's* national health summary on the opioid crisis (source).

- **Dependency: 1 in 3 prescription opioid users show signs of dependency; 1 in 10 become fully dependent** (The Guardian, 2024).
- **Australia:** New paracetamol restrictions began February 2025 after a sharp rise in overdoses among adolescents and young adults (News.com.au).

Recreational & Escapist Drugs

Whether for pleasure, rebellion, or escape, these substances reflect a society desperate to feel something—or *nothing at all.*

- **Cannabis (U.S.):** Legal in 24 states, with 48.2M users in 2023—up from 26M in 2012 (Statista).
- **Psychedelics:** LSD, psilocybin, and MDMA use up 33% since 2020, especially in 'healing retreats' (NIH, 2024).
- **Cocaine & Methamphetamine:** Meth seizures up 60% in 5 years; cocaine overdoses cause 15,000+ deaths annually (DEA, 2024).
- **Fentanyl:** Increasingly laced into recreational drugs, driving spikes in accidental overdoses—even among casual users.

These aren't just statistics—they're proof that society isn't facing its problems. It's numbing them. A culture that turns to chemicals to cope is a culture that has already surrendered its Resilience.

The Decline in Modern Society: The Loss of PV²

For centuries, strong societies were built upon PV²—the building blocks of strength and unity. People often point to honor, respect, and admiration as the foundation of greatness. But as we clarified in the Tutorial Primer, those are not the drivers of the PB² system—they are byproducts. They emerge only when people live in alignment with self-evident truths like the following:

- Responsibility → Accountability → Integrity
- Sacrifice → Commitment → Selflessness
- Facing Fear → Courage → Bravery
- Perseverance → Fortitude → Resilience

That's PV² in action: Principles drive Values. Values shape Virtues.

From there flow honor, respect, and trust are the fruits of a principled life, not the roots. But today, we've traded timeless Principles for fleeting opinions and cultural moods. Instead of practicing Consistency, we get distracted by shiny objects. Instead of living with Responsibility, we surround ourselves with excuses. Instead of exercising Perseverance, we quit or opt for quick fixes at the first sign of crisis. Without PV², people are unprepared for life. A culture that values comfort over challenge produces individuals who fold under pressure. A culture that glorifies self-indulgence over sacrifice breeds entitlement instead of resilience. This is where the PB² system comes in.

Lesson Box: PV² → PB²

- **PV²** = Principles, Values, Virtues. The foundation.
- **PB²** = Principle-Based Breakthrough. The system for applying PV² to business, fitness, family, and life.
- **PV²** provide the universal foundation. PB² system provides the framework for execution.
- When you apply the **PB²** system, the natural byproducts are the things we crave: honor, respect, admiration, trust—even love.

Impact of Pop Culture on Principled Living

Pop culture shapes values on a massive scale—often elevating fame, wealth, and image over Virtues like Integrity, Selflessness, and Resilience.

The very foundation that once built strong societies is being eroded.

- **Music:** Once a medium for inspiration and social commentary, much of it now glorifies violence, materialism, promiscuity, and fleeting relationships. Uplifting messages have been traded for shock value.
- **Movies:** More adrenaline, less meaning. Spectacle has replaced substance. Depth has been sacrificed for cheap thrills and hollow one-liners.
- **Fashion:** From elegance to exposure, fashion now mirrors our obsession with self-gratification over dignity.
- **Institutional Ideology:** When identity categories are elevated above Principle, coherence and excellence suffer. In some universities and corporations, ideology has begun to outweigh merit—stifling free thought and sidelining Principle-driven growth.

Entertainment, fashion, and ideology don't exist in silos—they feed one another. Together, they create a culture that prizes false image over grounded substance. That's why the erosion runs so deep: it doesn't stop at what you think you consume—because what you consume shapes who you become, and who your children will be allowed to become.

Today's popular culture is insidious and relentless. It's everywhere and unforgiving. It doesn't care who it harms. It has no purpose other than to propagate. It comes at you from all sides—sounds, images, storylines— gradually reshaping value systems that once nurtured and strengthened societies. The consumer doesn't even know it's happening; they are being reprogrammed. The music you sing shapes your emotional makeup. The clothes you wear feed a false ego and dull true character. The movies you watch define what you think life should be. The games you play inflate who you think you are. And the final judge and jury—the lens through which all of it is measured—is falsely calibrated through social media.

When my kids were growing up, I fought this battle every day. I remember them playing music in their rooms—dancing, singing, and laughing. But if I heard cursing or nasty lyrics, I'd barge in and make them turn it off. They'd say, "Dad—but we're not singing the bad words!" And I'd tell them, "You don't understand. By dancing to it, by singing it—even without the foul language—you're consuming it. You're letting it into your emotional fortress, and your spirit drinks from that toxic well. And whether you realize it or not, you're becoming it."

I've never allowed that thug-rap garbage in my house, my car, or my gym. I know they sneak it in when I'm not around—but not in my presence. I refuse to be a witness to it. My children have always known what their father stands for, and I've tried to live it to the best of my ability. Now, they thank me for it.

They tell me I was right. They tell me they'll teach their kids the same lessons. That's what this is all about—protecting the next generation from being programmed by noise and helping them build their own frequency, grounded in Principles, Values, and Virtues. Because the world will always try to define you. But, **when you live by Principle—it is you who defines the world.**

Lesson Box: Ideology in Disguise

- Pop culture and institutional ideologies transmit values—some affirming, some corrosive.
- When entertainment or policy promotes **identity categories** over principle, it erodes PV^2.
- **Guarding Principles means recognizing when ideology is dressed up as progress but actually erodes the moral fiber of society.**

The Social Media Coliseum

If pop culture is the soundtrack volume of society, social media is the amplifier. It doesn't just reflect values—most of which are broken—it manufactures and enforces them at scale. Platforms have become the new Coliseum, where attention is the currency and outrage is the blood sport.

- **Addiction Over Awareness:** Algorithms reward extremes. The more shocking, divisive, or indulgent the content, the wider it spreads. Principles don't trend—provocation does.
- **Influence Without Accountability:** A teenager with a phone can now shape global opinion faster than any statesman or philosopher. *Influence is cheap when wisdom is absent.*
- **Comparison Culture:** Every scroll measures your life against filtered illusions. Gratitude and fulfillment are replaced by envy and dissatisfaction.
- **Cancel Over Conversation:** Dialogue has been traded for digital mob justice. Mistakes aren't corrected—they're weaponized.

Social media didn't invent narcissism, envy, or deception—but it supercharged and weaponized them. It is the delivery system for cultural decay, feeding the masses distraction and division while eroding principles beneath the surface. Gratitude fades. Humility disappears. And without Humility—the first Principle—there is no foundation for growth.

Why PV² and the PB² System Matter

The erosion of PV² leaves society unstable, divided, and fragile. In times of crisis, only those grounded in Principles can stand firm.

- **Sacrifice** leads to Commitment, which produces Selflessness.
- **Facing Fear** leads to Courage, which produces Bravery.
- **Perseverance** leads to Fortitude, which produces Resilience.

The PB² system is the engine that takes those inner foundations and turns them into real-world strength. It's how Integrity shows up in business decisions, how Responsibility plays out in parenting, how Perseverance fuels training, and how sacrifice sustains leadership.

Without PV², there's no stability.

Without the PB² system, there's no transformation.

Lesson Box: Restoring Balance Through PV² → PB²

- PV² builds the foundation.
- PB² applies that foundation for real-world breakthrough.
- Together, they restore accountability, resilience, and collective strength.

Conclusion: A Return to PV² and the PB² System

Returning to foundational Principles doesn't mean resisting progress—it ensures progress is built on truths that don't expire. When we realign with Principles, we revive our Values. When we live those Values, Virtues follow—and society begins to heal. We all have a moral obligation to be good stewards of society and its moral fiber, so that healing falls on you.

The PB² system is the framework that turns that alignment into transformation. It bridges the gap between belief and behavior, between inner conviction and outward impact.

This isn't about nostalgia for the past—it's about reclaiming the Discipline, Sacrifice, and Courage that every strong culture has been built on. In the chapters ahead, I'll show you how PV² lays the foundation—and how the PB² system unleashes breakthrough in fitness, business, family, and leadership. Together, we can rediscover the power of a principled life—and live it forward.

"What is a church, if not a place where bodies come to build, minds come to share, hearts come to heal, and spirits come to soar?"

~ JCS

05

MY CHURCH:
THE INSTITUTE
OF HUMAN
PERFORMANCE (IHP)

The Institute of Human Performance (IHP) was born from a vision—not just of a world-class training facility but of a community built on timeless Principles. The PB² Principles of Responsibility, Facing Fear, and Consistency—combined with Values like Courage and Discipline—transformed an idea into reality and continue to guide IHP's journey. This chapter explores IHP's creation, growth, and its role as a professional home for personal trainers, strength coaches, therapists, and scientists.

Pre-IHP: The "I Can Do It Better" Phenomenon

The seeds of IHP were planted in the wake of my personal and professional rebuilding after bankruptcy in 1992. At that time, I returned to Florida Atlantic University (FAU) to complete my bachelor's degree while enrolling in a six-month certification program at the Fitness Institute International. My long-term goal was a career in fitness, but my immediate priority was providing for my one-year-old son, Rio. Grants and loans weren't enough, so I began working as a personal trainer while continuing my education.

By 1996, I was teaching at FAU and pursuing a doctoral degree. A pivotal opportunity came when I began working at a friend's personal training studio. Within a year, I transformed that part-time job into a thriving business, attracting FAU's top students as interns and maintaining nearly sixty weekly client appointments. I even wrote a local newspaper column and developed a presence on the national lecture circuit. Success came rapidly, but it also came with a recurring thought: "I can do this better."

Driven by that belief, I hired two of FAU's top interns and moved to a small location while planning a larger facility. Three of my clients believed in my vision enough to co-finance and oversee the purchase of land and construction of a 7,200-square-foot facility. I designed IHP exactly as I wanted it, from the ground up. In April of 2001, IHP opened its doors— a physical embodiment of vision and Principles put into action.

The Lessons of My Father—AND MOM TOO

Reflecting on the journey to IHP, I recognize how profoundly my father's example shaped my path. His relentless dedication to our family, his ability to face challenges with Courage, and his Commitment to securing a better future left an indelible mark on me. He worked tirelessly, saved for a house with patience, and invested in his children's growth—from sports to music lessons to education. His actions taught me the importance of Sacrifice, Resilience, and service.

As much as my father role-modeled the male persona of life, my mother was a force to be reckoned with. When we needed a wrecking ball, we called Dad; when we needed a laser-guided missile, we called Mom. She was the matriarch of the family (well over forty-five people in the U.S.), complementing my dad's brute force with negotiation and interpersonal skills. When Dad's screams and curses were over the top, in came Mom—the sniper—to calm everyone down, resolve the conflict, and offer a win-win solution.

How lucky was I? I had the best loving parents teaching me how to live by Principles, then demonstrating in real time how that was done. Dad was all about the brawn: Responsibility, Sacrifice, Facing Fear, Perseverance, and Finishing Big. Mom was the master of finesse. She personified Humility, Self-Reflection, Self-Awareness, Strategizing, and Consistency.

The story of IHP is more than a tale of business success—it is a story of family culture manifesting into business culture. It's a testament to the enduring power of lessons passed from one generation to the next.

Lesson Box: Foundational Lessons in Action

- **Courage:** The belief that "I can do it better" was not just ambition but the Courage to pursue something greater, even when the odds were uncertain.
- **Dedication and Patience:** The journey from bankruptcy to building a thriving business was rooted in consistent effort and unwavering Commitment, echoing the Virtues my father demonstrated.
- **Resilience:** Overcoming personal and financial challenges required Resilience, a refusal to be defeated by circumstances.
- **Vision and Service:** IHP was not just about a gym but about creating a space to serve others—professionals and clients—through principles that transform and elevate lives.

IHP Operates by Old Principles and Forges a New Era in Fitness

When I founded IHP in 2001, my vision was clear: to create a training center that transcended conventional fitness, much like Bruce Lee transcended traditional martial arts with Jeet Kune Do. The fitness industry was focused on bodybuilding and general health routines. I believed true physical performance extended far beyond academic dogma and wanted to pioneer training that bridged the gym and the field.

Apart from our physical training system, our coaching is unique because we frame ancient life Principles into the training at IHP. Relating the journey of life to the journey of fitness sets us apart and became the impetus for this book.

The Birth of Functional Training at IHP

I was well-versed in bodybuilding, Olympic weightlifting, and powerlifting. I also knew how Speed, Agility, and Quickness (SAQ) training enhanced athletic performance. Yet something was missing. That 'missing bridge' became clear when I attended a seminar by Gary Gray, the father of modern Functional Training. This revolutionary approach emphasized whole-body movements that mimicked real-life activities, contrasting with bodybuilding's focus on isolating individual muscles.

Functional Training prioritized efficiency, economy, and coordination—Principles aligned with Bruce Lee's philosophy of precise and effective movement. It was transformative. Functional Training wasn't about making a muscle scream, but about teaching the entire body to sing in harmony. I embraced it immediately, integrating it with traditional training techniques to create programs that delivered safe, efficient, and highly effective results. IHP quickly became the spearhead of Functional Training, not only nationally but worldwide.

Standing out in the Fitness World

In those early days, I was a paradox: a muscular 5'9" and 220 pounds, moving with balance, grace, and power. My ability to demonstrate what I taught, paired with a deep technical understanding, set me apart from many other leaders in the fitness industry. Those skills allowed me to bridge theory and practice, solidifying my reputation as a world leader in human performance.

IHP was a center for innovation, education, and transformation. Every piece of equipment, exercise, and program served a clear purpose rooted in function and movement. As I refined our systems, I began sharing them with other fitness professionals through books, articles, and lectures. Growing demand led to the creation of IHP certifications—groundbreaking programs that emphasized practical application. Trainers who earned these certifications didn't just learn exercises; they understood how to integrate them into meaningful, results-driven programs.

Lesson Box: Principles Driving IHP's Success

- **Innovation:** Challenging industry norms by integrating Functional Training into traditional strength and conditioning.
- **Practicality:** Developing systems and certifications that prioritized real-world application over theory alone.
- **Education:** Creating a culture of continuous learning and sharing knowledge globally to advance the fitness community.
- **Service:** Designing every aspect of IHP to serve a clear purpose—enhancing human performance with integrity and precision.

The Role of Principles in IHP's Growth

IHP's rise wasn't a straightforward path. Success came with challenges, uncertainty, and doubt. Clients saw my Integrity, Clarity, Execution, Tenacity, and Resilience—Virtues living out the PB² Principles. That conduct inspired confidence not only in clients but also in their network of bankers and contractors who helped build IHP.

Taking clients' money to fund IHP wasn't just a financial obligation—it was a moral one. Losing their trust would have been far worse than losing their investment. Fear of failure whispered constantly in the background, but Courage wasn't about silencing those whispers; it was about coexisting with them—sitting with fear in calm neutrality, all while Strategizing.

The Value of Courage is often less about bold action and more about the absence of reaction to FEAR (False Evidence Appearing Real). Fear, at its core, is not a fact—it's a feeling. When you see fear for what it truly is, without assigning it weight or value, you can simply be with it. That presence allows you to move forward—not frantically, not recklessly, but with a disciplined plan and unwavering resolve. Courage isn't the absence of fear; it's looking fear in the eye, shaking its hand, and saying: *"Nice to meet you. You can come along for the ride if you want, but you need to get out of my way—I have work to do."*

Introducing Functional Training to a skeptical industry required every ounce of that Courage. Bravely moving forward with Clarity meant standing firm in my beliefs while facing pushback, embracing inevitable mistakes, and learning from them. I learned to see errors as bridges to growth and wisdom—if I had the Courage to cross them. At IHP, this isn't just theory—it's lived daily. Our PV², such as Responsibility, Courage, Integrity, and Resilience, built IHP and continue to drive it forward.

Lesson Box: Courage as a Foundational Principle

- **Courage in Action:** Facing fear and uncertainty head-on, whether in accepting financial support or pioneering new training methods.
- **Integrity Under Pressure:** Building trust by staying true to Principles, even when doubts arose.
- **Resilience Through Fear:** Understanding that Courage is not the absence of fear but the willingness to act honorably in its presence.
- **Adapting Through Errors:** Recognizing mistakes as bridges to knowledge and growth rather than obstacles.

IHP's Culture of Excellence: Building a Community of Growth

While practical methods and scientific knowledge were essential to our success, it's our culture that defines us. From the start, I wanted IHP to be more than just a training facility. Our first slogan—"IHP Is Where the Best Come to Train, and Professionals Come to Learn"—was accurate, but it didn't capture the spirit of the place. When people walk into IHP, they feel something. It's hard to explain at first, but sooner or later clients use words that go deeper than just "great workouts" or "amazing trainers." That feeling—that vibe—has become our true point of differentiation. As I always say...that's our JAM!

Over time, clients started calling IHP "the Church"—not in a religious context, but because something transformational happens inside its walls. Over the years, we've shaped bodies, sharpened minds, and forged spirits. It's no coincidence that our formal name includes "Institute" and our nickname is "the Church."

Lesson Box: IHP's Culture of Excellence

- **Culture defines success:** Methods and certifications are tools, but a strong, authentic culture is what sustains and elevates an organization.
- **Spirit matters:** A place that fosters transformation in body, mind, and spirit leaves an impact that words often can't describe.
- **Legacy starts with intention:** Building something special requires a commitment to values that endure over time.

Institute Meets Church

An institute and a church have much in common. Both are organized communities centered around shared Purpose, Values, and guiding Principles. Their goals may differ—education vs. spiritual growth—but the parallels are striking:

- Both cultivate Understanding, shape Behavior, and improve lives through Commitment and Sacrifice.
- Both create a community of like-minded individuals, fostering belonging, shared purpose, and camaraderie.

Principles Set in Stone

The culture at IHP is rooted in the PB² Principles that shaped my life and career: Responsibility, Facing Fear, Consistency, and Perseverance. These Principles shape Values like Accountability, Courage, Discipline, and

Fortitude. When lived out, they produce Virtues like Integrity, Bravery, Tenacity, and Resilience.

These aren't just words—they're the bedrock we build on. At IHP, we live the PB² system: train hard, think deeply, and hold each other to standards that don't move when life gets messy. High standards build trust, forge respect, and form the backbone of every strong team, family, and mission. I run IHP like I run my family: with laughter, Discipline, and unwavering love. Fun without standards leads to chaos, and standards without heart lead to burnout. The balance keeps the spirit alive.

Lesson Box: Principles Set in Stone

- **The basics build greatness:** Respect and Accountability create stability; when paired with clear expectations, they form the foundation for sustained growth
- **High standards never fail:** They foster trust, cultivate respect, and elevate every interaction, whether in a family, team, or business.
- **Balance is key:** Play while staying disciplined - that's the secret to working hard while having fun.

The Hard Truth About Standards

Don't think for a second that setting and holding high standards is easy. Explain a rule, a policy, or a law once, and you might think it's a wrap—but it never is. People are human. People are flawed. Anyone who's parented children or managed a group knows this universal truth: humans don't always follow the rules, even when they're crystal clear. Why not? A few of the big reasons:

- **They're not used to it.** Acting or thinking a new way takes time—it's a process. Habits don't change overnight.
- **They genuinely forget.** Let's be honest—it happens to the best of us.

- **They're testing you.** Some will test your Integrity and Commitment— do you really stand by your Principles?
- **They think they're above it.** A few feel rules don't apply to them— Principles don't care how anyone feels.

I wish I could offer you a magic trick, a secret formula, or some revolutionary method for making people stick to high standards, but here's the truth: it doesn't exist. Like most solutions, the answer is old, simple, and known to everyone: it starts at the top.

Show me a team that lacks unity, stability, or direction, and I'll show you a leader who isn't leading. I see it all the time—business owners with companies raking in cash, but their staff is miserable, turnover is through the roof, and nothing feels stable. It's a classic sign of missing standards. And want to know something even more telling? Their personal lives often mirror their businesses. They live undisciplined, scattered, and disconnected lives. Their relationships are shallow at best and insignificant at worst, their friendships few, and their money is used as a desperate Band-Aid for every crack in their foundation. They throw money at problems, thinking it'll buy PV^2, but it never will. Principles, Values, and Virtues can't be bought—they have to be built by adhering to them, by living a Principle-driven life.

Lesson Box: The Hard Truth About Standards

- **Standards require consistency:** Explaining a rule or policy once isn't enough; leadership demands constant reinforcement.
- **It starts at the top:** A team's unity, stability, and success reflect its leadership. Accountability begins with the leader.
- **Virtue can't be bought:** Integrity, Clarity, Execution and Resilience are built through consistent action—not money. They're the foundation of real leadership and every leader must role-model them to form a winning culture.

Leadership Is Human

Working with young people will test every ounce of your patience and leadership. You'll hear every strategy, reason, and excuse for not following standards—it's no different than raising children or leading a corporate team. That's why I try to lead by example and expect my staff to do the same. When I slack off, I admit it. I explain what happened, why it happened, and what I'm going to do to prevent it next time. My staff sees my imperfections and the hardships I go through, but they also see me fighting every day to get better. Leadership isn't about being perfect—it's about being authentically human. It's about navigating your flaws and your humanity while still setting and following the highest standards possible. At IHP, we don't expect perfection, but we demand CORRECTION (Accountability and Growth).

"In the absence of perfection, we aim for correction."

Lesson Box: Leadership Is Human

- **Lead with authenticity:** Great leaders show their humanity—admitting mistakes, striving for growth, and leading by example.
- **Perfection isn't required:** Leadership is about showing up and doing the work, not about being flawless.
- **In the absence of perfection, aim for correction:** Growth thrives in a culture of humility and accountability.

IHP—A Ship with a Destination

One of the key elements that sets IHP apart is our emphasis on respect and camaraderie. In many gyms, competition creates a cutthroat mentality. At IHP, we see each other differently. We are crewmates on a ship at sea, and the ship has one mission: to reach its destination port. For that to happen, every one of us must support and serve the ship. It's not just a place where we work or train; the ship is our professional home. It provides for us, supports our lives, and gives us purpose. Its health and stability are paramount to everyone's well-being and success.

There is no room for selfish egos that operate through the lens of "What's in it for me?" We are a team, a unit, a family. We cover for one another, support one another, and defend one another—no matter what. We clean the ship, we take care of the ship, we love the ship, and we defend the ship.

And this analogy doesn't stop at IHP. It applies to any group you're trying to lead—a family, a sports team, a corporate department, an armed forces unit, even a nation. A collaborative environment fosters genuine connections, allowing people to thrive without the burden of constant comparison or competition. At IHP, this sense of team and family extends beyond our staff. It includes our clients, our visitors, and anyone who sets foot inside our doors. Once you step into IHP, you are part of the crew, you are par of the ship, and if only for an hour - we are all heading to the same destination. Perhaps as simple as a better day. That mentality and spirit is why IHP is our church.

Lesson Box: IHP–A Ship with a Destination

- **Every role matters:** Success depends on the contribution of every individual. When everyone supports the mission, the ship reaches its destination.
- **Unity is strength:** Selfishness sinks the ship; teamwork lifts it. Prioritize the health and stability of the group over ego.
- **Your environment is your home:** A thriving team, family, or business starts with care, love, and defense of the space that supports you.

Spreading the Spirit

IHP's culture draws a beautifully diverse community of clients—from professional athletes chasing their peak to everyday individuals reclaiming their health. Everyone at IHP is treated with the same level of respect and dedication, no matter their background or fitness level. Inclusivity isn't just something we do—it's who we are. It's one of the cornerstones of our community, making IHP a place where anyone—whether a beginner or a seasoned athlete—can come to improve, learn, and grow.

Our approach to training is rigorous yet empowering. We don't just push limits; we help clients and trainers reach beyond the limits they thought they had. And this is only possible because of the unwavering support of the IHP community. The culture here doesn't just build stronger bodies—it sharpens minds, strengthens hearts, and inspires people to carry lessons of Resilience, Discipline, and Perseverance into every corner of their lives.

As word of IHP's unique training and professional culture spread, trainers from around the globe came to IHP to 'feel the vibe'. Our certifications became more than technical training—they became immersive journeys into the IHP way of life. Trainers left with more than skills; they left with a deeper connection to the timeless Principles that underpin effective and impactful training, as well as the human connection we know as 'coaching'.

The ripple effect of IHP's culture can be felt across the world. Thousands of trainers have carried this ethos back to their own gyms and training centers, spreading Discipline, Humility, and principled growth far beyond our walls.

IHP has become a beacon for those seeking more than physical transformation. It's a home for personal growth, and a deeper connection to the Principles of Humility, Responsibility, Sacrifice and Perseverance —a legacy built withing a culture of excellence.

Lesson Box: Spreading the Spirit

- **Inclusivity creates strength:** A culture that embraces everyone fosters both individual and collective growth.
- **Empowered people empower others:** By helping individuals grow, you create leaders who carry the spirit forward.
- **Culture creates ripples:** A strong ethos transcends its walls, impacting communities far beyond its origin.

"The right to your opinions is paid
by responsibility for their results."

~ JCS

06

WHEN OPINIONS FORM FAULTY PRINCIPLES

The Illusion of Opinion as Truth

One of the most common sayings is, "Everyone is entitled to their own opinion." That's true—but it doesn't mean everyone is entitled to good outcomes for crappy opinions. Opinions that run against self-evident truths never lead to the right results. For example, the PB² Principle of Facing Fear gives rise to the Value of Courage—the willingness to act despite fear. That, in turn, produces the Virtue of Bravery—taking meaningful action in the presence of fear. Here's how that aligns in PB² 'chain'—a Principle, its matching Value, and the Virtue that flows from them.

Principle: Facing Fear | **Value:** Courage | **Virtue:** Bravery

Now imagine someone forms the opinion that they should avoid anything that makes them nervous or uncertain. They justify it by saying they don't want stress because stress can cause physical ailments like anxiety, depression, or even cancer. They decide fear is a cue to retreat in order to maintain calmness. By rejecting the Principle of Facing Fear and prioritizing comfort, they condition themselves to avoid stress, pressure, and challenge. That opinion doesn't just change how they feel—it rewires how they behave. And eventually, it changes who they become—at best, an uninvolved and incompetent citizen; at worst, a coward. What would you think of that person? Would you want them in a leadership position of any kind? Would you hire that person or want then on your team? Would you even want them around you?

This chapter explores how faulty opinions can corrupt your Values and harden into misaligned Principles—and the havoc that creates in every area of life. When a person's Values (personal beliefs or preferences) become their Principles (guiding rules for behavior), but those Principles don't align with self-evident truths, conflict, dysfunction, and stagnation always follow.

Many people hide behind opinions, mistaking the right to have an opinion and the right to act on it as proof that the opinion is right. But a right does not necessarily entitle you to righteousness. When subjective Values replace universal truths, chaos is inevitable.

There is no clearer way to expose the problem with the idea that "everyone is entitled to their opinion" than the wave of senseless crimes we see today—the murder and assassination of innocent people. Setting aside those suffering from psychotic disorders, every killer held an opinion that, in their mind, justified their actions. Did they have the right to those opinions? Yes. Does that mean they had the right to act on them? No—the way they chose to act on them was against the law. Does society as a whole agree with those opinions? No. Do they deserve protection just because they are "opinions"? No. Why? Because although you are free to have any opinion, you are not free to act on any opinion without being responsible for the consequences. Freedom has a price—and it's Responsibility.

The freedom to have and express an opinion—in words or actions—carries the burden of being responsible for adhering to Principles, specifically the Principle of Responsibility. Responsibility is the currency one pays for the freedom to think, speak, and act while still being accepted by society. If you choose to voice or act on your opinion, you must exercise Accountability and act with Integrity. Only then will your opinion-based actions benefit you and those you touch.

Conversely, when opinion and action abandon Responsibility, reject Accountability, and ignore Integrity, consequences are inevitable—legal, social, and even spiritual. That's the cost of treating opinions like truths. And that's why, in the sections that follow, we'll pull back the curtain on some of the most destructive misalignments between opinions (Values) and Principles—how they play out in real life, and why ignoring the PB² system always leads to collapse.

Act on opinions that violate Principles and life will invoice you a bill that drains your life's bank account.

In the section that follows, we'll look at some common ways life invoices you when opinions don't line up with universal truths. Some carry a personal cost, others damage relationships, and some ripple out to create wider social impact. Each case will be explained using a PB² chain.

With 10 Principles, there are 10 chains. This '10 × 3 setup' keeps the PB² system organized, simple, clear, and practical.

Now, keep this in mind: while we try to simplify the complex topic of Principles, that doesn't mean the topic itself is simple. Principles, Values, and Virtues constantly interact, and a single bad choice can break several chains at once—multiplying the damage. The PB² system should be seen as a guide for clarity, not a rigid formula. It's a framework that helps you find your way back when you're lost or troubleshoot a situation when misalignment happens.

As we go through some of our misalignments we tried to organize things in an order of how misalignment can impact you. We start with consequences that are more of an internal and immediate in nature. We then work our way outward to illustrate how internal misalignments impact the external environment, which ends up impacting your place in the world. However, understand the when we say 'internal', this can mean internal to a person, but also internal to a group. Likewise, when we say external, this can mean another person, another group, and even another country. That's the beauty of Principles: THEY ARE UNIVERSAL and apply across the spectrum of humanity, community and social behavior.

We also want to mention that for the sake of simplicity we will apply the PB² system in a very general term, just so you can get a feel for how to use it. Suffice it to say, Humility is a form of awareness, and is probably that first step in the turning point in people's perspective and the initiation of change.

So we don't turn this into a 100-page chapter, let's make some generalities. If you don't come clean with Principles, this doesn't end up well—for a person, group, company, team, town, city, or country. Below are examples of how the breakdown of the PB² system can impact not only the individual but also the collective moral compass. One great way to see Principles is through the Butterfly Effect, a concept introduced by MIT mathematician and meteorologist Edward Lorenz. In his now-famous 1972 lecture, "Does the flap of a butterfly's wings in Brazil set off a tornado in Texas?" Lorenz explained how tiny changes in initial conditions can create massive, unpredictable consequences. In the same way, even the smallest compromise in

Principles can ripple outward—first unsettling the individual, then destabilizing families, organizations, and eventually entire nations—until the world begins to see and treat them according to the storms they have created. Let's start with generalities and the individual (butterfly's wings) and then work our way outward into immediate member of our group, then out to society and the world.

Personal Breakdown of the PB² System

Can't contemplate being wrong
Humility → Openness → Coachability

Refuse to accept ownership for your misaligned views
Responsibility → Accountability → Integrity

Ignore how your views are seen by others
Self-Reflection → Analysis → Clarity

Fail to take inventory of what has to change
Self-Awareness → Recognition → Objectivity

Don't create a plan for change.
Strategizing → Prioritization → Execution

Avoid paying your dues.
Sacrifice → Commitment → Selflessness

Unwilling to face failure or challenges
Facing Fear → Courage → Bravery

Absent participant - not 'showing up'
Consistency → Discipline → Tenacity

Quitting when things get hard.
Perseverance → Fortitude → Resilience

Start everything but finish nothing.
Finish Big → Dynamic Mastery → Integrated Reps

This personal break down will not only impact your ability to live in peace and move forward with minimal issues, but it will also impact how those in your immediate circle sees you. That could be your family, neighbors, co-workers, team, or your community.

The same thing happens in a group (Unit). If you are part of group, or lead a group, how the group adheres to Principles impacts the collective psychology of everyone in the group, but is also has a huge effect how the group is seen by the immediate community outside of that group. As the circle of impact gets larger, the impact on the interaction with the external community grows. If the group adopts **Principled Values** and **Virtuous** behavior then they are accepted and admired by the larger external community. If the group does not follow a Principled path, I don't care what their opinion is and how they rationalize their Values and Virtues, there will be dire consequences!! Life's invoice will come in the way of isolation, profiling, discrimination, and all negative words that end with "ism" and "phobia." Now let's take a wider lens to the PB² system breakdown at the group level. At this level all consequences fall on the hands of the leaders. Period, hard stop.

Group breakdown of the PB² system

Adoption of a fanatical ideology and incapable of collective introspection
Humility → Openness → Coachability

Refuse responsibility and defer to history, religion, or factors for justification
Responsibility → Accountability → Integrity

Ignore the preponderance of negative feedback and external resistance
Self-Reflection → Analysis → Clarity

Fail to consider possible solutions, suggestions, or negotiations
Self-Awareness → Recognition → Objectivity

Don't create a plan for change.
Strategizing → Prioritization → Execution

Not willing to pay the price for change
Sacrifice → **Commitment** → **Selflessness**

Fear the ugly things that change often requires
Facing Fear → **Courage** → **Bravery**

Absent of the staying power and time change usually requires
Consistency → **Discipline** → **Tenacity**

Can't withstand strong pockets of strong resistance
Perseverance → **Fortitude** → **Resilience**

Lack the will to see things to their end
Finish Big → **Dynamic Mastery** → **Integrated Reps**

Does some of this sound familiar? Do you have friends who act this way? Do you work in a place that resembles this? How about the news? Do you see groups, communities, and countries that fit the breakdown of the PB² system?

As you will see, the PB² system applies to the individual as well as the group. No matter how it's viewed, it's clear that change comes from within and starts with you—then it trickles from the top down.

Now, let's look more specifically at how the breakdown of Principles always starts within—then spreads outward. We'll illustrate common ways the PB² system breaks in various scenarios. With this information, you can prevent a collapse of your principled living and better understand and help others. That, in itself, spreads your love and impact through your family, friends, community, and the world.

1. Cognitive Dissonance—the Mental Scramble

Cognitive dissonance occurs when your thoughts, beliefs, or actions don't line up with each other. It creates that crappy feeling in your gut, the mental tension you can't shake. To get rid of it, the mind scrambles—change the belief, change the behavior, or make up a story so things seem to fit.

Example: Identity Rejection and Projection

An individual resents being born into a certain race, gender, or sexual identity. They mask it with smiles, success, and material goods, yet project that resentment toward others, even close members of their social group (e.g., family members and close friends). This creates dissonance between professed happiness and hidden resentment, between forgiveness and persecution. To cover up the misalignment, money and accomplishments are often used to show themselves and the world that nothing is wrong. This cover-up perpetuates the misalignment.

Example: Group Blame Displacement

A minority sector may feel anger toward either the identity they were born into or the conditions surrounding their community. Instead of examining internal shortcomings, they project blame onto outside sectors of society (e.g., institutions or other groups). This dissonance lets them claim victimhood while avoiding humility and responsibility. To cover up the misalignment, narratives of oppression and external persecution are emphasized to explain all struggles, showing the group and the world that nothing is wrong internally. This cover-up reinforces the misalignment.

Example: Individual Fitness & Diet Conflict

An individual claims that fitness and health are central to their life, yet repeatedly skips workouts, chooses unhealthy foods, drinks, and smokes. They present themselves as committed to fitness and health, but their actions expose the inconsistency of their claims. This creates dissonance between their stated Values and lived behavior, between self-control and indulgence. To cover up the misalignment, they display or show off "markers" of fitness—stylish gym clothes, supplements, the latest in anti-aging, or social media posts of them "living the healthy fit life"—to convince themselves and others that nothing is wrong. This cover-up sustains the misalignment.

Example: Group Fitness & Health Conflict

This occurs in many minority communities throughout the world, especially when government funding is sought to deliver fitness and health programs. A community asks for subsidies to promote fitness and healthy living, making that central to its identity. Yet, collectively it embraces habits of inactivity, poor nutrition, and convenience culture. Outwardly, the group projects pride in its Values, but its actual practices contradict them. This creates dissonance between the stated Values of fitness and health and the lived reality of neglect, between collective responsibility and collective indulgence. To cover up the misalignment, visible symbols—such as new facilities, slogans, or program announcements—are emphasized to signal progress, even while daily practices of sedentary living and indulgence remain unchanged. This cover-up prolongs the misalignment.

Lesson

No matter where you run, there you are! You can't run away from truth, from Principles. You can't make a lie disappear by explaining it away, hiding it under money, or even by career or economic success. Principles are the last thing that visit you right before you fall asleep. If everything is aligned—ahhh...*good sleep!* If there is unresolved conflict due to a misalignment of Principles—arrgh! No sleep. Stay grounded in Humility so you are at peace with being human. Be guided by Self-Reflection so you can bring Self-Awareness to bear. And always practice Clarity so you can enjoy many nights of good sleep and a life of peace.

Lesson Box: Cognitive Dissonance

- **Truth always surfaces:** No amount of money, success, or excuses can cover misaligned Principles—conflict shows up in your gut and in your sleep.
- **Humility clears the fog:** Honest Self-Reflection exposes where beliefs and actions clash, creating the opening for change.
- **Alignment restores peace:** When Responsibility and Integrity match behavior to Principles, the mind rests easy—ahhh...good sleep.

2. Lack of Accountability: When Responsibility Is Replaced by Excuses

Lack of accountability is the absence of the Principle of Responsibility. Making excuses, passing blame, and the default escape phrase "I don't know" are three common ways people manifest a lack of accountability. The fact that it takes Courage to be accountable is an example of how all PV² elements are intertwined. If you don't have the Courage to own or take control of a situation, you will either pass the buck to someone else or make excuses and shift blame for failures. Blame is only blame when nobody is willing to take Responsibility for a bad situation—otherwise, it's called credit. Everyone wants the credit for something good; nobody wants to be accountable when things get heavy.

Example: Blame (Corporate)

A project deadline is missed, and instead of owning their role, a manager says: "My team dropped the ball." "If upper management had given us more resources, this wouldn't have happened." "The client kept changing their mind—it's their fault we couldn't deliver." Here, the manager deflects Responsibility onto others instead of acknowledging their own leadership gaps in planning, resource allocation, or communication.

Example: Excuses (Marital Infidelity)

One spouse violates the marriage commitment by cheating. Instead of owning the immoral act, they attempt to justify it with excuses such as: "I travel too much, and I get lonely." "The kids take up all our time, and my spouse and I don't have enough private time." "I've always been attracted to [XYZ type], and my spouse just isn't like that." "It just happened—I couldn't help myself."

Each of these excuses shifts the Responsibility away from the choice to betray and onto circumstances, preferences, or external factors. This rejection of the PB² Principle of (Responsibility) corrodes (Accountability) and weakens (Integrity), leaving the relationship fractured.

Example: I Don't Know

Say an employee is in charge of a division of a company, like Janitorial Services. Every time anyone asks where cleaning supplies are (e.g., a mop, a pail, cleaning solution), the knee-jerk answer is, "I don't know." Even if they do know, they might add: "I don't know—try the back closet, I saw it there last." If this becomes consistent and patterned, researchers describe it as a learned helplessness cue—a conditioned way of saying: "Don't put responsibility on me; I don't want to be accountable."

Multi-level Breakdown

Sometimes, the breakdown happens at multiple levels simultaneously—excuses, blame, and the "I don't know" response all at once. Consider a married individual who, during a night out with friends, decides to visit an adult night-club. This action directly violates an agreement within their marriage. Instead of honoring that commitment, they follow their friends and later deflect blame with excuses like the following: "It wasn't my idea." "I wasn't driving." "There was nothing I could do." "I didn't even know where we were going until I was inside." "My friends pressured me by telling me I would be ruining the night for everyone." These excuses, blame-shifting, and pleading ignorance reject the PB² Principle of

Responsibility by refusing to say, "I chose this, and it's on me." Alternatives were available—taking an Uber, refusing to go inside, or simply walking away. By shifting blame, they abandon Accountability, weaken Integrity, and corrode the foundation of the relationship.

Lesson

Accountability is not about perfection—it's about ownership. Excuses, blame, and the reflexive "I don't know" all serve one purpose: to protect a fragile ego in the short term while destroying credibility in the long term. Whether in business, marriage, or any leadership role, the unwillingness to accept Responsibility erodes Accountability and eventually kills Integrity.

When you stand up and say, "This was my choice, and it's on me," you do more than own the moment—you strengthen the foundation of trust that every relationship, team, and organization is built on. The stronger your Accountability, the stronger your credibility. And credibility is the currency that buys loyalty, trust, and respect. So, **"Own the moment early and fully, and you'll never have to ask for trust or respect—they'll be given freely."**

Lesson Box: Lack of Accountability

- **Excuses erode trust:** Shifting blame or saying "I don't know" protects ego short-term but destroys credibility long-term.
- **Ownership builds strength:** Saying, "This was my choice, and it's on me," reinforces Responsibility, Accountability, and Integrity.
- **Credibility earns respect:** Own the moment early and fully, and trust and respect will follow freely.

---

3. Toxic Behaviors: When Misaligned Principles Enable Harm

Toxic behaviors emerge when Principles are abandoned and replaced by subjective Values—personal opinions that are not grounded in universal truths. Once detached from Principles, these opinions can be twisted into rationalizations that justify unethical, unfair, or unprofessional actions. This is the breeding ground for corruption, manipulation, and abuse. No excuse-making, blame-shifting, or clever storytelling can prevent misaligned Principles from producing damage. Left unchecked, they harm individuals, corrode trust, and destabilize communities, organizations, and relationships. For example, power without Principles breeds manipulation and abuse. Authority becomes a weapon instead of a responsibility, and leadership collapses into control, fear, and exploitation.

Example: Toxic Behavior (Corporate)

An employee feels insecure and jealous of what they see as a model manager. Instead of leveling up in competency and professional conduct, the jealous employee tries to lower the manager's Value by secretly spreading defamatory gossip. This misalignment of the PB² Principles erodes decency, respect, and Integrity. If such behavior is tolerated, it destroys the company's ability to build a culture rooted in Principles. Over time, more people adopt toxic patterns—proving the old truth: "One bad apple spoils the bunch."

Example: Toxic Behavior (Family)

A father grew up in a rough and unloving household, never learning the Principles needed for healthy parenting. Now, as he raises his own son, he loves him deeply but carries insecurity and fear that his son might 'do better' than he did. Instead of celebrating his son's growth, he withholds praise, never says he is proud, and resists passing down the wisdom his son needs to excel. This behavior is not as outwardly obvious as physical abuse, but its silent and insidious nature can be even more detrimental—eroding encouragement, stifling potential, and weakening the bond between father and son over time.

Example: Toxic Behavior (Country/Nation)

A nation's leadership may claim to Value justice, stability, and honor, yet secretly authorize the elimination of a political critic on foreign soil. The act is denied publicly, wrapped in excuses and misdirection, but the truth eventually emerges. On the surface, order and strength are projected; beneath, the silent and insidious abandonment of Responsibility, Accountability, and Integrity corrodes the nation's moral standing.

The same pattern unfolds domestically. A country celebrates freedom and unity as its core Values, yet within its own borders a reformer, activist, or civil rights leader is silenced through assassination. Leaders and citizens mourn publicly, but behind the grief lies a deeper truth: the misalignment of Principles that allowed hatred, fear, and ideology to outweigh Responsibility, Accountability, and Integrity. Because when Principles are misaligned, power and ideology replace truth as the highest Value, making silencing opposition through violence seem justified. History shows that when voices of truth are silenced—whether abroad or at home—the cost goes far beyond one life. It destabilizes communities, deepens divisions, and signals that might is Valued more than Principles.

Lesson

Toxic behavior is the inevitable result of misaligned Principles. Power without Responsibility, Accountability, and Integrity always rots from within. True leadership doesn't silence truth or shift blame—it owns the moment, lifts others, and builds trust that lasts. Anything less may look strong for a season, but collapse is guaranteed. Stay grounded in Humility, Responsibility, and Self-Reflection so power never corrupts. Adopt Accountability, Commitment, and Courage so blind spots don't become excuses. Lead with Integrity, Clarity, and Resilience so trust multiplies. Align with the PB² system—for it is the antidote to human toxicity.

Lesson Box: Toxic Behaviors

- **Broken promises fracture trust:** Sacrifice and Commitment are abandoned when ambition outranks love.
- **Hidden agendas destabilize:** When self-interest is masked as protection, Accountability and Integrity vanish, leading to disillusionment and division.
- **Opportunism poisons unity and strength:** Responsibility, Accountability, and Integrity are the only foundation strong enough to resist collapse.

4. Erosion of Trust: When Self-Interest Overrides Selflessness

Erosion of trust is the absence of the Principle of Sacrifice, the Value of Commitment, and the Virtue of Selflessness. Putting self-interest—personal gain, recognition, or comfort—above the collective good slowly corrodes the bonds that hold relationships, teams, and communities together. Broken promises, hidden agendas, and opportunistic actions are three common ways people manifest this erosion. The fact that it takes Discipline and Integrity to remain selfless is an example of how all PV^2 are intertwined. If you lack the Discipline to be willing to Sacrifice for others, you will eventually prioritize yourself at their expense. Trust is only trust when people are willing to put others first—otherwise, it's manipulation.

Everyone wants to be trusted when it benefits them;
few are willing to be trustworthy when it costs them something.

Example: Erosion of Trust (Family—Broken Promises)

A father promises his daughter he'll attend her school recital. She practices for weeks, counting on him to be there. On the night of the event, he doesn't show up—not because of an emergency, but because he stayed late at work to network for a promotion. When she asks why, he says, "I was working—I'll make it next time." The only problem is that this was not the first time or an isolated event. The repeated pattern of broken promises sends a clear message: her trust and time don't matter as much as his ambition. What do you think happens to that daughter's trust in her dad's word?

Example: Erosion of Trust (Government—Hidden Agendas)

Citizens place their trust in government to act in good faith—protecting borders, safeguarding health, managing resources responsibly, and upholding freedom of speech. But when policies are presented one way and later revealed to serve hidden agendas, the trust that holds a nation together begins to unravel.

In recent years, citizens have been told one story while another reality unfolded. Immigration policies were framed as compassion, yet underlying motives hinted at political advantage. Wars were justified in the name of security, while questions of profit and accountability lingered. Public health measures were promoted as science-driven, only to later reveal layers of politics and conflicting data. Even free speech—the cornerstone of democracy—was strained, as media narratives narrowed and government attempted to censor or pressure social media platforms into compliance.

The betrayal of trust here is profound: what was presented as leadership and protection is not often revealed as manipulation and control. Hidden agendas corrode Accountability and Integrity, leaving citizens disillusioned and communities divided. You see the social division today—it's all due to a lack of trust in our government.

Example: Erosion of Trust (Corporate—Opportunistic Actions)

A senior executive promises transparency and fairness in promotions, but quietly uses their position to advance personal allies while sidelining more qualified employees. On paper, the process looks fair; behind the scenes, decisions are driven by favoritism, politics, and self-interest. Those who are overlooked see the pattern clearly, and morale begins to collapse. What appears to be leadership is really manipulation. The opportunistic abuse of authority corrodes Accountability and Integrity, replacing merit with mistrust. Once trust in leadership is gone, teams disengage, performance deteriorates, and the culture fractures.

Lesson

Trust is earned through Sacrifice, Commitment, and Selflessness—and it unravels quickly when lack of commitment and selfishness take over. In families, broken promises send the message that ambition matters more than love and the welfare of family members. In government, hidden agendas turn protection into manipulation and give breath to social distrust and apathy. In corporations, opportunistic actions replace merit with favoritism.

The only way to restore trust is through Responsibility, reinforced by Accountability, and proven with Integrity. Responsibility doesn't dodge failure—it owns it. Accountability doesn't assign blame—it admits it openly. Integrity doesn't let failure fade—it corrects course through consistent action. Without these, trust collapses. With them, trust not only returns—it strengthens and builds a culture of excellence.

Lesson Box: Erosion of Trust

- **Broken promises fracture trust:** Sacrifice and Commitment are abandoned when ambition outranks love.
- **Hidden agendas destabilize nations:** When self-interest is masked as protection, Accountability and Integrity vanish, leading to disillusionment and division.
- **Opportunism poisons unity and strength:** Responsibility, Accountability, and Integrity are the only foundation strong enough to resist collapse.

5. Social Fragmentation: the great multiplier of descent

When misalignment spreads from one person to a community, then to an entire society, the result is the same—only the scale multiplies. When justice ignores truth and fairness, fear, bias, and abuse of power corrode trust and stability. Once a group adopts misaligned Values, the descent begins. Social fragmentation is never sudden. Even fast revolutions are fueled by decades of unseen erosion. It begins quietly, **one person at a time**, as Sacrifice is traded for comfort, Responsibility for excuses, and Integrity for convenience. Each compromise seems small, but together they unravel the moral fabric of the community.

Once erosion reaches critical mass, the group disintegrates under its own demoralization—no matter the justifications. People may blame politics, economics, or outside forces, but the true cause is internal: the decay of Principles. Without Responsibility, Accountability, and Integrity to anchor it, society cannot hold. What looks like sudden collapse is usually the slow harvest of neglected seeds of Principles.

Example: Toxic Fragmentation: (Family)

A family begins to fracture when parents lose track of their own Principles and allow misalignment to trickle downward. When children see parents consumed by careers or personal pursuits and neglecting family responsibilities—promises broken, meals abandoned, conversations replaced by screens—they will eventually start neglecting theirs. Over time, children feel disconnected, trust erodes, and resentment builds. The home becomes a house full of misaligned individuals rather than a family anchored in shared Principles. Fragmentation doesn't happen overnight—it grows quietly, one neglected moment at a time, and lives to propagate to future generations.

Example: Toxic Fragmentation: (Corporate)

A company abandons Integrity for profit and Responsibility for expediency. At first, it seems small—cutting corners on quality, hiding data from clients, rewarding political loyalty over competence. Employees notice. Those who once felt proud of their work and part of a team become disillusioned and apathetic. High-Value employees leave, unwilling to work in an environment not guided by Principles. The ones who stay either disengage—seeing the job as nothing more than a paycheck—or become absorbed into the toxic culture. Some may even slip from wasting time surfing the net during work hours into theft or sabotage. What began as isolated compromises grows into systemic decay. By the time customers lose trust and the brand collapses, the seeds of fragmentation were planted years earlier

Example: Toxic Fragmentation: (City-Country)

History is full of countries that were once thriving and modernizing their societies, only to decay into instability and chaos. Entire regions in the Middle East and South America have imploded under the misalignment of

Principles. Even within the U.S., once-charming cities have become places people avoid. Fragmentation begins one home at a time, but accelerates when leaders prioritize ideology and self-interest over Responsibility for the welfare of their citizens. Justice becomes inconsistent, institutions bend to politics, and people lose faith that their lives matter. At first, citizens adapt—choosing silence, cynicism, or retreat into smaller tribes or gangs. Over years, divisions deepen, trust evaporates, and unity is replaced by suspicion and hostility. What looks like a sudden collapse is really the end of a long rot, where neglected Principles finally buckle under accumulated decay.

Lesson

Over time, internal rot leads to the collapse of social structure—what we call toxic fragmentation. This decay always progresses from the inside out and usually reflects the character of its leaders (parents, executives, or politicians). As with all misalignments, when Responsibility is sacrificed for self-interest, moral chaos ensues. Accountability disappears, Integrity crumbles, and distrust takes over. Families fracture, companies corrode, and nations disintegrate.

The formula is clear: Responsibility + Accountability + Integrity = justice, trust, and unity. Abandon them, and collapse is guaranteed. Live them, and you create families that thrive, organizations that last, and societies that endure.

Lesson Box: Toxic Fragmentation

- **Families fracture without Responsibility**: When parents choose self-interest over Sacrifice, promises break and trust erodes.
- **Companies corrode without Accountability**: When leaders hide behind favoritism or expediency, employees disengage and cultures collapse.
- **Nations disintegrate without Integrity**: When truth is sacrificed for power, division deepens and societies fall.

---

6. Cultural Decline: Misaligned Principles Erode Group Dynamics

Often times, within a large geographical location, there are smaller cultures living. These smaller cultures can be different nationalities, religions, or ethnicities. I separated this from the social fragmentation because these subsets of society serve as a perfect test tube to see how a culture within a society behaves and what the outcome is. If you see a consistent pattern—it's not a coincidence. You will see many neighborhood, towns, cities, and even countries erode due to their misaligned cultural Values. Sometimes, the struggling culture operates within a successful society— so society can't be blamed. Sure, the culture has their opinions, sometime grounded in deep religious faith. But, religion and faith does not guarantee the adherence to Principles, especially if the interpretation of a Principle becomes fanatical. When religion, spiritual customs, and ethnic rituals do not fall within accepted, universal Principles, you will have dissent, revolt or defection.

Like social fragmentation, cultural decline rarely starts with a dramatic collapse—it begins with small lapses, short cuts, and excuses. Over time, inconsistency erodes unity, lowers standards, and eventually brings the entire culture down.

Example: Cultural Decline: (Religious)

Some religious systems push extreme rules that go way past universal Principles. Women are denied basic rights—education, freedom of dress, opportunities, even the right to choose who they date or marry. Gay people are punished brutally, sometimes even killed. Freedom to practice another religion is shut down. These restrictions are enforced as if they are protecting faith, but in reality, they are crushing Responsibility, Integrity, and Selflessness.

Over time, this doesn't just drive people away on the outside—it wears down the inside. Younger generations start asking hard questions. Women push for education and opportunity. Even people inside the culture see the damage and want change. That's the thing about misaligned Principles: it may look strong for a while, but sooner or later, the culture begins to crack from the inside out.

Example: Cultural Decline: (Racial)

Racial groups can decline when they let anger, blame, or entitlement replace Principles. Instead of building on Responsibility, Sacrifice, and Integrity, some groups fall into patterns of excuses, a victim mindset, or over-reliance on political favoritism. At first, it shows up as missed opportunities or a lack of unity. Over time, the pattern grows—families break down, education is neglected, and crime or dependency replaces growth.

Decline doesn't happen overnight. It builds slowly, one compromise at a time, until the group starts losing credibility from the inside out. Even when leaders try to justify it with slogans or blame outside forces, the truth is simple: no group can rise without aligning to universal Principles. Each group must take Responsibility for its own situation, and only then can things improve. It all comes back to auto-regulation and taking individual action for a Principle-driven life—because when Principles are ignored, decline is inevitable.

Example: Cultural Decline: (Ethnicity)

Ethnic groups can erode when pride in heritage drifts into isolation, resentment, or superiority. Instead of drawing strength from Principles, some groups cling to traditions in ways that block growth, or lean on grievances and favoritism to explain stagnation. At first, it shows up as lost opportunities to integrate, innovate, or build unity with others. Over time, the pattern grows—education lags, economic progress stalls, and the culture turns inward on itself.

This erosion doesn't happen overnight—it's a slow burn. It festers one compromise at a time, until the ethnic identity that once gave meaning and resilience becomes a crutch and a barrier to growth. Leaders may try to justify decline with cultural slogans or by blaming outside forces ("the system"), but the truth is simple: no ethnic group thrives without aligning to universal Principles. When they are ignored, decline is inevitable.

Lesson

Cultural decline is not the same as corruption or injustice (as in Section 2). It doesn't come from abuse of power, prejudice, or discrimination—it comes from internal neglect. This doesn't mean there is no injustice or discrimination in society; unfortunately, those are part of the human condition. But Principles always prevail, and the PB² system will always add strength to any group.

Success rarely disappears in one dramatic moment—it dies slowly, as families break promises, communities lean on excuses, or cultures cling to traditions and excuses that block growth. Over time, education slips, opportunities fade, and unity erodes from the inside out. The cure is simple: Principles. Choose what is necessary over what is convenient. Align with PB², and groups won't just endure—they'll thrive.

Lesson Box: Cultural Decline

- **Religions weaken without Responsibility:** When extreme rules crush Integrity and Selflessness, faith loses its strength from within.
- **Races falter without Sacrifice:** When excuses, victimhood, and entitlement replace Responsibility, families break down and growth stalls.
- **Ethnicities erode without Discipline:** When traditions and excuses harden into isolation and resentment, education lags and progress fades.

---

7. Isolation and Polarization: When Nobody Wants to Play

If the first six misalignments don't lead you to change, the world will put you in time-out. I don't care why you act the way you act or what your opinion is. Results tell the truth. Either your beliefs and behavior align with Principles—or they don't. When they don't, the invoice is discrimination—in its truest sense: being judged and separated by outcomes—and eventual isolation.

If you believe one way but act another, you live with dissonance. If you double down on misaligned Values, you'll see the same outcome everywhere: people keep their distance, opportunities dry up, and your circle shrinks. This pattern shows up in neighborhoods, towns, cities, and countries across the world.

Example: Isolation and Polarization: (Family)

Even in a strong, principled home, one member can drift. A teenager influenced by anger, poor coping skills, or negative peers begins to reject Responsibility. Excuses, blame, broken promises, and defiance erode trust. Over time, parents, siblings, and even extended family stop depending on the member who has drifted away from Principles. Invitations fade, communication becomes scarce, and eventually that family member feels 'cut out.'

A person adrift may believe they are being actively targeted for isolation by the family—but in truth, it is their lack of Principles that separates them. The family does nothing but hold true to Principles. It is the unprincipled member who isolates themselves. The truth is simple: when a family member abandons Principles, even a loving family will allow a drifter to create distance.

Principles are not up for negotiation—not even for love.

Isolation and Polarization: (Corporate and Market)

Many corporations have learned the hard way what happens when marketing directors push campaigns that elevate ideology over Principles. Most of society is tolerant of different communities and lifestyles. But when inclusion is forced as an agenda rather than lived as a Value, it collides with the worldview of the majority. The result? Organic rejection—boycotts, disengagement, and customers simply stop buying. No leader has to organize it; society reacts on its own

What looked like "progressive branding" quickly turns into isolation. Customers withdraw support, shareholders lose confidence, and brand loyalty evaporates. When corporations abandon Responsibility and Integrity in pursuit of trends or politics, they polarize themselves. Society responds by putting them in time-out—not with speeches, but with their wallets. The result is silence, distance, and lost sales.

Example: Isolation and Polarization: (Community)

Communities thrive when people live principled lives. But when any group moves into a space and acts without regard for universally accepted Values— ignoring laws and traditions, neglecting property, or embracing conduct unbecoming—they quickly become unwanted. Neighbors move out, businesses pull back, and property values drop. Over time, the wider community builds a kind of 'jail,' and that pocket of the community becomes a 'prisoner of isolation.'

History shows this pattern everywhere—whether in a neighborhood, a town, or even on a cruise ship at sea. When a group acts with disorder, disrespect, or aggression, others instinctively avoid them. It's not about race or ethnicity—it's about conduct. Act like a thug, and you'll be treated like one. Communities protect themselves by withdrawing from—or isolating—those who reject universal Principles.

Example: Isolation and Polarization: (Global)

Nations, like communities, thrive on shared Principles. But when large groups migrate into a country and refuse to assimilate—choosing instead to import Values and behaviors that clash with the host culture—they quickly create tension. Locals see disrespect for laws, traditions, and order, and the result is resentment, division, and eventual isolation. When the push-back comes, it's often labeled "discrimination," but in reality it is the natural consequence of misalignment with universal Principles.

This pattern repeats worldwide. Extremist factions within certain cultures have allowed violence, corruption, and radical ideologies to define them. Over time, these groups become unwanted wherever they go. Borders close, visas are denied, and entire populations are left without a safe place to call home. Why? Because they tolerated misaligned leadership and destructive behaviors within their own communities. A nation—or a people—that refuses to align with Responsibility, Accountability, and Integrity will always find itself isolated on the global stage.

Lesson

Isolation and polarization are not random—they are line items on life's invoice for misaligned Principles and faulty ideologies. In families, excuses and broken promises push even loved ones away. In corporations, forced agendas erode trust and trigger boycotts. In communities, disorder and disrespect drive neighbors out and businesses away. On the global stage, nations that reject Principles find themselves cut off from allies, trade, and opportunity.

By facilitating an organized plan to live a Principle-Driven life, the PB² system becomes an antidote to isolation. Responsibility builds trust, Accountability keeps relationships honest, and Integrity sustains unity. Live by Principles, and trust multiplies, unity strengthens, and doors open at every level—home, marketplace, community, and nation. Abandon them, and isolation is inevitable.

Lesson Box: Conflict and Polarization

- **Families drift without Responsibility:** Excuses and broken promises cut bonds, even in loving homes.
- **Corporations collapse without Integrity:** Forced agendas erode trust, trigger boycotts, and destroy loyalty.
- **Communities fracture without Accountability:** Disorder and disrespect drive neighbors out and leave pockets isolated.
- **Nations disintegrate without Principles:** When cultures refuse alignment, borders close and isolation follows.

Conclusion: The Cost of Misalignment

Across the seven breakdowns we covered in this chapter, the pattern is clear: when opinions drift from universal Principles, collapse and separation follow. You may have the right to your opinion, but you don't have the right to self-evident truths. Principles always prevail—whether you acknowledge them or not, the majority of humanity does. Pride, denial, and ignorance only make the consequences of misalignment hit harder. Alignment isn't optional—your survival depends on it. And when you do fall out of alignment, as we all do, the PB² system can offer a way back to alignment. The path is simple, but never easy.

Parachute Lesson: How to Rebuild When You Fall out of Alignment

I wish that reading this book could align your life so closely with Principles that you'd never fall out of step. But that's not real life. Everyone stumbles. Everyone falls from grace—usually more than once. And the truth is, our biggest lessons often come from those falls. That's why I taught my children a simple '1–2–3' sequence: a ripcord you can pull to open a safety parachute when you've blown it and find yourself out of alignment.

1. **Admit it → Responsibility**

   Own what you did on the spot, without excuses.

2. **Express it → Accountability**

   Offer a genuine apology—through words, but even more through actions—that prove you understand the consequences of your actions.

3. **Change it → Integrity**

   This is the most important step. Apologies without behavioral change mean nothing. In fact, they can be insulting. But change, even without words, speaks volumes. People believe what you do far more than what you say.

When your words and actions line up—that's Integrity in its purest form. This is the lesson I drilled into my kids and the one I work to live by myself. May it serve you the same way—in those moments when you need a parachute to land softly, reset, and get back into alignment with Principles.

Lesson Box: The Parachute

- **Responsibility:** Admit it. Own it.
- **Accountability:** Express it. Show it.
- **Integrity:** Change it. Prove it.

07

"*To live life aware is
the highest form of learning.*"

~ JCS

THE MERGER
OF EXPERIENCES IS
HUMAN EVOLUTION

In this chapter we cover the process of merging and how it adds productivity with less effort. I share how merging impacted my career and how it influences physical training. I could have used other examples, but the coach in me couldn't resist using fitness—especially for those of you who work out and may have heard of Functional Training. I slipped in the kind of examples, wordage, and explanations we would give a client at IHP. Now you get a feel for what it's like to walk into IHP and hear firsthand what we do and why it works so well. Enjoy.

Life as a Mosaic—Merging Experiences

Life is very much like a mosaic—a perfect example of how the whole is greater than the sum of its parts.

A mosaic is composed of small, individual pieces called tesserae, which can be made from various materials, including:

- **Stone**—Marble, granite, or limestone.
- **Glass**— Colored glass, often used in Byzantine mosaics.
- **Ceramic**—Glazed or unglazed tiles.
- **Porcelain**—Smooth and durable, ideal for intricate details.
- **Metal**—Gold, silver, or bronze for striking highlights.
- **Shell**—Mother-of-pearl or other iridescent elements.
- **Pebbles**—Used in ancient and rustic designs.

These tesserae are then embedded into different surfaces, such as:

- **Mortar or Cement**—For floors and outdoor mosaics.
- **Adhesive on Mesh or Wood**—For modern, portable mosaics.
- **Plaster or Concrete**—For architectural masterpieces.

At first glance, each **tessera** seems **insignificant**—just a fragmented piece of stone or glass. But in the hands of an artist, **these scattered fragments merge into breathtaking masterpieces**, telling stories, forming patterns, and transforming mere materials into works of art. Now, imagine that mosaic represents your life:

- **The Mosaic (Life):** The grand masterpiece of your existence, formed over time.
- **The Tesserae (Experiences):** The individual moments—joys, struggles, relationships, and achievements—that shape you.
- **The Surface and Binding Medium (Principles, Values, and Virtues):** The foundation that holds everything together, giving structure, meaning, and coherence to your beliefs and actions.

Each experience in life is a tessera—some smooth, some jagged, some brilliant, some dull. Individually, they may seem trivial. But step back, and their meaning is revealed only when seen as a whole.

Every single piece matters. Change just one tessera, and the entire mosaic shifts. Every challenge, every triumph, every failure is a distinct piece—so powerful that it can reshape the entire landscape of your life.

So, what makes a mosaic a masterpiece?
What gives it its beauty, coherence, and depth?

The Merger

At its core, merging—bringing together diverse elements to create something better, more efficient, and more valuable—is the very essence of human evolution. By merging experiences, we develop a broader, more resilient perspective, which is why we grow wiser over time.

Each new challenge or opportunity doesn't replace what came before—it integrates with it. The key to this integration is using universal principles to process different experiences, fueling personal growth and collective progress in any field.

The Evolution of Training: My Journey of Merging Disciplines

In the 1990s, the world of performance training and strength training was highly segmented:

- **Bodybuilders** trained for size, sculpting physiques like statues.
- **Powerlifters** obsessed over maximal strength, measuring success in pounds lifted.
- **Olympic lifters** trained for explosive power, perfecting snatch and clean and jerk.
- **Rehabilitation specialists** focused strictly on post-injury recovery.
- **Mind-body disciplines** like Pilates and yoga stayed in their own lanes.

A few of us stood in the middle—watching all sides, seeing what many could not. My foundation began in martial arts, and I later layered on bodybuilding, powerlifting, and Olympic weightlifting. Just as I studied the systems of martial arts pioneers, I also studied the methods of the strength and bodybuilding legends. In college and early in my career, I was deeply influenced by functional training pioneers like Gary Gray and Vern Gambetta, who were reshaping how athletes trained.

From childhood, I had one foot in movement and the other in strength. That gave me a perspective few in either camp fully understood: Strength without movement is limited. Movement without strength is weak. The answer wasn't one or the other—it was both. This was the same principle Bruce Lee brought to martial arts. Instead of being confined to one rigid style, he took the best from each, creating Jeet Kune Do—a "systemless system" built on efficiency and effectiveness. What Bruce Lee did for martial arts in the 1970s became my mission in personal training in the late 1990s and early 2000s: to merge bodybuilding, powerlifting, speed, agility, quickness, yoga, rehabilitation techniques, and functional training into one seamless hybrid system.

The IHP Hybrid Training System Was Born.

The training system we created at IHP is a mosaic. It wasn't about choosing one method—it was about building a system, creating a masterpiece, that took individual disciplines and combined them into something greater than the sum of each separate discipline. By merging these disciplines, we created one of the most complete training methodologies in the world—one that continues to evolve, adapt, and push the limits of human performance.

Lesson Box: Merging for Growth

- Life's journey is about merging experiences to build growth and resilience.
- Each lesson layers onto the last, creating wisdom through integration.
- Practicing the principle of merging drives both personal and collective evolution.

A Range of Skills: The Power of Range

The value of **merging experiences** extends beyond personal growth—it is also a fundamental driver of exceptional performance and achievement. In his book Range, David Epstein presents compelling evidence that broad experiences often lead to superior outcomes in specialized fields. Epstein contrasts the developmental paths of two world-class athletes: **Tiger Woods and Roger Federer.** Woods exemplifies early specialization, dedicating thousands of hours to a single domain to achieve mastery. Federer, on the other hand, played multiple sports before committing to tennis. This broader athletic foundation gave him a wider range of biomotor skills, sharper visual processing, and greater adaptability. His success demonstrates that diverse experiences can enhance specialization rather than hinder it.

This principle extends far beyond sports. Organizations like **NASA** assemble think tanks by merging experts from multiple disciplines—AI, aeronautics, physics, and policy—to accelerate innovation. The same concept applies to individuals. By integrating diverse skills and experiences, a person becomes more adaptable, resourceful, and capable of excelling in any pursuit.

How Hybrid Training Proves the Power of Range

At IHP, I've seen the power of merging disciplines firsthand for more than two decades. Clients often arrive from traditional training backgrounds— competitive athletes shaped by bodybuilding, powerlifting, or Olympic lifting, or general fitness enthusiasts raised on machine-based workouts in big-box gyms. They expect progress to come from lifting heavier, log- ging more hours, and isolating muscles—because that's what they were taught. When we introduce them to Hybrid Training, those expectations get challenged. By merging traditional strength work with Functional Training and mobility, they discover a different kind of transformation:

- They get stronger while lifting less.
- They move better with less wear and tear on their body.
- They become more powerful and efficient without excessive weight training.

The surprise doesn't last long once they understand the principle: strength isn't only about how much force a muscle can generate—it's about how efficiently the body coordinates movement. A strong but inefficient body is like a high-performance car without a steering wheel—you can't use the power you can't direct.

By layering Functional Training into traditional strength programs, we teach the body to synchronize and coordinate muscle systems and develop neuromuscular efficiency. The result isn't bigger lifts necessarily —it's faster speed, sharper agility, and explosive power. Gains don't always come from bigger muscles, but from coordinated muscle systems.

Strength + Coordination = Higher Performance with Less Effort

That's the power of merging disciplines. By combining traditional training with Functional Training, the whole body becomes greater than the sum of its parts.

Lesson Box: The Power of Range

- Broad experiences enhance performance in specialized domains.
- Merging diverse skills creates adaptability and innovation.
- Combining disciplines often leads to better results than early specialization alone.

Principles Cross Boundaries

The principle of merging isn't confined to fitness or sports. It applies everywhere—in relationships, business, education, and personal decision-making. Universal principles cut across professions, cultures, and life experiences. When applied correctly, they create synergy, allowing you to do more with less. At IHP, I've seen how merging training disciplines unlocks superior performance. But this principle doesn't stop at fitness—it applies to every corner of life.

Merging Households: The Smartest Decision a Family Can Make

Take a common scenario: two single parents decide to build a future together. One has one child, the other has two. They live in separate homes in the same city, each carrying the full load of rent, utilities, groceries, childcare, and transportation. Their combined cost of living? Roughly $12,000 per month. But by merging households, they eliminate major duplications—housing, food, babysitting, gas, and other expenses. The payoff is huge: a higher quality of life, less financial stress, more resources, and better opportunities for their kids. For this couple, merging delivers:

- **More Financial Stability:** They save money that can be invested in the kids' education, better food, or experiences.
- **More Time & Convenience:** With shared responsibilities, they reduce stress and create more family time.
- **A Stronger, More United Family:** By merging traditions, values, and routines, they create a stronger support system.

This mirrors what happens in business mergers, where two companies combine resources to boost efficiency, cut waste, and expand opportunities. The same principle that drives athletic training drives life: when systems work together instead of separately, the results multiply, mostly through efficiency.

Lesson Box: Principles that Transcend

- Merging creates synergy and systems work together resulting in exponential output and production
- Efficiency combines efforts, frees up resources and cuts waste, opening up space for growth, opportunity, and stability
- The universal principle of merging applies to all genres; fitness, family, or business, turning separate parts into a stronger whole.

Merging Skill Sets

For most of my career, my focus was coaching, personal training, and education. Naturally, I gravitated toward teaching what I knew best—training clients and lecturing worldwide. The business side of IHP was never my primary focus. I saw it as an extension of my work, not as a business that needed my leadership.

As my international lecturing and educational enterprises took off, I dedicated more time to international consulting and less time to IHP. I treated IHP like my office—a very expensive office. But a 7,200-square-foot facility with 11–15 employees doesn't run itself. The more money IHP needed, the more I traveled to generate income. Instead of fixing the root issue, I threw money at the problem and ignored the reality of running a business.

Then, COVID hit.

Within one month, my entire educational and international business vanished. Hundreds of thousands of dollars disappeared overnight. I had no choice but to face the truth—I had neglected the Principle of Responsibility in regards to IHP. The lesson was clear: you can't throw money at a lack of Responsibility. Sooner or later, the jig is up. The solution? Merge my skills, take ownership, and rebuild IHP from within.

1. **Pivot to Online Business:** We focused on online equipment sales, home workout programs, and digital certifications. Trainers needed and wanted education, and we created virtual seminars to meet that demand.
2. **Team Leadership & Administration:** My son, Rio, and I took full ownership of IHP—learning bookkeeping, sales, and staff training while building a stronger team culture. IHP actually taught us what culture really was.
3. **Hands-On Leadership:** We personally took on 40+ hours of training per week, cutting payroll costs while leading by example on the gym floor.

One thing I noticed during this time was that when you merge one group of people into a larger group, not only does the group itself become bigger and stronger, but each individual within it grows stronger too. The same applies to skills. When we merged all of our skills together at IHP, we became more familiar with each because we had to use them more often. We also saw how every skill related to the others, as well as to the bigger picture of the business. That makes perfect sense in hindsight, but it's not always obvious before the merger.

The biggest impact merging had on IHP wasn't just financial recovery—it was cultural transformation. The online business developed a new look and flow. Rio and I learned processes we had never dealt with before—licensing, taxes, payroll, retirement funds, insurance, and more. When we returned to full-time training, we came back as better trainers, which elevated our methods. Our constant presence on the floor created an energy shift that raised accountability and professionalism. That rubbed off on younger trainers, and clients immediately noticed the stronger vibe in the gym. The merging of IHP's skill sets was the key to our survival after COVID—and the reason for our strong position in the community 25 years later.

Lesson Box: Ignoring Principles Has Consequences

- Ignoring a principle won't make it disappear—it will come back with consequences.
- Throwing money at a problem never solves an issue rooted in responsibility.
- Merging skills, leadership, and direct involvement creates lasting success.

Wisdom isn't just knowledge—it's the ability to apply principles in real-time over various genres. True wisdom emerges when experience forces you to merge old ways with new approaches, and realize the synergy that exists outside of a single domain (your small world). In simple words, merging different skill sets into your life allows you to become a more complete version of yourself.

Merging Principles

If you think merging companies, people and skill sets is powerful, you will realize merging Principles is the juggernaut of personal evolution. It's akin to merging a few soldiers on a battlefield versus merging the world's armies on the global stage. Why? For the same reason we keep mentioning: **PRINCIPLES APPLY TO EVERYTHING.** *Master Principles, and you master life.*

We are all born with different aptitudes and gravitate to different skill sets. Some of us are good at math and gravitate toward engineering, others are more literal and move toward the literary arts, while others have a natural knack for the sciences and pursue medical professions.

As we alluded to during our discussion of personality and character, we are born with a certain personality—how we are wired to think, feel, and behave. It's our natural style of interaction with the world. In contrast, character is what we create through choices, upbringing, and Principles. It reflects our moral compass and how we decide to act.

In essence, your character becomes the way your aptitudes and personality interpret and apply Principles. And here's where the AHA moment comes: all three are pliable. As your awareness, understanding, and implementation of the PB² system increase, so does your ability to live a Principle-driven life. Therefore, if you see Principles as separate skills shaped by both genetics and upbringing, then consistently honing those skills—and merging them through the PB² system—can transform you just as it transforms organizations worldwide.

IHP Example—Clients

Let's say a shy young man is timid by nature and raised in a noncom- petitive, non-aggressive family. His character may align with Principles like Humility, Responsibility, Self-Reflection, Self-Awareness, and even Strategizing. We've all met kids like this—sweet, respectful, considerate, and bright—but they struggle in life because they weren't raised with the "action" Principles that require a more aggressive energy: Sacrifice, Facing Fear, Consistency, Perseverance, and Finish Big.

You wouldn't believe how many parents bring kids like this into IHP. I can spot them before they even walk through the door—the body language gives them away, and their look confirms it. Their whole presentation screams "gardener in a garden," and their parents don't want them to become "a gardener in a war" when they step into the real world. They see IHP as a place that lives by Principles, capable of teaching all of them—especially the ones that build tenacity.

Most of these kids love boxing. It gives them controlled aggression and the confidence they're missing. Our training is demanding, and the intensity allows them to experience Sacrifice, Facing Fear, and Perseverance. Over time, Consistency gets lived out in real practice within our IHP environment. At IHP, exercise is our prayer. Intense efforts mimic the fear often encountered in real life, and our coaching teaches the very Principles found in the PB² system to push through our workouts. Not only does the kid become a more competent young man in his physicality, he is also coached on how that applies to the outside world. The parents LOVE this aspect of IHP—our church.

Here's the key: these kids' natural aptitudes and personalities give them a way to process thoughts and experiences. As they're exposed to new Principles, they use their natural wiring to make sense of them. They learn how the new Principles connect with the old ones. This happens with the help of mentors (their parents and our trainers), a stimulus that mimics life's challenges (training itself), and the confidence that comes from knowing they can defend themselves (boxing).

They start by leaning on the Principles that come naturally, and from there, they expand. Their PB² system becomes more complete as each new Principle merges with the ones already in place. Over time, their PV² framework grows more synergistic. This is how IHP helps everyone who walks in the door move toward a more Principle-driven life.

This is why I always remind my trainers: part of their job is helping parents raise their kids. Parents are always looking for 'third-party endorsements' of the Principles they're already trying to instill. If a parent tells a boy to eat vegetables and lean meats, nothing happens—doughnuts remain the food of choice. But if, in the middle of training, as the kid feels stronger, more confident, and more hopeful about his future, a trainer they look up to says the same thing—suddenly, vegetables and lean meats make sense. The same goes for doing homework, showing respect, or staying out of trouble. Every one of these behaviors (Virtues) connects to Values, and those Values connect back to Principles. That's the connection we make at IHP. That's how we teach the merging of Principles through the fitness journey. Pretty cool, right?

IHP Example—Corporate

We see the merging of Principles at the corporate level at IHP as well. New employees come to us in their 20s—great people. I always say, just to work at IHP, "You have to have good bones." At the very least, Humility and Responsibility. We can work on the rest.

I'm willing to guess some of these kids don't even make their beds when they're first employed. At first, many don't understand what being on time means. They don't clean their stations. They don't fill out their charts. They don't turn their payroll in on time, and they don't grasp the importance of a proper uniform—just to name a few of our pet peeves.

Whether they were never taught or they refused to learn doesn't matter to me. What matters is that they are not doing it now. At the start, all I demand is effort. The effort to be humble enough to know they need to evolve—that they need to change. I also want effort in taking Responsibility for their shortcomings and recognizing how those shortcomings are not serving them—or IHP. Then, I expect repeated attempts at correction and improvement.

In other words, practice adding principled behavior to their life (merge) and caring about the place that's nurturing them (Selflessness). As they add new Virtues (behavior), they better understand their corresponding Values (beliefs), and then they learn how they align with universal truths (Principles). That merge organizes more Principles, and they become competent, responsible, and respectful adults—worthy of respect from their community. Every single employee who has left IHP has said something like this: "*I will never be the same again. This place has taught me more about life than fitness—thank you. I will forever be aware and pick up the piece of paper.*"

Conclusion: The Merging Experience

Traditionally, we think of merger in the context of business—companies combining resources to maximize efficiency. But the universal principle of merging is far broader. At its core, merging is about combining models, methods, and experiences. Whether in training, business, parenting, or leadership, the act of merging creates a synergistic effect, where the whole becomes greater than the sum of its parts.

So ask yourself: "What experiences have I integrated into my decision-making process? Can I spot how a person, a family, a sports team, or a business became stronger by combining resources, skills, systems, and wisdom that were once separate?" That's the essence of growth, adaptation, and evolution. Merging isn't just about efficiency—it's about creating something new, something greater, and something transformative.

If you see PV² as a set of skills (Virtues) performed out of a set of beliefs (Values), guided by ideals (Principles), then you've got your models, methods, and experiences of merging right there. When you use the PB² system to merge PV², there is no way your life doesn't improve.

"A great leader doesn't aim to do great things; he aims to embody greatness."

~ JCS

08

HARD-WON LESSONS OF LIFE AND LEADERSHIP

Adversity doesn't always knock—sometimes, it kicks down the door unannounced. In those moments, it's not what you know but what you do that counts, and what you do is usually a function of who you are. Needless to say, when the rubber hits the road, you actions are what determine whether you rise or fall, and at time whether you live or die.

Life teaches lessons in ways that no book, seminar, or mentor can fully capture. Experience is the ultimate teacher, and the most profound insights are often forged in the darkest of times.

In this chapter, I'll share challenges that shaped me as a person, professional, and industry leader. We'll explore how adversity deepens understanding and strengthens commitment to Principles. By the end, I hope you'll see that the toughest challenges yield the deepest knowledge. And when you merge the lessons from your greatest struggles, wisdom emerges. That's why the fundamental Principle chain needed to respond when fear is present is:

- **Facing Fear** (the foundational **Principle** that confronts fear)
- **Courage** (the **Value** tied to Facing Fear)
- **Bravery** (the **Virtue** that puts courage into action)

This chain is the 'just do it' action chain from the old Nike commercial. Of course other traits like respect, dedication or wisdom may emerge as relational expressions, but they are not part of this chain, they are the result of this and other chains.

Growth Through Adversity: Catalysts for Growth

If there's one thing life has taught me, it's that growth rarely comes from comfort. Adversity has been my greatest teacher, and I believe this is true for all of us. When a challenge stops us dead in our tracks, we're forced to step outside our comfort zone. The very things that once brought us success are suddenly unavailable, and we must find new solutions. The strategies we develop to overcome obstacles become part of our experience and skillset, refining our knowledge until it transforms into wisdom. This is a universal Principle—one we all recognize instinctively. Our culture is filled with expressions that reinforce this truth:

- **Whatever does not kill you makes you stronger.**
- **Absence makes the heart grow fonder.**
- **Steel forges steel.**
- **No pain, no gain.**

Most people accept that adversity builds strength, but few can articulate why—or apply this principle intentionally. If you don't understand why something works, how can you fully embrace it and use it with purpose? Here's a breakdown of the principle behind the phrase "whatever does not kill you makes you stronger."

The ABCs of Facing Fear (Confronting Adversity)

The Principle of Facing Fear aligns with Newton's Third Law of Motion: for every action, there is an equal and opposite reaction. When life applies the action or 'force' of adversity, our reaction can be adaptation, growth, and strength. Just as a physical object pushed by force responds in kind, human beings pushed by challenges have the opportunity to respond with proportional transformation. Without the action of adversity, there is no reaction of growth. Because it is objective and timeless, the Principle of Facing Fear applies across cultures, industries, disciplines, and generations. It forms a foundational framework for personal growth and evolution.

At the Value level, Courage represents the belief that fear must be confronted in order to transcend beyond the limitations it creates. It is a mindset—a choice to act when most don't.

Finally, the Virtue of Bravery puts Courage into action. It is the consistent willingness to confront fear through decisive behavior. Persistence transforms belief into behavior, making Bravery a lived experience that others recognize and respect.

Lesson Box: Facing Fear

- **Principle: Facing Fear** (often expressed as Confronting Adversity)—Growth comes from facing and overcoming challenges.
- **Value: Courage**—The belief and commitment to act despite fear.
- **Virtue: Bravery**—Consistent action that confronts fear in real situations. Other traits like respect, dedication, and wisdom may emerge as relational expressions, but they are not part of this triad.

By organizing Facing Fear as the Principle, Courage as the Value, and Bravery as the Virtue, we create a clear framework that captures the natural progression from:

1. **Universal Truth (Principle):** What governs the world
2. **Personal Belief (Value):** What you choose to embrace
3. **Actionable Trait (Virtue):** What you consistently live by

Together, these concepts offer a powerful lens through which to understand, embrace, and grow through those times when you feel like the world is against you, when it seems you can't catch a break, or when life throws you a 100 mph fastball. During these moments of despair, the monsters in your head start whispering, "You can't do it." The Santana song "Put Your Lights On" (written by Everlast, performed by Santana featuring Everlast on the album Supernatural) expresses how the Value of Courage works through the presence of an angel:

"...there's a monster living under my bed
Whispering in my ear.
There's an angel, with a hand on my head
She say I've got nothing to fear..."

Lyrics by Everlast, ©Sony/ATV Music Publishing LLC

The principles of growth through adversity aren't just theoretical—they manifest in real, tangible ways, and can be recounted in the annals of human history. When one thinks of Facing Fear, Courage, and Bravery, many war stories come to mind—from the famous stand of the 300 Spartans during the Battle of Thermopylae (480 BCE) to D-Day during the Normandy invasion (June 6, 1944). It's easy to understand how fear could take over in the face of certain death. Events like these require a level of Courage most of us will never have to contemplate, and we are grateful for that. For that reason, I always thank ALL of the members of our military and law enforcement for being the ones who choose to contemplate such a destiny so we don't have to.

Now, there are other instances in life we see every day that require a different type of Courage and Bravery—for instance, the story of an immigrant father...

Adversity in Action: An Immigrant Father's Story

Imagine a young family immigrating to the U.S., starting from nothing. With limited funds, the father moves his family into a cramped one-bedroom apartment in a rough neighborhood. They endure long walks through dangerous streets, face harsh weather, and rely on public transportation to get by. Yet, despite these hardships, the father's resilience shines through. He juggles two jobs to keep food on the table and spends three nights a week at vocational school, determined to build a better future as an electrician. Through years of Perseverance, he rises to become an electrician and eventually the foreman of a six-man crew. With his improved financial situation, he moves his family to a safer neighborhood, upgrading to a three-bedroom apartment and purchasing two modest vehicles. This progress not only provides his family with greater stability but also serves as a testament to the power of persistence and the Principles of Sacrifice, Facing Fear, and Perseverance. Now, consider this father's new standard of living:

- He no longer fears for his family's safety in a high-crime area.
- His family is no longer crammed into a small, uncomfortable space.
- They no longer depend on public transportation, gaining freedom and security.

As progress is made, PV² don't change—the circumstances under which it operates does. Take the Facing Fear chain of the PB² system as an example. Just because you no longer need to brave crime-ridden streets on your way to work doesn't mean you won't need to Face Fear in life again. As long as you are alive, there will always be challenges that require Courage and Bravery—from facing a disease like cancer to risking your savings on a new business.

The same applies to the Sacrifice and Consistency chains. Just because you endured the persistent discomfort of staying in a cramped apartment while you increased your financial capacity to move to a bigger and safer place does not mean you won't need to 'go without' for a prolonged period of time to reach a goal. PV² are forever; only the stakes and circumstances change.

As time passes, your application of PV² and the PB² system becomes more sophisticated. It's no different than playing baseball. The game and rules don't change (PB²) from Little League to the pro leagues. The core skills don't change either—you still have to hit, catch, and throw (PV²). What does change over time? The size of the field and the speed of the game. In Little League, you're dealing with pitches at 40–70 mph. In the pros, it's 80–100 mph.

The rules never change—only the level of play does.

Translate that to life and you can see how a problem, a threat, or a sacrifice to a 10-year-old can't be compared in absolute magnitude to what is a problem, a threat, or a sacrifice to a 50-year-old. Yet, the relative magnitudes can be the same. A level 9 problem to a 10-year-old may be losing a $10 bill; to a 50-year-old it may be a $50,000 lawsuit. To overcome the challenge, both have to exercise level 9 PV².

A person's ability to fundamentally understand the universality and application of PV² is directly proportional to their evolutionary bandwidth. This phrase means you will intellectually evolve to the extent you can identify, organize, and live by a systematized order of PV². It's not easy, it is a work in progress, and that's why I decided to develop the PB² system. It is my attempt to identify, organize, and systematize PV² into a workable format. The living part—that's on you.

Lesson Box: The Consistency of PV²

- Principles, Values, and Virtues remain unchanging across all of life; it is the circumstances under which they exist that change.
- The level of application of a system, such as the PB² system, becomes more sophisticated over time.
- A person's evolution is directly dependent on their ability to apply PV² consistently throughout life.

The Modern Conundrum of Comfort vs. Growth

In our pursuit of comfort and progress, we often overlook a critical reality: Avoiding adversity robs us of the growth that hardships potentiate. This is where modern convenience culture faces a unique challenge.

I've encountered younger individuals who have never faced real adversity—in my town, they're often called 'silver spooners'. When you talk to them, you quickly notice what's missing:

- They lack the stories, experiences, and struggles that shaped their parents and grandparents.
- Their conversations center on shallow values—material possessions, social media status, and entitlement.

- They have never developed the character that life's challenges cultivate— they are not intimately familiar with the Principles of Humility,
Sacrifice, or Perseverance.

The value that our modern culture has place on convenience has exac-
erbated this issue. From on-demand services to apps that eliminate effort,
we've created a world where discomfort and hardship are actively avoided.
While technological progress has undeniably improved our quality of life, it
has also dulled our ability to confront and overcome challenges. Yet, struggle,
problem-solving, and tenacity are seeds for growth—and increasingly sacrificed at the altar of convenience and comfort. The dilemma before us is this:

**How do we embrace progress and comfort while still
instilling the principles that only adversity and struggle teach?**

The answer lies in teaching Principles, recognizing them in daily life,
and reinforcing them consistently within their current environment and
circumstance. Although your kids may never work a coal mine job they
have to walk to, that doesn't mean they can't get a summer job and ride
their bike (or the used car you provide) to get there. We're not asking them
to relive the life we lived—we're asking them to live life as we did: learning
and adopting Principles along the way.

Instilling Principles in a Comfortable World

A self-made businessman who built an empire from nothing may have
a son in medical school who will never experience his father's struggles
firsthand. But that doesn't mean he can't learn the principles:

- Instead of handing him everything, the father can have him work sum-
mers in the family business to understand the value of labor and money.
- Instead of gifting him a luxury car at 16, he can encourage him to
save for his first vehicle.

- Instead of letting him spend hours on video games, he can involve him in training for a charity 5K, teaching him resilience and communal generosity.

Through conversations and role-modeling, the father can instill:

- **Responsibility**—Owning your actions and choices.
- **Consistency**—Showing up consistently and following through.
- **Perseverance**—Pushing through obstacles without quitting.

From these, relational expressions like respect, consideration, and delayed gratification naturally emerge. By framing school as a quest for competency, he reinforces the Principle of Perseverance and eventual growth, ensuring that comfort does not weaken character but instead serves as a platform for development. This balance exemplifies a critical truth:

Principles are not optional—they are universal laws that govern the consequences of our actions and outcomes of our lives.

Whether we embrace them or not, life will eventually force us to confront self-evident truths. Comfort and convenience may blur our perception of PV², but life has a way of pulling us back to reality. Challenges inevitably force us to confront the unyielding truths of Principles, much like gravity—unavoidable and indifferent to our preferences and opinions. The question is not if we will face this reckoning, but how we will rise to meet it.

**Will we adapt, grow, and strengthen our character?
Or will we succumb to the false allure of comfort and convenience, leaving ourselves unprepared when adversity strikes?**

The choice is ours, and the stakes couldn't be higher.

> **Lesson Box: Comfort and Growth**
>
> - **Shielding others from hardship denies them growth;** protecting others too much limits their ability to develop Tenacity and Resilience—the Virtues that flow from the Principles of Consistency and Perseverance.
> - **Wealth and privilege cannot bypass life's laws**—Comfort and resources do not exempt anyone from the universal truths of character building.
> - **Principles prevail, always**—Those who honor principles are uplifted; those who don't are exposed when adversity comes.

Principles Are a Stubborn Thing—They Always Come Around

Even the most spoiled person is not exempt from life's adversities. I often say, "Life is a map with bridges of adversity connected by small islands of triumph." Challenges eventually visit everyone. Sometimes they arise from straying from principles; other times, they are simply life's way of testing and training us.

The people I've known who lived by Principles weathered life's storms and came out stronger. Those who avoided challenges, however, crumbled when misfortune struck. Tragedy often consumed them, branding them as victims for all to see. Instead of being defined by how they responded and grew, they became defined by what happened to them.

No matter how challenges present themselves, the PB^2 chain under Perseverance is a way through: the Value of Fortitude and the Virtue of Resilience in action. Life doesn't discriminate when it delivers hardships; but it judges you on how you respond. Principles are what separate survivors from those who allow tragedy to define them and keep them in victimhood. Ironically, in striving for a better quality of life, we often stray from principles. We buy bigger homes to impress other, fancy gadgets to make us feel special, and supplements to offset our crappy lifestyle, believing they'll improve our lives without us doing the hard part—the real internal work involved in living a Principle-driven life. Deep down, we know these pursuits are hollow—they distract rather than fulfill. Vanity often drives them more than practicality, and this creates cognitive dissonance:

No matter how cool people think we are because of our material possessions, if we know it's all a facade, we don't think we are cool—and that becomes the problem!

Take weight loss, for example. Many turn to pills, wraps, shakes, or even cold plunges, believing they're taking control of their health. In truth, they're avoiding the real issue—the neglect of basic health Principles. Their physical presence—sloppy and unfit—screams "lazy, weak, and fake," no matter how expensive their clothing or the car they drive. Even worse, I've seen millionaires pull up to IHP in $200,000 cars filled with trash. That sight screams, "Sure, he's a millionaire, but he completely lacks character—and he's certainly unaware of Principles."

There's nothing wrong with wanting the finer things in life, but they should highlight your best qualities, not compensate for a lack of PV². *Quick fixes can never replace the hard work and consistency required for true transformation that always increases your intrinsic value.* This Principle is especially evident in the world of fitness, where simplicity and consistency reign supreme.

Lesson Box: You Can't Fake Principles

- **Adversity is inevitable;** Principles, especially under Perseverance, provide the path through with Resilience and Tenacity.
- **Those who live by Principles grow stronger through hardship;** those who avoid challenges fall into victimhood and let tragedy define them.
- **Quick fixes and vanity pursuits distract from real transformation—** discipline and consistency remain the only lasting way forward.

Fitness Mimics Life—
The Rules May Change, but the Game Remains the Same

Humility, Sacrifice and Consistency are universal truths that transcend industries and markets, and fitness is no exception. As a personal trainer, I learned firsthand how these Principles shape not just physical transformation, but life itself. My journey navigating the ever-changing trends in health and fitness revealed one constant: the timeless power of staying grounded in the basics.

When I graduated from college in the mid-90s, the career of personal training was in its infancy. Everyone was still high on Pumping Iron and the bodybuilding methodology; people went to a gym to get big and strong. However, there was an undercurrent of new methods and technologies being popularized by various disciplines and companies in the allied health professions.

As the fitness industry evolved in the late 1990s, technology promised to revolutionize health and performance. Quick methods for measuring body composition, oxygen consumption, reflex time, and other attributes started to trend. Each new device came with a promise of precision and progress—but often at the expense of the timeless principles of simplicity and consistency. The allure of innovation was undeniable, yet it often distracted from what truly worked.

We were sold the dream of quick measurements and specialized training equipment that promised instant results. As a new personal trainer eager to stand out, I dove headfirst into the latest developments, spending thousands of dollars on tools and gadgets. At the time, it seemed like the key to delivering cutting-edge results. But over time, I began to realize a hard truth: these quick fixes rarely addressed the fundamental principles that truly drive success. The excitement of innovation often overshadowed the simplicity and consistency that actually produce lasting change.

This mindset wasn't unique to me—it mirrored a broader cultural obsession with quick fixes. Crash diets, extreme fitness challenges, and biohacking trends all promise transformation without foundational effort. But as I learned, these shortcuts rarely address the principles that actually lead to sustained progress. They're distractions from the real work: consistency, discipline, and mastery of the basics.

I quickly found out that many of these gadgets were inaccurate and unreliable, at best. For example, bioelectrical impedance equipment had huge error margins depending on factors like hydration status, pregnancy, menstrual cycle timing, and body-fat profile. Tapping flashing lights on a target did not improve athletic reaction times since reaction to a light sequence and reaction to a three-dimensional moving environment are two different things.

One of the most eye-opening lessons I learned was the gap between gym-based metrics and actual athletic performance. I invested heavily in the latest power-measuring equipment, convinced it would give me an edge. Over time, however, it became clear that improving numbers in the gym didn't always translate to success on the field. Training for power in a controlled environment often overlooked the complex, dynamic demands of real sports. That's right: our training numbers looked great, but we got our asses beat by people who were nowhere near as impressive as we were in a gym.

I began to ask myself hard questions: Why did less knowledgeable trainers have fully booked schedules? Why were athletes with less strength outperforming mine on the field? Why were competitors with seemingly inferior conditioning outlasting us? These questions led me to take a step back and reassess the timeless truths of fitness, health, and performance. The answer wasn't in more complexity or advanced tools—it was in re-discovering and applying the Principles that have stood the test of time. I found the secret sauce was...

Train the Principles that change the mind
more than methods that change the body.

The Basics Beyond Fitness

The healthiest populations on the planet don't rely on the latest gadgets, supplements, or quick fixes. Instead, they thrive by living in non-toxic environments, maintaining low-stress lifestyles, eating unprocessed foods, and avoiding overeating. Their longevity and health are rooted in timeless PB² Principles—eventually expressed in simplicity and balance—a reminder that true wellness doesn't come from trends but from enduring truths.

Who are the best coaches in sports? Rarely are they Hall of Fame athletes, as elite players often struggle to translate their physical talents into the mental game of coaching. Great coaches are not defined by their technical or tactical knowledge alone—they excel because they understand people. They know how to inspire, motivate, and instil Principles that transcend the sport itself.

Vince Lombardi, for example, wasn't great because of his football expertise. He was a teacher of PV², like Accountability, Discipline, and Resilience. Similarly, Phil Jackson in basketball, Béla Károlyi in gymnastics, and Angelo Dundee in boxing achieved greatness not through superior knowledge of their sport, but by building the character that allowed different athletes to think and play as a team. At the core of their success was teaching Principles of character.

How about the world of business and technology? Take the most cited man in business, Napoleon Hill. Hill was a journalist—he wasn't even a rich businessman. Yet, his book Think and Grow Rich is the most cited and recommended book in business history.

Tony Robbins in the world of self-help is a similar story and parallels that of Napoleon. Like Hill, Robbins emphasized PB²-aligned themes—the Value of Discipline, the Virtue of Clarity, and the Principle of Perseverance—over quick-fix strategies or luck. They and many other self-help gurus focus on timeless Principles, Values, and Virtues we all recognize as self-evident but often fail to follow because we haven't identified or organized them into a system for living.

The examples are endless, but they all lead back to one undeniable truth: it's not just the information or techniques that matter—it's the Principles that guide them. Living a principled life transcends context and circumstance, whether in fitness, business, relationships, or personal growth.

Principles and Values provide a constant foundation, no matter the challenges you face. Facing Fear and Courage, for instance, remain essential whether you're confronting a tough training challenge, a difficult business decision, or a personal trial that ignites fear. By filtering your actions through the lens of PV², you ensure that your response reflects the actions of a competent, good, and decent person. Working through the PB² system, the relational expressions of living a Principle-driven life naturally manifest themselves.

Lesson Box—Simplicity of Principles

- Embrace Simplicity and Practical Over Theoretical align with the Consistency → Discipline → Tenacity chain, emphasizing practical application over complexity.
- Learn People, Not Just Products reflects the Responsibility → Accountability → Integrity chain, focusing on understanding and serving others responsibly.
- Benefits Over Features ties to the Humility → Openness → Coachability chain, suggesting a humble approach to meeting personal needs and fostering buy-in.

The Unpredictable Nature of Growth

I also spent years studying biomechanics, earning certifications, and mastering assessment systems. Each system claimed to pinpoint movement deviations and predict outcomes based on muscular imbalances. Yet, after two years, I couldn't diagnose or predict success any better than a coin flip. Perfectly symmetrical people often suffered injuries, while those with glaring asymmetries often thrived and even achieved world-class success. The lesson? **Humans are inherently asymmetrical, and no one truly knows the 'acceptable' level of imbalance.** The key wasn't a complicated assessment but effective communication: relating what I saw to the client's symptoms and explaining how my training could help. It's much like taking a car with a clicking noise to a mechanic—clients don't need overly complex diagnostics; they need clarity and actionable solutions.

Growth, I've learned, is a process of acquiring and letting go. We gain knowledge, skills, and perspectives while shedding outdated beliefs, habits, and limitations. Yet, many people mistake this shedding for failure. It's not. If you lost 15 pounds, your old clothes wouldn't fit anymore, and you'd happily replace them. Would you mourn the discarded clothes? Of course not—they symbolize progress. Plateaus and purging are not defeats; they signify success, growth, and evolution. Over two decades, I've returned to the simple Principles that existed long before this industry. There's no magic trick to changing body composition: **nutrition dictates how you feel and look, the scale reflects your weight, and your clothing tracks your progress.** These realizations became catalysts for change, compelling me to reevaluate and dive deeper into the science and philosophy of training.

Adversity taught me the value of resilience—not just in physical training but in life. It's easy to stay motivated when everything goes smoothly, but true Resilience, the Virtue under Perseverance, emerges when we face obstacles head-on. **Adversity demands we persist, adjust, and keep sight of our goals.** Every challenge has been an opportunity to refine my approach, strengthen my resolve, and deepen my understanding of what it means to live by Principles.

> **Lesson Box—Game and Rules Remain the Same—Skills Must Evolve**
>
> - **Simplicity and consistency always win:** Whether in training, business, or life, the basics outlast gadgets, trends, and quick fixes.
> - **Principles transfer across domains:** The same Accountability, Discipline, and Resilience that build athletes also build leaders, businesses, and relationships.
> - **Methods evolve, but Principles remain timeless:** Technologies and tactics shift, but true success always flows from the PB² foundation of living a principled life.

The Repercussions of Breaking Principles

In both my personal and professional life, I've witnessed the cost of compromising Principles. Early in my career, I remember a time when I tried to take shortcuts in my professional evolution. Driven by the desire for faster results, I bought and implemented the latest trends in fitness. At first, everyone was excited about the new modalities and techniques. However, over time, the results we were ultimately expecting never came. Eventually, we lost interest in continuing the fads we employed and went back to the basics. My clients appreciated my open mind and willingness to try new methods, but what they valued most was that I stood on Principles when evaluating our program. My clients appreciated that:

- I was humble enough to see we were not heading in the right direction.
- I took responsibility for the decision to embark on a new training direction.
- I reflected on what led us to try a new program.
- I figured out what it was about the program that did not work.
- I designed a new program, and off we went with confidence.

That's just 50% of the PB² system. Only using half of this great system turned the direction I was taking with several clients. They respected me more for correcting course than they would have if I'd stuck with a program that wasn't optimal for the sake of my ego. Admitting an error—or the need for a change of plans—is a huge sign of strength. As the younger generation says, "It's such a gangster move."

This experience taught me the importance of honoring some of the basic axioms of training: progression, safety, and sustainability. Breaking these Principles had clear consequences—it destabilized the foundation of my practice and jeopardized the well-being of those I was responsible for. Since then, I've made a steadfast commitment to never compromise on these Principles, regardless of the hype of new training methods, equipment, or supplements. It was a hard-won lesson, but it deepened my respect for the natural laws that govern success and Integrity.

Lesson Box: Respect Comes from Correcting Course

- Admitting mistakes and making changes shows strength, not weakness.
- People value Humility, Responsibility, and Perseverance far more than ego-driven stubbornness.
- Realignment with Principles always earns lasting respect.

A Plateau Is Not a Sticking Point—It's an Inflection Point

Through my years in training, life, and business, the word plateau has always carried a negative connotation. The most common phrase when someone hits a plateau is, "I'm stuck." That phrase alone implies stagnation, frustration, and even desperation. But think about it—a plateau, by definition in regards to an uphill path, represents the terminal stage of a successful process. You don't just appear on a plateau; you either climb to reach it or descend to stop a fall. Both scenarios involve movement before the pause.

Plateaus should be celebrated and viewed as inflection points. When carefully analyzed, they can lead to further progress. It's all a matter of perspective—and if your perspective is guided by Principles, you'll be prepared to deal with them. When you hit a plateau, ask yourself:

- Am I truly stuck, or have I reached diminishing returns where more effort won't produce better results?
- Is pushing forward worth the potential repercussions?
- What other areas of my performance or life could benefit from focused attention right now?

The ultimate goal is not always about acquiring more, breaking through, or charging forward. The goal is optimization—the 'sweet spot' where more is not better. In strength and conditioning, this is called optimal strength—the point where extra gym gains don't carry onto the field and only add wear and tear that shortens a career. I've personally heard seasoned coaches say, "You can never be strong enough." Taken literally, it suggests every lift should forever increase. But we know that's not realistic. A plateau often signals tremendous progress, maybe even reaching genetic potential. That's a moment to celebrate, not lament. Pushing beyond it must be approached with caution.

Ask yourself: Does the strength you've built already exceed what's required for peak performance in the activity you are preparing for? If the answer is yes, why risk injury for no additional benefit? That's when you step back, redirect focus, and develop other qualities that may be lagging. A plateau is often the threshold where reckless pushing leads to injury. Why play with fire if there's no reason to be near it?

Just as ignoring an athletic plateau leads to physical breakdown, ignoring life's plateaus leads to burnout. The consequences may differ—torn ligaments versus a fractured sense of purpose—but the principle is the same: more is not always better.

This concept of optimal strength applies to every arena. In a career, it may mean scaling back when further growth diminishes quality of life.

In business, it may mean pausing expansion before product quality and customer service collapse. In relationships, it's about investing enough to sustain meaningful connections without losing yourself or suffocating others.

I've sat with millionaires who confessed, "I hate my life. I feel like a prisoner to everything I've created." How tragic is that? The very thing they worked so hard to achieve consumed and enslaved them. Like athletes ignoring their physical limits, these executives ignored their plateaus—pushing past "enough" until wealth became bondage. In both cases, they failed to recognize the sweet spot—the inflection point where more stops being better and starts becoming destructive.

Everyone wants more—money, power, attention, respect. Most hard driving people accept the sacrifice required. But there comes a point where more no longer improves life. Even something as beautiful as peace, when overindulged, can stifle productivity and leave you purposeless.

If you overemphasize peace, you risk losing all the spice in your life.

I've come to see Principles as laws of physics—they operate regardless of our desires. Ignore them, and the price is paid in ripple effects beyond the moment. Breaking a Principle may offer short-term relief, but the long-term cost is heavier. Likewise, when you've lost your way, the only path back is through the very Principles you violated.

This has shaped me as an industry leader, citizen, trainer, and a father. It taught me that Commitment and Courage lie not in avoiding falls, but in rising after them. Wisdom doesn't come from never failing—it comes from comebacks. Ultimately, optimum isn't about doing more; it's about finding the sweet spot, where more is not better.

Recovery and growth are never separate from Principles—they are governed by them. Just as over-training can cause injury, and unchecked ambition can lead to burnout, ignoring truth brings setbacks. But realignment with Principles always resets the path forward.

Lesson Box: Learn to Miss

- **Honor plateaus**—they are not failure, but proof of progress.
- **Celebrate the sweet spot**—the goal is optimization, where more is not better.
- **Reflect and recalibrate**—use plateaus as opportunities to reset for sustainable growth.
- **Enough is enough**—know when to shift focus or accept 'enough' to prevent misery.

Reflection and Growth

As you reflect on this chapter, ask yourself:

- As you've grown, have your views changed?
- Has your standard of living improved?
- Have your circles of friends shifted?
- Have your goals and expectations evolved?

The answer is almost certainly yes—as it should be. The key question is: do you see your PV² woven through those changes? You remain the protagonist of your life, but the way you apply PV² improves with experience. My hope is that you now make even greater strides with a system—the PB² system—that organizes and guides that application. With the PB² system, you gain control, moving forward with Integrity, Clarity, Bravery, and Resilience—while staying mindful of the sweet spot, where more is not better. At that point, the PB² system will prevent you from going overboard and remind you why you work so hard: not for 'more', but for a productive, balanced, and meaningful life.

> "Knowledge is born when information meets experience. Wisdom is born when knowledge lives through many experiences."
>
> ~ JCS

09

FROM INFORMATION TO ACTION:
How What We Do Defines Who We Are

Learning doesn't just shape what we know—it shapes who we become. It's not a passive collection of information but an active journey of applying, refining, and embodying the knowledge extracted from out experiences.

This chapter explores how learning moves from understanding to application and, ultimately, to wisdom that governs our actions. We will examine:

- Why a 'miss' is not a failure—and how this reframing changes everything.
- The role of setbacks in learning and why mistakes are essential for growth.
- The power of mentorship and collaboration in accelerating understanding.
- How repetition and deliberate practice reinforce learning and transform information into lived Principles.
- Why teaching deepens mastery by forcing us to organize and apply knowledge in practical ways.

Whether in fitness, family, or business, learning—and living—by Principles forms the foundation of a meaningful, impactful life.

The Purpose of Learning

Learning isn't just collecting information—it's an evolutionary, experiential progression. This chapter doesn't aim to introduce new information; it reorganizes familiar ideas into a logical framework that's easier to relate to and practice. The sequence here guides readers in turning raw data into actionable behavior that aligns with Principles. We'll explore how we learn, how we practice what we learn, and how that practice becomes the cornerstone of who we are.

True learning doesn't happen in classrooms or seminars—that's information acquisition. It begins where structured teaching ends: the trial-and-error of applying what you've learned to real-world challenges. Learning happens when you test information. You discover what works (and what doesn't), why it works, and how to apply it across scenarios. If you don't use information, you lose it to fading memory—"use it or lose it."

For example, a 5th grader learns multiplication through repeated attempts and countless corrections, while an Einstein-level thinker uses mathematics within formulas that make physics applicable across domains. Mathematics works because it follows universal Principles; repetition is what gives information its application and creates knowledge.

How Knowledge Becomes Wisdom

When information is taken for a test run in the real world, it transforms fleeting information into lasting, applicable knowledge. Filtered through experience, knowledge gains context. With more context, you can apply that knowledge more and more. Eventually, this knowledge becomes so applicable that it can be used outside the domain that created it. At this point, knowledge becomes wisdom—a universal model that applies across different domains. That's true wisdom—and no matter how much or how little you have, it eventually governs how you behave and live. Now, let's step back and dig a little deeper into the entire learning process.

From Words to Understanding:
Data, Information, Knowledge, and Wisdom (DIKW)

The journey from raw data to actionable wisdom is the foundation of effective learning and decision-making. While schools and traditional learning environments often focus on the accumulation of information, true mastery requires a deeper and more practical process. This progression—commonly referred to as the DIKW model—illustrates how we move from raw data to wisdom that shapes our decisions and actions. Let's break it down:

- **Data (D):** The raw, uncategorized elements we encounter, like "a degree in temperature." On its own, it lacks context or meaning.
- **Information (I):** When data is contextualized, it becomes useful. For instance, "Temperature tells us how hot or cold it is outside."
- **Knowledge (K):** Applying information to make decisions forms knowledge. "When the temperature drops below a certain point, it's wise to dress warmly."
- **Wisdom (W):** Wisdom extends knowledge by connecting concepts across broader applications and unrelated domains. "Temperature isn't just for weather—it's vital in cooking, cleaning, propulsion, and survival."

While DIKW is valuable, it's rare to encounter data entirely without context. Data is almost always accompanied by some level of context that gives it meaning. That's why we often simplify it into a more practical model:

- **Information (I):** Gathering usable information
- **Knowledge (K):** Applying that information
- **Wisdom (W):** Broadening its application through experience, across different domains

Learning starts with collecting information, but mastery comes from action—until information becomes knowledge. Once knowledge is conceptualized at its highest level, it can be applied or generalized to unrelated domains. Only then can it become wisdom. Wisdom isn't the end of learning; it's the beginning of refined behavior. It's the understanding of how PV^2 apply across the domains of your life. Therefore, Wisdom writes the playbook of who you are and how you engage with the world.

Lesson Box: From Data to Wisdom (DIKW)

- Information is collected, but knowledge comes only when it's applied in real-life scenarios.
- Knowledge matures into wisdom when experience broadens its use across multiple domains.
- Wisdom isn't the end—it's the bridge between Principles and action, shaping who we are and how we live.

Does School Teach?

Does the above model remind you of school? YUP—except the knowledge and wisdom parts. Perhaps our educational system expects knowledge and wisdom to come after graduation. Fair enough, but why waste time on courses that have nothing to do with the career one is choosing? A balanced education? Perhaps. But is that "balanced education" retained at all after a 16-week course that has nothing to do with one's career? I can tell you, "did not retain it"—and neither has anyone else I've asked.

Yet, we continue to think we go to school to learn—but are we truly learning, or mostly memorizing and test-taking with little long-term retention? Without repetition and reinforcement, most learning fades—and fades surprisingly quick. Regular exposure to the same information facilitates consistent reflection, refinement, and retention. So, when we say we're "learning" in school, it's worth asking: are we actually learning—or just proving we can jump through informational hoops?

Now, I'm not saying school is useless. A hard curriculum designed to thin the herd of applicants to medical school may be used exactly for that—to thin the herd. Very much like hell week for the Armed Forces. You go through a bunch of stuff whose only purpose is to break your spirit and make you quit. Perhaps school is that—a way to thin the herd from scholastically-oriented individuals to practically-oriented people. That separation would funnel some into important professional careers like law, engineering, biotech, IT and medicine, while others pursue the valuable trades the world depends on—carpentry, electrical, construction, metal work, etc.

Regardless of what the real purpose of school may end up being, there's no doubt about it: if you want more effective teaching, there has to be a repetitive, applied, and practical process to retain the information you're learning. Science has shown that to be true. Following this, we provide a summarized count below.

Memory & Retention (The Forgetting Curve)

Returning to 'use it or lose it', memory is central to learning, and repetition is central to memory. By extension, forgetting is the enemy of learning—and it feeds on single exposure. This means that in order to learn, we must understand retention and how to prevent losing it. Hermann Ebbinghaus' Forgetting Curve shows that without review, recall drops rapidly after exposure—unless the information is refreshed.

We're not going into the full science here. Retention varies with many factors—genetics that influence memory, the personal importance of the material, associations with knowledge you already have, repeated exposure, and whether you're required to retrieve and use the information periodically. So, we'll keep this general and use approximate values; the goal is practical application, not lab precision.

Following is a general Forgetting and Retention Curve graph. It illustrates how recall decays over time and how repeated exposures increase retention.

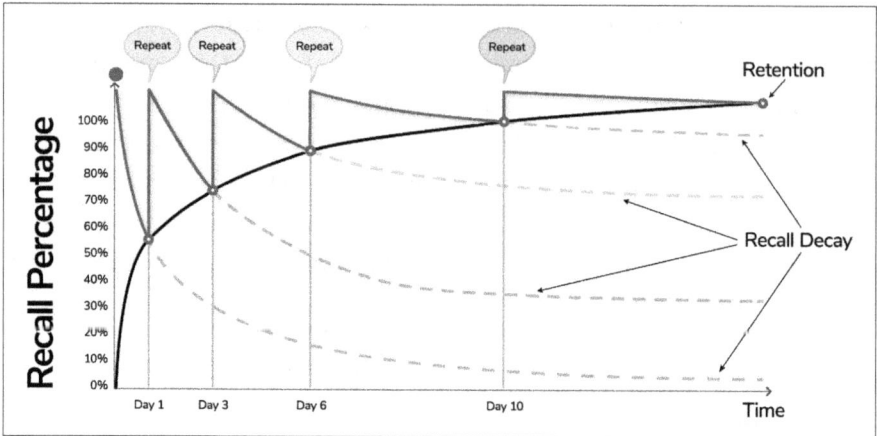

As you can see, the Forgetting Curve shows rapid loss within minutes of exposure to new information. The decay of recall is shown in the dotted lines and indicates how retention continues to decline when there's no attempt to reinforce it. Roughly:

- **After Day 1:** You can forget ~60% of new information (you retain ~40%).
- **After 3 days and beyond:** You can forget ~80% of new information (you retain ~20%).

Ebbinghaus also discovered that regular repetition dramatically improves recall, especially when spaced out over time—spaced repetition. Spaced repetition is the process of reviewing material at repeated intervals to strengthen recall and consolidate memory. Each repetition flattens the Forgetting Curve and lifts the Retention Curve (the thick black line). For example: For example:

- 1st review: Day 1
- 2nd review: Day 3
- 3rd review: Day 6
- 4th review: Day 10

As the figure shows, these repeated exposures can boost recall from 10–20% to about 90% after just two weeks. That's an insane improvement—and it proves how critical regular repetition is for retaining and mastering anything.

For more information on learning and forgetting curves, please refer to: Thalheimer, W. (2006, February). Spacing learning events over time: What the research says. Retrieved November 30, 2006, from https://worklearning.com/wp-content/uploads/2017/10/Spacing_Learning_Over_Time__March2009v1_.pdf

Retention Through Repetition

The Ebbinghaus Forgetting Curve provides the self-evident truth that repetition is the foundation of mastery. That's where the old saying "practice makes perfect" comes from. The Forgetting Curve shows how quickly we lose what we've learned without repetition and practice.

Everyone knows practice is essential, but not everyone knows what good practice is. Is it just a function of putting in time and repetitions? Can it be non-physical practice—like visualization, mental rehearsal—or other methods of skill acquisition and refinement? These are all factors that determine the kind of repetition you need.

As you can imagine, methods and strategies are almost too many to count. Therefore, I'd like to present the body of work that nails down how to look at practice, how to organize it, and how to manage it so it evolves as you do. I present to you the concept of deliberate practice.

Now, can we apply this model of learning and retention to how we live? Can we enhance our adherence to a way of life if we repeat specific actions regularly? The answer is obvious: YES. We see it in training, we see it in skill acquisition, and we see it in structured lifestyle scenarios like the armed forces. Therefore, if we treat life and the practice of specific habits the same way we treat other learning models, then learning new habits and evolving into a competent human being becomes a very doable objective.

Lesson Box: Learning and Retention

- School, without experience, remains just information.
- The more frequently you recall information, the more you retain it.
- Repeated exposures can increase retention from 10–20% to about 90% in just 10–14 days.

The BEST Repetition—Deliberate Practice

Now that we've established "you have to get your reps in," the question remains: what kind of practice is best? This topic has been studied extensively.

Deliberate practice, first studied rigorously by Anders Ericsson and later popularized by Geoff Colvin (Talent Is Overrated), emphasizes that improvement comes from targeted, structured work—not just time spent doing reps. Unlike regular practice or simply logging hours, deliberate practice is systematic and purposeful: specific goals, immediate feedback, and targeted work on weaknesses. It transforms effort into mastery through disciplined, intentional engagement. It doesn't just counter the "use it or lose it" problem—it elevates learning to a durable, high-performance level, whether physical skills or knowledge.

To maximize the benefits of deliberate practice, first establish a solid foundation: know exactly what you're working toward and which gaps matter most. Start with a clear vision of the desired outcome, then create a logical path to get there. As you can see, deliberate practice and our PB² system have much in common—both are based on Principles.

Highly focused practice often requires sacrificing comfort for growth— Commitment to the process. Consistency builds Discipline and fosters Tenacity to push through obstacles and achieve mastery. The structure ensures your effort moves in the right direction, builds on what's retained, and addresses gaps highlighted by the Forgetting Curve. Identifying what needs to be learned, designing a solid practice plan, and engaging in refined repetition becomes the path to mastery. Learning isn't luck—it's design. That's why deliberate practice beats random trial and error every time. The more deliberate the practice, the more gaps you address. With deliberate practice, you also learn to manipulate and organize knowledge across domains, which adds to the Wisdom that becomes part of who you are and how you behave. Living a Principle-driven life is no different from playing golf—or mastering any other skill.

Take golf. A young player trying to master putting breaks it down—stance, grip, reading greens, and handling pressure. He schedules deliberate practice, repeats, analyzes, and refines until the misses get smaller and smaller. An elite golfer, by contrast, isn't learning how to putt anymore. He's folding the short game into his overall strategy, adjusting in real time across 18 holes. Practice evolves with you—from fixing fundamentals to refining mastery.

The same process applies to Principle-driven living. Understanding what Principles are, aligning your Values with those Principles, and practicing the Virtues consistent with those Values is the deliberate practice of living a Principle-driven life. Below is an outlined summary of the essential and key characteristics of deliberate practice.

Deliberate Practice—The Essentials

1. **Highly Structured and Goal-Oriented**
   - Sessions are planned to address specific misses (i.e., weaknesses or challenges).
2. **Focused Effort and Concentration**
   - Requires intense mental engagement. Unfocused reps don't count.
3. **Feedback is Essential**
   - Immediate feedback—via a coach, mentor, or video—is critical for refinement.
4. **Challenges Current Abilities**
   - Pushes you past your comfort zone and forces growth.

5. Repetition with Refinement
- Repeat, refine, repeat again—with each iteration improving the last.

6. Not Inherently Enjoyable
- Often strenuous and mentally taxing—but highly effective for growth.

And here's where misses enter the picture—because no deliberate practice works without them.

Lesson Box: Deliberate Practice

- Effective practice goes beyond time and reps; it's not about volume, it's about quality.
- Deliberate practice is systematic: specific goals, immediate feedback, and targeted work on weaknesses.
- This method of practice is hard work—it's not fun or enjoyable. *FOCUS IS DIFFICULT!*

MISSES—The Pathway to Mastery

A miss, or mistake, is not a failure—it is a repetition with context. When you miss, you add layers of context to an action. Let's look at how missing opens the floodgates of knowledge.

Suppose you want XYZ as your outcome. You design your best attempt, A, to get XYZ. But you miss and only get X. You refine your design and come up with AA, certain this change will work. But no—it gets you XY. Finally, you make a third adjustment, AAA, and bingo—AAA produces XYZ.

So what did you learn? On the surface, you'd say, "AAA produces XYZ." True—but that's not all. You also learned:

A produces X   AA produces XY   AAA produces XYZ

Along the way, you also discovered the methods, processes, and variable interactions revealed by each adjustment. Multiply that over years, and the knowledge gained from misses becomes exponential. This cycle—recalibrating misses and reaffirming wins—is the learning process. Each miss sharpens cause and effect, providing the feedback improvement needs. Without misses, there's no refinement. Without refinement, there's no mastery. One could say mastery is built on misses. That's why we say, "We're not looking for perfection—we're looking for correction." The corrections are where knowledge resides.

A Personal Story: Learning Through a BIG Miss

I remember the first time I hosted an elite group from the Navy's DEVGRU (SEAL Team 6) at IHP. Wanting to impress, I spent a week preparing a thick manual on combat physiology—covering the neurological, hormonal, and psychological responses to warfare. When the day came, I handed out the manuals and started lecturing. Within minutes I saw it—the blank stares, the disengaged body language. They weren't here for theory. In that moment, I dropped the manual to the floor with a loud thud and said, "Alright guys, talk to me—what do you actually need?" Instantly the energy shifted. They leaned in. One of them said, "We just want to train hard—we want to learn how to train in the desert at our base." That pivot changed everything. The rest of the week was all practical training—coaching, working, refining techniques, everything explained while doing. Kinesthetic learning, not slides.

The result? A brotherhood that still lasts. IHP became their go-to place for training, I was invited to DEVGRU HQ multiple times, and we even developed the exercise band package they'd take to bases across the Middle East. And that big manual I made? It wasn't wasted—it became articles and presentations that strengthened the theory behind my practical techniques. The miss added brains to my brawn.

Misses—'Stairway to Heaven'. Every miss built a step that carried me higher—turning failure into feedback, and feedback into mastery.

Lesson Box: Learning Through Misses

- **Schooling isn't always learning**—true retention comes from repetition, reinforcement, and practice, not just memorization.
- **A miss is not failure**—it's feedback. Each miss provides context, data, and a chance to recalibrate toward mastery.
- **Action over theory**—real growth happens when you pivot from abstract knowledge to experiential learning that sticks.

Deliberate Practice and Misses in the Armed Forces
Focus: Standardization, Stress Inoculation, Immediate Feedback

Deliberate practice is at the heart of how recruits transform from civilians into disciplined soldiers. From the first day, routines are precise—wake-up times, uniforms, drills, inspections. At first, it feels forced, but immediate feedback from instructors ensures mistakes are corrected and habits are ingrained.

As training progresses, that same model applies to conditioning, marksmanship, and technical skills. Drills are run under fatigue and time pressure to harden execution. Over weeks and months, what began as awkward becomes automatic and reliable under fire.

Now take that general scenario and laser into a highly skilled role: the sniper. In training, he doesn't land a perfect shot the first time. He misses his way to success—adjusting, recalibrating, dialing in until the process is locked. Then he keeps perfecting smaller and smaller misses until he can hit the mark with precision anywhere, every time. If every miss were labeled failure, he'd have quit after a few shots. Treating each miss as a calibration point is how he became a sniper. Owning each miss without excuses—and seeing it as an opportunity for growth—is the first step to personal evolution.

Deliberate Practice and Misses in Music
Focus: Variability, Nuance, Discovery Through Misses

In the late 1980s, researcher Anders Ericsson studied violinists at the Berlin Academy of Music, one of Europe's top conservatories. Here's what he found:

- By age 20, the elite group had logged about 10,000 hours of deliberate practice.
- The 'good' group averaged around 8,000 hours.
- The future teachers? Closer to 4,000.

But it wasn't just about hours. The elites kept strict practice logs and attacked their weaknesses with laser focus—intonation, bowing, phrasing—broken down into deliberate, goal-driven sessions. Ericsson proved the top violinists didn't practice more casually—they practiced deliberately.

And here's where it connects back to misses. Music is the perfect example: a mistake is often new ground for exploration. Each miss opens new possibilities, which is why misses are essential to learning. Take a new musician struggling with a chord progression. That struggle highlights an area for targeted practice—but in working through it, they also discover transitions, variations, and related chords they might never have explored otherwise.

Each mistake (miss) shows you where to adjust—finger placement, timing, or transitions. In the process, the musician not only masters the original chord but also deepens their overall knowledge. Without the miss, none of this refinement would happen. Misses aren't just teachers—they're off-ramps to experiences you wouldn't have found otherwise.

Back in the old days of touring with my band, our rehearsals were full of 'mistakes'—wrong progressions, wrong tempos, wrong transitions, even the wrong measure count in certain parts of a song. And without exception, those misses turned into impromptu jam sessions that gave birth to something new: maybe a twist on the song, a new section, or sometimes a whole new song. As with everything in life, there's a time for precision and a time for play. Live by Principles and follow your heart, and you'll find the sweet spot between the two.

Lesson Box: Mastery Through Deliberate Practice

- **Repetition ingrains mastery**—what feels forced at first becomes automatic through consistent, deliberate practice.
- **Misses are teachers**—each mistake provides feedback, context, and a roadmap for refinement.
- **There's a time for both**—precision and play. Discipline means embracing misses, because they open unexplored territory.

The Role of Mentorship and Collaborative Learning

Learning is not a solitary journey. Mentors, peers, and collaborators play a vital role in transforming knowledge into wisdom. A mentor provides guidance, shares practical insights, and accelerates learning by offering "shortcuts" they've discovered through experience. Mentors help contextualize the "why" behind Principles, giving learners a deeper understanding that enhances deliberate practice.

Mentorship evolves over time. Early on, mentors serve as teachers—guiding you through foundational Principles and offering tools to overcome challenges. As you grow, the mentor-mentee relationship transitions to collaboration, where ideas are exchanged and learning becomes mutual. For example, a young entrepreneur may start out relying on a mentor's advice to navigate business strategy. Years later, the two may collaborate on a new venture, each bringing their own insights to the partnership.

Collaboration with peers also strengthens learning. Sharing perspectives, debating ideas, and solving problems together reveals blind spots and opens new avenues of understanding. For example, a medical student in a team-based learning scenario gains a broader perspective on patient care by analyzing cases collaboratively. Similarly, in fitness, peers who co-design strength and conditioning programs often produce more effective solutions than working alone—the group's collective wisdom is greater than the sum of its parts.

By combining deliberate practice with mentorship and collaboration, learners create a dynamic feedback loop that accelerates learning and deepens understanding. This interconnected approach ensures that the knowledge gained is not only retained but also enriched through collective insight.

From Student to Teacher—Meeting Dr. Anthony Abbott

This progression isn't theoretical—I lived it.

When I transitioned from bar-owner to college student, I met the man who would transform my life—Dr. Anthony Abbott, CEO of the Fitness Institute and creator of one of the most comprehensive training certifications in the industry. At the same time, I enrolled at Florida Atlantic University in Exercise Science and joined Dr. Abbott's certification program. I still remember reading his résumé before class: commandant of the U.S. Army Special Forces Airborne School, leader of the Underwater Swimmers and Para/Scuba Rescue School, gym manager, founder of a certification school, legal expert. My immediate thought was, "I want to be like this man!" I had found my guru.

Fast forward: I graduated from all three of Dr. Abbott's courses while finishing my bachelor's degree. I earned my master's in just three semesters and quickly rose through the ranks of the National Strength and Conditioning Association (NSCA), eventually serving as Florida State Director, Vice President, two terms on the Board of Directors, and receiving NSCA Fellow status. Along the way, I published books, built IHP, and began my worldwide lecture circuit. Dr. Abbott recognized my growth and asked me to design and teach a fourth course in his curriculum—the Functional Training Certification. I taught it for over a decade until COVID shut it down. And when the course first launched, who was in the front row taking notes? Dr. Abbott himself.

Over the years, mentorship evolved into collaboration—and eventually role reversal. Dr. Abbott and I built a relationship of admiration and respect. To this day, I consider him the most influential professional mentor I've had. He once said of our journey: "It is with great pride that I, the teacher, have become the student." Imagine that—the man who ignited my career now learning from me. That cycle—student to peer to teacher—is the essence of lifelong learning. My journey with Dr. Abbott wasn't just about fitness or certification; it was a masterclass in humility, growth, and giving back. The greatest success isn't just reaching the top—it's pulling others up with you.

Lesson Box: Mentorship and Growth

- Mentors accelerate growth by sharing wisdom, offering shortcuts, and contextualizing Principles that shape deliberate practice.
- Collaboration multiplies insight—peers reveal blind spots and co-create solutions greater than any individual effort.
- The cycle comes full circle when the student becomes the teacher, passing on wisdom and lifting others just as they were lifted.

The Evolution of Wisdom across Life Stages

Wisdom isn't static—it evolves as we move through life.

- **Early adulthood:** *Wisdom draws from external sources—mentors, books, structured experiences. Deliberate practice focuses on mastering foundations and aligning actions with Principles.*
- **Midlife:** *Wisdom becomes reflective. Personal wins, misses, and lessons begin to guide bigger arenas—relationships, leadership, fulfillment—beyond any single domain.*
- **Later life:** *Wisdom turns to legacy. The focus shifts to teaching and mentoring—distilling decades of experience into actionable guidance for the next generation.*

Bottom line: *Wisdom isn't what you know—it's how you use what you know to navigate complexity, contribute to society, and lift those you come in contact with.*

Lesson Box: The Evolution of Wisdom

- **Early adulthood:** Wisdom grows through mentors, books, and deliberate practice—laying the foundation for skill and Principle alignment.
- **Midlife:** Wisdom shifts inward—shaped by wins, losses, and lessons—guiding leadership, relationships, and fulfillment.
- **Later life:** Wisdom matures into legacy—teaching, mentoring, and passing down Principles that outlive the individual.

Personal Legacy in Action: IHP as 'Church'

Wisdom shows up everywhere—at home, at work, and in sport—which is why legacy matters more than titles or trophies. I call IHP my "church." One of its miracles has been the constant synthesis, resynthesis, and sharing of wisdom and life experience. I raised all four of my kids within IHP's walls. They worked every role—from custodial to management. At home and at the gym, the lessons were the same. At dinner they'd laugh: "Being at IHP is just like being at home—we get the same lectures!" Of course—why wouldn't they? Principles are universal truths. If they apply to raising a family, they apply to running a business.

Take my oldest son, Rio. As a teen, he didn't always align with the Principles he was raised with, and life delivered some hard lessons. At one time, I doubted he'd ever be ready to run IHP. But through consistent role-modeling and a positive, structured environment, he realigned his Values with the Principles. Today, at 34, he's IHP's General Manager—leading meetings and teaching the very lessons I drilled into him growing up.

The same process I went through with Rio, I go through with every young trainer at IHP. Many call me "Pops." Even those who've moved on still come back—giving hugs that say, "Thank you for what you taught me." If you can build a culture of Principles at home, you can build it anywhere—in a team, a company, or a gym like IHP. The most beautiful part? I watch my trainers mentor their clients—often people older than they are—through universal Principles:

- **Respect for the space**: put equipment away and clean up—just like at home.
- **Discipline and perseverance**: celebrate the work in training and the carryover into life.
- **Coaching through hard moments**: connect athletic progress to personal Resilience.

In my coaches, I see a little bit of me. In IHP, I see my home. This is why IHP is my church.

Lesson Box: Principles Create Legacy

- **Principles are universal truths**—what works at home also works in business, on teams, and in communities.
- **Principles empower leadership at any age**—when lived out, they allow anyone to lead, teach, and influence.
- **Principles build legacy**—when modeled consistently, they ripple outward through family, peers, and future generations.

Teaching, Integration, and Practicing What You Preach

Stephen Covey said the best way to learn is to teach. Teaching forces deeper engagement—it turns passive information into active knowledge. To teach well, you must clarify, organize, simplify, contextualize, and tie concepts to real life. That process exposes gaps you didn't even know were there.

I've seen this all over the world. People ask, "As a fitness expert, who do you learn from?" My answer: "I learn from you." Audience questions revealed where I hadn't explained clearly enough. Each question became a slide or bullet in my deck. Over time, that constant feedback refined my material and pushed me to master my subject at a deeper level.

The same thing happened later when I decided at 66 to learn investing. I opened a brokerage account, made mistakes, and realized I wasn't applying the same structure I used in fitness. So I went back to basics—courses, fundamentals, reps. Teaching my kids about investing forced me to break concepts down into simple, digestible steps. And the more I taught, the more I learned. Courses bring in information; teaching turns it into knowledge. That transfer across domains is where wisdom begins to emerge.

But teaching doesn't stop at knowledge—it creates accountability. When you teach, you're pushed to live what you preach. A coach teaching Consistency must embody it personally. A leader emphasizing Prioritization must show it in their decisions and time management. People spot disconnects instantly, and that gap destroys credibility.

When your words and actions align, authenticity takes root. That alignment builds trust, cultivates Integrity, and eventually hardens into Virtue. Over time, living what you teach becomes second nature. It creates a feedback loop: the more you live by Principles, the more your habits reinforce your Values, and the more your Virtues emerge.

Lesson Box: Teaching as a Learning Tool

- Teaching reveals gaps and sharpens clarity—forcing you to organize, simplify, and apply knowledge in real life.
- Teaching accelerates wisdom—sharing across domains deepens understanding and drives growth.
- Teaching creates accountability—living what you teach reinforces credibility, trust, and authenticity.
- Alignment builds Integrity—when words and actions match, your message gains power and respect.
- Consistency reinforces Virtue—the more you embody Principles, the more your Values and Virtues align.

Wisdom as the Pinnacle of Learning

Learning isn't a destination—it's a journey of discovery, practice, and transformation. To live a Principle-driven life, we must move from:

Information → Practice → Wisdom.

Wisdom isn't pursued for its own sake—it's sought to live better, lead better, and teach others to do the same. When Principles become habits, and habits shape character, wisdom emerges as the highest form of learning and human evolution.

Consider a coach refining programs over decades. At first, they rely on textbooks and certifications. Over time, trial and error, client feedback, and reflection turn that into wisdom that extends beyond training—into coaching, leadership, equipment design, and speaking. Or a parent raising kids. At first, they lean on outside advice. Over time, through reflection and persistence, they balance boundaries with love. That wisdom shapes family, then spills over into business, leadership, and community.

Wisdom doesn't arrive passively—it develops through practice, misses, mentorship, and teaching.

Each miss is feedback. Each practice sharpens skill. Each mentor accelerates growth. Each teaching moment crystallizes knowledge. Together they forge wisdom—the force that shapes who you are and what you pass on.

Lesson Box: Principles, Teaching, and Wisdom

- **Wisdom grows from practice**—Principles lived out as habits shape lasting character.
- **Misses refine wisdom**—failures and adjustments provide the deepest lessons.
- **Wisdom transfers across domains**—what's forged in one area enriches leadership, family, and life.

Closing Challenge

Wisdom shapes who you are, aligns your actions with universal Principles, and defines the legacy you leave. So ask yourself:

- What Principles will guide you?
- How will you integrate them daily?
- How will you pass them on?

These questions lead to wisdom—and to a life rooted in enduring truths.

Lesson Box: Building and Passing on Culture

- **Culture transfers everywhere**—a strong home culture can be recreated in teams, businesses, and communities.
- **Mentorship multiplies impact**—today's students become tomorrow's teachers, carrying principles forward.
- **Principles unify life**—respect, Discipline, and Perseverance apply at home, in training, and in every relationship.
- **Let Principles pave the way**—even when your lost, Principles will always bring you home

*"Humility is the faithful servant
of strength."*

~ JCS

10

OWN IT AND FIND A WAY OUT
(Principles 1–4)

Core Principles, Values and Virtues for Fitness, Business, and Life

Make no mistake about it—these next three chapters are the engine of this book. Organizing these sections in a meaningful, sequential flow was the biggest challenge I faced while creating this system.

The following three chapters explore the foundational Principles that drive success across every area of life—Humility, Responsibility, Self-Reflection, Self-Awareness, Strategizing, Sacrifice, Facing Fear, Consistency, Perseverance and Finishing Big. These are the cornerstones of meaningful progress, whether in fitness, business, or personal relationships. Relational expressions like patience, loyalty, honor, and respect will naturally emerge when you practice these Principles.

Each Principle horizontally follows the Principle–Value–Virtue (PV^2) chain: a structured approach to identifying the universal truth behind each Principle, the Value that supports it, and the Virtue required to put it into action. By understanding how a Principle turns into action, we develop a mechanism that turns an ideal into a Value and then into a habit. Once we understand how a chain works, we can organize the chains into a sequential vertical system—something like a personal breakthrough flowchart.

We call this vertical model the Principle-Based Breakthrough (PB^2) System.

The PB^2 System is a no-BS method that allows you to break through personal plateaus and live a Principle-driven life. It doesn't just explain the difference between Principles, Values, and Virtues—it walks you through applying them in real life, in a logical sequence. When followed honestly, the PB^2 system helps you identify where you are, what's holding you back, and the exact steps you need to break through—whether in fitness, business, relationships, or any other area of life. Since the 10 steps of the PB^2 System can be hard to keep organized, we've separated them into three phases that make more sense—identify the issue, plan and execute solutions, and finish big. It's the 1-2-3 of fixing issues in your life. It doesn't get simpler than that. This is a closer look at the three phases of the PB^2 System:

- **STAGE 1**—Take Responsibility and identify the next best step.
- **STAGE 2**—Create and execute the plan to move forward.
- **STAGE 3**—Stay the course and Finish Big.

Stage 1—Principles 1–4: Own the Problem & Find the Way Out

√ Humility—Admit it

√ Responsibility—Own it

√ Self-Reflection—What caused it?

√ Self-Awareness—What will fix it?

Stage 2—Principles 5–7: Create & Execute the Plan

√ Strategizing—The plan to fix it

√ Sacrifice—Be willing to pay the price

√ Facing Fear—Just do it—Prioritization

Stage 3—Principles 8–10: Stay the Course & Finish Big

√ Consistency—Stay with it

√ Perseverance—Push through obstacles

√ Finish Big—Integrate your learning

RINSE & REPEAT—You'll cycle these stages continuously as you grow.

Don't sweat the small stuff. The PB^2 framework isn't about semantics—it's about transformation. The PV^2 Chain on the PB^2 Chart always keep their fixed names and chains. What matters is applying them in a vertical sequence, living them in action, and allowing relational expressions like patience, empathy, and respect to naturally emerge as byproducts of living a Principle-driven life.

One thing I want to point out: this book, or model, is a theoretical framework, but it's a tool for real transformation. The model, and everything in this book, is not meant to become a semantics competition where we get stuck on technicalities. The PV^2 always use the exact names from the official PB^2 Chart. Don't get bogged down in labels—what matters is how you apply them in sequence to organize your life. Focus on what the framework is asking you to do, not just the words themselves. Don't sweat the small stuff by getting lost in meaningless details. Stay focused on practice and forward progress, not scrambling your brain swapping words or redefining categories. The following is a summary table of the PB² system:

PRINCIPLE UNIVERSAL TRUTH— WHAT MUST BE UNDERSTOOD	VALUE WHAT DEFINES IT & GUIDES THINKING	VIRTUE HOW IT'S APPLIED— DEMONSTRATED IN ACTION	
1	**Humility** Recognizing you don't have all the answers.	**Openness** Willingness to learn from others and situations	**Coachability** Receiving feedback without ego and applying it
2	**Responsibility** Owning all of it; no blaming others.	**Accountability** Accepting your role in what happened	**Integrity** Committing to fixing what is broken; no excuses
3	**Self-Reflection** Understanding how it broke	**Analysis** Analyze how your actions shaped the outcome.	**Clarity** Seeing cause and effect— actions to outcomes.
4	**Self-Awareness** Identifying needed changes	**Recognition** Recognizing best choices for action	**Objectivity** Taking the best course of action from the best solution
5	**Strategizing** An organized plan is needed	**Prioritization** Prioritizing structuring the plan for effectiveness	**Execution** Implementing the plan without hesitation
6	**Sacrifice** There is a price to pay for growth and change.	**Commitment** Willingness to make sacrifices	**Selflessness** Paying the price without resentment
7	**Facing Fear** Fear is unavoidable, but must be faced.	**Courage** Willingness to act despite fear	**Bravery** Taking action in the presence of fear
8	**Consistency** Success comes from repeated right actions.	**Discipline** Doing the work regardless of emotions	**Tenacity** Staying on course despite distractions
9	**Perseverance** Growth requires enduring hardship.	**Fortitude** Courageously working through difficulty	**Resilience** Bouncing back from setbacks
10	**Finish Big** Be the closer.	**Dynamic mastery** Applied mastery— wisdom is synthesized	**Integrated reps** Each rep integrates experience wisdom into life experience.

As you go through the PB² system, don't get bogged down in overthinking the 10 Principles. Apply them honestly and allow your own relational traits to emerge along the way. What matters most is that your personal Values align with universal Principles, and that your Virtues show up in action. At the end of the day, it's about how you live and how you act—not renaming the system. The PB² terms never change, but how you express them in your life will be unique to you. This book is meant to educate you on how to associate and align your thoughts and actions with universal truths. So, if your own vertical list of actions is a combination of principles, values and virtues—FINE! Work that program! So, your list of 10 personal actions may look like any one of the following options:

	LIST #1	LIST #2	LIST #3
1	Humility	Coachability	Openness
2	Integrity	Responsibility	Accountability
3	Self-Reflection	Self-Awareness	Self-Reflection
4	Self-Awareness	Self-Reflection	Self-Awareness
5	Prioritization	Prioritization	Prioritization
6	Sacrifice	Prioritization	Sacrifice
7	Courage	Courage	Perseverance
8	Discipline	Perseverance	Discipline
9	Perseverance	Discipline	Courage
10	Finish Big	Finish Big	Finish Big

Even though the PB² system always uses the same 10 Principles, 10 Values, and 10 Virtues, the way you work the system can be customized to your situation. What matters most is that each step triggers the right behavior. If "Humility" doesn't click for you, and the word 'blue' reminds you to stay humble, then 'blue' works—because it pulls you into the right action. The official names don't change, but your triggers can be personal. The order can also shift depending on circumstance. In a crisis, you may have to start with Courage and Face Fear immediately. Maybe you stay there for weeks, relying on Discipline and Resilience just to survive. Later, when the smoke clears, you may move into Self-Reflection, which humbles you, and then into Self-Awareness and Strategizing to make sure it doesn't happen again. The map stays the same, but the road you take through it can change. And if working with all three categories—Principles, Values, and Virtues—feels too complicated at first, simplify it. Start with just the Virtues. In that case, your program becomes a 10 x 1 instead of a 10 x 3. You focus only on living the ten Virtues in action: Coachability, Integrity, Clarity, Objectivity, Execution, Selflessness, Bravery, Tenacity, Resilience, and Integrated reps. And if these Virtues don't trigger you into the right action, you can lean on relational expressions that resonate with you. Later, if you feel it's necessary, you can always connect them back to their Values and Principles.

How to Use this Guide

All of the principles we'll cover have a huge perspective component. Your mindset at the moment of a decision can massively affect how things turn out. One bad call can block major progress. So when you ask yourself a deep question, and ask your maker for help with the answer—do what Jordan Peterson suggests: "Sit at the edge of your bed, ask the question, and sit and wait for the answer." If you sit long enough, the answer will come. It may not be the one you want—but it'll be the one you need. With that in mind, here's how to get the most out of this book and the Principles in this chapter:

1. Read each principle and reflect on how it applies to your journey.
2. Answer the self-assessment questions honestly to get clear on what's holding you back.
3. Apply the principles in fitness, business, and family using real examples and insights.
4. Review the lesson boxes to reinforce key lessons.

This process will show you where you're stuck—and how to break through.

Stage and Principle Chain Structure.

At the beginning of each stage, we'll dive into a more in-depth discussion of the main Principle—really exploring its meaning and significance. After that thorough breakdown, we'll present the Principle Chain within the PB² System. This section reviews each component of the chain and how they connect to one another.

You may feel that revisiting the main Principles is a bit redundant—but that's by design. These short reviews serve as deliberate repetition, which is essential for retention. Remember, you've never seen this system before, and much of what you're learning here is new. Repetition isn't filler—it's reinforcement.

Following the review of each Principle Chain, we'll examine common difficulties people face at that stage and how to navigate them. Every Principle Chain concludes with reflection points and practical applications you can implement immediately.

Stage 1—Own the Problem and Find the Way Out

Stage 1 consists of the first four Principles: Humility, Responsibility, Self-Reflection, and Self-Awareness.

This Stage is where we take ownership of our current situation. Ownership starts with Humility—the surrender of ego and the realization that we don't know everything and sometimes need help. Humility transitions into Responsibility, where we fully own the moment. Through Self-Reflection, we understand how our actions created our situation, and through Self-Awareness, we identify what actions will get us out of it.

Stage 1 sets the tone for growth and prepares you to start building a plan—the focus of Stage 2.

STAGE 1, PRINCIPLE 1—HUMILITY
You Don't Have All the Answers

Humility is the starting line of all learning and change. It's the recognition that you don't know it all—and that's okay. Some people find that realization uncomfortable; others find it liberating. Either way, Humility opens the door to every breakthrough that follows.

The PB² Alignment - The Humility Chain

- **Principle: Humility**—Recognizing you don't have all the answers.
- **Value: Openness**—Willingness to learn from others and situations.
- **Virtue: Coachability**—Receiving feedback without ego and applying it.

Let's dive into the first—and perhaps most crucial—step in this stage: Humility.

Principle 1—Humility: Admit you are in over your head, you don't know everything, and you are open to learning.

Humility isn't weakness; it's strength—the Courage to admit you don't know and stay open to learning. The world doesn't reward arrogance. It rewards adaptability and competence. Those who refuse to listen, refuse to grow.

One of my favorite analogies for Humility is the beach ball. Just because you can't see the colors on the other side doesn't make you weak or stupid—it just means you're not in the right position. That's what Humility is: recognizing someone else may have a better angle. Drop the ego. Listen to the person who sees what you can't. Then, turn the ball—and you'll see what you were missing.

One turn of the ball reveals everything.

From now on, when you think of Humility, think: *TURN THE BALL!*

Why this Is the First Step

Humility is the launching pad of change. Nothing takes off without it. Even acknowledging that change is needed—whether you're stuck in something you can't escape or reaching for something you haven't yet attained—requires a serious bite of humble pie. The biggest conundrum with this principle is that to be humble, you have to be vulnerable. And vulnerability is still wrongly seen as weakness. But here's the truth:

Vulnerability takes strength; it takes self-confidence.

These are two qualities rarely associated with Humility—but essential to it. Putting Humility first in the PB^2 system wasn't just strategy. It was a stroke of luck and coincidental genius, because Humility isn't just the beginning of change—it's the door to everything that follows. It's your first encounter with quiet strength, Discipline, and the self-confidence we'll rely on throughout this entire transformation process. This is also where a lack of Humility becomes a straight line to self-sabotage and guarantees you will never make any significant progress.

Show me a man who's been lost in a crowded city for 20 minutes and refuses to ask for directions, and I'll show you someone sabotaging himself. You know the type: "I know what I'm doing!" He's had dozens of chances to ask for help—and now he's out of time. He misses the monument he wanted his family to see. Because of his ego, they all miss something beautiful. What do you think the rest of his life looks like? That's pride running the show—at the cost of everyone around him.

Only the strong who value wisdom are humble enough to ask questions. Only those who truly seek competence chase knowledge. Real competence isn't about having the final say—it's about recognizing when someone else has a better angle and having the Humility to ask questions. It takes confidence to see the gaps. It takes Humility to close them. And nothing commands more respect than a leader willing to learn from anyone—regardless of status. That's the kind of strength that transcends titles and status.

One of my favorite analogies for Humility is the beach ball. Just because you can't see the colors on the other side doesn't make you weak or ignorant—it simply means you're not in the right position. That's what Humility is: recognizing that someone else might have a better angle. Drop the ego. Listen to the person who sees what you can't. Then, turn the ball—and suddenly you'll see what you were missing.

The Truth About Humility

- You're stuck and don't have the answers.
- You're willing to accept help.
- You check your ego at the door and listen.

In fact, accepting your limits and seeking others' input follows one of the most important personal development models ever created:

Stephen Covey's Stages of Growth

1. **Dependence**—You rely on others for survival (like a baby).
2. **Independence**—You gain self-sufficiency (like a young adult).
3. **Interdependence**—You reach your highest potential by working with others and leveraging community.

Why does **interdependence** come last? Because it's the most advanced—and it requires strength and Humility. Sometimes, you'll never be able to change enough on your own to break through a stage in life. You can't kick the addiction. You can't write the code. That's when you outsource the block—you bring in help. Maybe it's a therapist. Maybe it's a colleague. Maybe it's a family member or friend. Maybe it's a support group. Maybe it's a hired professional.

When it's external and non-personal—like a business system or a car repair—most people have no issue calling in a specialist. That's easy to justify. The ego says: "It's not my fault. I didn't do anything wrong."

But when the block is personal—when the issue is you—that's a whole different ballgame. The ego gets involved, and when the ego shows up, Humility runs for the hills.

When was the last time you heard someone proudly announce: "I'm going to therapy to fix my self-sabotaging habits!" You don't. Why? Because business problems are external and feel like they're not your fault. Personal problems? Those are yours to own—and they feel like failure. That's the trap: Ego. Pride. Insecurity. The gatekeepers of stagnation.

That's why Humility is the first order of business when change is needed. It's the only way forward.

Humility is the antidote to stagnation—in all its forms.

How the Value of Openness and Virtue of Coachability Relate to this Step

The Value of Openness and the Virtue of Coachability bring Humility to life. Openness allows you to listen, learn, and consider perspectives beyond your own. Coachability turns that openness into growth by applying what you've learned with action and discipline.

Value: Openness
Willingness to Learn from Others and Situations

Openness is the practical side of Humility. It's not just knowing you don't have all the answers—it's willingly and actively seeking them. Much of the time we learn through interpersonal communication. Whether it's a conversation, a training session, or a formal college class, we often learn through communication with others. Therefore, interpersonal communication becomes paramount if you adopt the Value of Openness. Being open requires:

- Adopting the student mindset
- Closing your mouth and opening your ears—staying quiet while others talk
- Seeking to understand—before being understood
- Asking questions instead of acting like you know it all
- Learning from those with greater knowledge, regardless of their status or title

Competent and impactful people are usually great students, and I don't mean in a school environment. As a matter of fact, a good student will never let school get in the way of his education. They are always open to learning new and better ways to do things. In simple words, a great student is always looking for a better way to think—and more importantly, a better way to feel. That's a powerful distinction because the way you feel dictates your attitude and outlook on life.

As you become aware of what Openness is and how important it is, you start adopting the value and becoming more coachable through practice. The more you practice Openness, the more Coachable you become. By default, you become a better student. You learn to stay quiet when others are talking—and you begin to notice the difference between hearing and listening, and between listening and understanding.

Nobody has taught me more about becoming a good listener than Stephen Covey. And I don't mean just being quiet and letting others talk. NO. I mean listening with the sole purpose of understanding what another person is trying to say. Here's what Covey says about listening and understanding: "Seek first to understand, then to be understood." (from *The 7 Habits of Highly Effective People*, 1989)

It's **Habit 5** in the book and it falls under interpersonal communication. Covey argues that most people listen with the intent to reply, not to understand or learn. They filter everything through their own lens. They don't listen to everything—they scan for confirmation of their own opinions.

Although listening quietly is a prerequisite, it's not the dominant factor. The dominant factor is **seeking to understand** what another person is trying to communicate. And remember: not everyone is a great teacher or communicator, no matter how much they know. When you're listening to understand, try to look beyond what's being said—and ask questions if necessary.

For example, when someone comes into IHP and we ask, "Why are you here and how can we best serve you?" The answer is often, "I wanna get fit." What does that mean? Nobody knows.

Our trainers are taught to listen and understand. When we hear "I wanna get fit," we ask follow-ups like, "If you were fit, what would change in your life?" or "What could you do that you can't do now?"

When these questions are asked, you usually get the answer you were actually looking for—not the generic "I wanna get fit" response. You now get something closer to the truth.

Virtue: Coachability
Putting Ego Aside

Where Openness is the mindset or ideal of Humility, Coachability is the action component. Coachability is what you practice from a mechanical standpoint. This is where you actively listen and understand. This is where you take in and apply feedback, then recalibrate your process. This is the essence of deliberate practice, and it starts with Humility, Openness, and being Coachable.

You hear it in sports all the time as a great trait to have—where an athlete lets go of the need to be right for the sake of improving and evolving. He can put his competitive ego aside and relinquish the need to be in control or be the dominant personality that's served him well during competition. Just being aware of this phenomenon alone can go a long way for those with very dominant and ego-driven personalities. Even people with strong personalities who aren't comfortable displaying any characteristic that might make them seem weak, inferior, or NOT ALPHA know an instinctual secret:

There is nothing weaker than incompetence.

When you step up to a higher level of execution and find yourself surrounded by people who could "take your lunch money," Humility becomes a necessity, not a choice. That's why it's ingrained in the culture of the armed forces.

We've all heard of the baddest men on the planet being humbled to the point of crying and quitting at the various levels of special forces training, such as SEAL Team 6 (DEVGRU). No better place to see Humility from would-be badasses than Hell Week at the Naval Amphibious Base Coronado, California. The biggest drop-off in SEAL training happens during the first phase of BUD/S, specifically during Hell Week, which is part of Phase 1: Physical Conditioning. This is the infamous point where 70–80% of initial candidates "ring the bell," leave their boots, and voluntarily quit.

Of course, if Hell Week doesn't humble you, there are many more stages of elite training that will teach you Humility—and that being coachable is the ONLY way to make it to the end and be awarded the famous SEAL Trident.

Principles can't be bullied or psyched out. They don't care who you think you are, what your opinions are, who you know, or what you've accomplished. You either come correct or you get beaten into correction. Principles have no feelings and no mercy—they only listen to facts. The ego says, "I know it all." Humility says, "I don't know enough." Openness says, "I'm willing to learn." Coachability says, "Please teach me."

Nothing destroys progress faster than ego and pride. If you can't put your ego aside, you set yourself up for stagnation. Trust me—sooner or later, life WILL check your ego. And unless you practice Humility, Openness, and Coachability, you'll be unprepared for that moment. The choice is yours: learn it now voluntarily or learn it the hard way when life smashes you. Your call.

Why Some People Struggle with this Step

- Soft, fake society—built on social media
- Bully or victim—no in-between
- Humility is seen as weakness.
- Learning from someone else lowers your social rank.

Two forces often destroy Humility, Openness, and Coachability: the ego and a culture addicted to image. The ego—what Jung called part of our Shadow—is wired to protect us from perceived weakness. It hates being wrong, corrected, or seen as less than. That's nature's resistance to growth. Left unchecked, the ego becomes defensive, arrogant, and obsessed with control. It rejects feedback, denies fault, and rationalizes poor choices—while convincing you you're just "strong, independent, and confident." Show me weakness driving confidence, and I'll show you the Shadow at the wheel. Now pair that with a culture addicted to image and external validation—and you've got the perfect storm.

Although social media has great applications, it also comes with deep traps. It doesn't teach Self-Awareness; it teaches self-branding and fakery.

Take social media influencers, for example. Their skill set is mainly limited to posing in front of a camera and influencing people through 15- to 30-second clips. That's not depth. That's learning how to front. Yet they influence millions who try to replicate what they see. I know many influencers—but not many I'd call deep thinkers, principled people, or individuals with a sophisticated philosophy of service. In that environment:

- Humility looks like weakness
- Coachability resembles incompetence

But in truth, those are the traits that lead to depth, competence, and wisdom. The more the world praises your fake image, the harder it becomes to build a real one. Everyone needs help, growth, and guidance. But in today's culture, asking for it is often misinterpreted as weakness and failure.

We're also living in a world of extremes—just like the middle class is disappearing, so is the middle ground of social behavior. Now, you're either a victim or a bully. Why? Because we've avoided the hard work that builds character. The result is a society full of posturing victims and over-compensating bullies—all jockeying for attention on a fake leaderboard.

Back in the day, you earned your rank in the neighborhood. You raced home from school, hit the playground, and found your place. You learned real social etiquette from the tribe of kids in your hood. You had to—there were no participation trophies, no "timeouts," and no parents stepping in to negotiate your problems. You had to:

- Share gear
- Handle wins and losses
- Deal with older kids
- Help the younger ones
- Stand up to bullies
- Earn respect—or lose it

There was no fronting. No faking. You were tested—on the spot—and everybody knew what you were about. Victims and bullies didn't last long. You had the freedom to move up or down in the tribe, depending on how you evolved. Those playgrounds forged real skills—social hierarchy, measured conflict, even Humility.

I still meet with the old neighborhood crew—the 'Callahan boys'. We sit around with cigars and rum, recounting the traits that stood out in those early years. Two always top the list: Humility and the willingness to learn. Right next to them? Courage.

It warms my heart when the stories turn to me. I was the quiet kid who didn't talk much—but I stood up to bullies when they showed up. I don't remember half the stories they recount, but the way they tell them cracks me up. Ten Cuban guys, all talking over each other—cigars in one hand, rum in the other—everyone trying to get their version in. Not a bad way to remember the Principles of Humility and Courage—50 years later.

But that's the thing: those Principles are *timeless*.

We've all heard the saying, "Knowledge is power." And it's true—for a reason. Knowledge applied is competence. It's the gateway to growth and respect within you community. But insecure people see learning as a power shift. If they learn from someone, they feel weaker—and view the other person as stronger. That's why so many people avoid therapy. They don't want to admit someone else can see their blind spots—especially if that person can call them out on it. I've seen this firsthand.

The people who suffer from recurring dysfunctions? They're usually the ones least willing to get help—or even admit they need it.

On the flip side, the strongest people I know are the most coachable. They put their ego aside. They hire mentors, therapists, and coaches. They bring in a third party to spot blind spots and help them fix what's broken—whether in business, life, or relationships.

The best don't avoid help—they invest in it.

Navigating this Step

- See where you are OBJECTIVELY—you are where you are.
  - o Stop denying, rationalizing, or blaming.

If something you want to change keeps recurring in your life, stop sweeping it under your conscious rug. It's not the outside world—it's you. If you have a history of abuse, violence, trauma, or just a lack of love—you might still find success in business, family, or other areas. But unless you've dealt with those issues—on your own or with professional help—you'll have loose ends that hold you back from full healing and a truly fulfilling life. It's no different than a functional alcoholic—someone who appears to be operating at a high level but is weighed down by a dark side they haven't faced. The same thing that drives the addiction also touches everything they do—and not in a good way. Even worse, the compensatory behaviors they've developed to hide the problem and project normalcy don't just mask the addiction—they bleed into every part of their life.

Their family.
Their friends.
Their work.

All touched by the same compensatory image. It's a beautiful life on the surface—but underneath, there's pain, shame, and sorrow. *That's not living. That's barely existing.*

Acknowledge that You Could Use Some Help

- Don't be the lost driver who refuses to ask for directions—get help and get there faster.

These are simple words that are hard to follow with actions. It's like telling a drug addict: "This drug is killing you. You have to stop. Don't be the guy who loses everything—please, stop now before it's too late." How often do those words work? Unfortunately, not often.

Here's the truth: Acknowledging the issue isn't the problem. Most people struggling already know something is wrong. The real barrier is admitting it to others—and that's what stops people from seeking help. Let me give you two examples of how this plays out:

1. I've seen people suddenly dive into self-help books. They don't just read one or two—they binge them. And yet, if you ask why, they'll insist everything is fine. They won't admit they're trying to understand something deeper. And they absolutely won't seek professional help. The books become a silent cry for help—a way to say, "I know something's off," without actually saying it. But their refusal to get outside support is front and center.

2. An amplified version of this can be found in the world of mental health and therapists in the field. There's actually some research and a fair amount of professional commentary supporting the notion that many people are drawn to psychology, therapy, or psychiatry because of their own unresolved issues or personal experiences with mental health. It's a common saying in both academia and clinical circles:

   - "Therapists are the craziest people you'll ever meet."
   - While an exaggeration, it reflects the cultural Self-Awareness in the profession.
   - Many therapists openly admit in interviews, podcasts, or memoirs that they got into the field to "figure themselves out."

Now don't get me wrong, self-help books are a phenomenal way to learn and improve your life. I've used books to educate myself and get ideas about what may be troubling me—but as a supplement, never as a substitute for therapy and coaching. I've always valued talking to a professional. I actually enjoyed it. I always went to therapy with a great attitude, **looking** for that one sentence—one new angle, one insight I hadn't thought of before—that could unlock the whole problem. And many times, that's exactly what happened. If I could give one piece of advice to anyone who feels stuck, it's this: Go to a *professional. It doesn't matter who. Just go.*

Think this: "One sentence could do it." One sentence could give you a perspective you've never considered before. One sentence could be the breakthrough. **One sentence could set you free.**

Don't be afraid to go to another therapist if you don't connect with the first one. Keep changing until you find one that speaks your emotional language. Don't choose one that tells you what you want to hear. Stay with the one who tells you the truth in a way you can understand and analyze.

See Yourself as a Highly-Skilled Person Perfecting Their Skill Set

- Many of the most elite go for help to finalize their evolution.

When contemplating getting help, don't see yourself as an inferior person with weaknesses and flaws that need to be addressed. How about if you see yourself as an elite athlete going to a professional to help you deal with the kinks in your armor? The best athletes in the world have sought sports psychologists, technical coaches, and other methods to deal with weaknesses or deficiencies. They did not see themselves as weak or less than—they were at the top of the heap and wanted to complete their arsenal to become the best. So be that athlete. You are NOT weak—you are at the final stages of perfection.

Personal Reflections
Self-Assessment (Demonstrating the Value of Openness and the Virtue of Coachability)

- Why do I act as if I have the answer when I know I don't?
- Do I avoid asking for help because I'm afraid people will think less of me?
- What would happen if I asked for help?

Application (Practicing the Principle of Humility, the Value of Openness, and the Virtue of Coachability)

- **Fitness:** Do I really listen to my coach, or am I competing against him just to be right?
- **Business:** Do I seek mentorship and wisdom from others in my company, or do I resist advice because I don't want someone else having authority or power over me?
- **Family:** Do I lack conflict resolution strategies where my ego and insecurities always lead me to weeks of silent treatment with my partner or family members—because I refuse to be the one initiating resolution?

Final Thought

The moment you believe you have nothing left to learn is the moment you stop growing. The moment you see yourself shying away from seeking knowledge and wisdom from others—so that you aren't seen as socially inferior—is the moment your prison stay begins with stagnation. Humility isn't about lowering yourself to the point where you need help—it's about knowing that during the process of getting help, you may be one sentence away from breaking through years of dysfunction. You are always a sentence away from freedom. If you never apologize, never initiate a resolution, never initiate "I love you," or never initiate intimacy with your partner—BOOM! There it is. You're that person who never needs help... but will always need help.

STAGE 1, PRINCIPLE 2—Responsibility
It's on Me—I Got Me Here

After Humility, Stage 1 moves into its second Principle—Responsibility. This is where ownership takes center stage. Below, we'll recap Stage 1 and then break down the Responsibility Chain that turns awareness into action.

Stage 1 Recap—Principles 1–4: Own the Problem & Find the Way Out

- **Principle 1—Humility:** Admit you are in over your head, you don't know everything, and you are open to learning.
- **Principle 2—Responsibility:** Own your role in your current situation—no blaming or excuses.

The PB² Alignment - The Responsibility Chain

- **Principle: Responsibility**—Owning your role. You are responsible for your current situation, regardless of external factors.
- **Value: Accountability**—Accepting your role in what happened.
- **Virtue: Integrity**—Committing to necessary changes without excuses, blame, or defensiveness.

Let's now dive into the second chain of this first stage: Responsibility.

Principle 2—Responsibility—Owning Your Role

Responsibility is not the same as admitting fault—though sometimes it can be. It's about owning your present moment so you can take control of your future direction. Many people resist Responsibility because they see it as blame or failure, especially during challenges. That's the wrong perspective. Taking Responsibility is a display of strength and an opportunity for Analysis and troubleshooting. You cannot fix what you are not willing to own.

Why this Is the Second Step

You stand where you stand because you walked yourself there. If you want to move forward, you have to own where you are now. That's why Responsibility comes second—after Humility, but before any real change can happen. Show me someone who blames bad luck, other people, or circumstances, and I'll show you someone who is stuck. Their excuses pile up, but their results don't. Responsibility isn't about guilt—it's about awareness and control. It's the neutral recognition that you got yourself here and you can get yourself out. That's where the power of Responsibility shows up—and where progress begins.

In life, the things most needed are often the hardest to give. You need credit to buy your first car but have none. You need experience to get a job, but no one will hire you without it. Strength and character are no different—they're most needed when you feel lost, tired, or ready to quit. Responsibility follows the same law: it's hardest to take when things haven't gone well, but that's when it matters most. Anyone can take credit when they're winning. True Responsibility is owning it when you're losing. When things fall apart because of what you did or didn't do, it's hard to face the mirror—but that's where character is built. Responsibility is the beginning of learning and growth. It's how you make sure the same mistake doesn't happen again. Without it, there's no value in the event and no lesson to learn.

> **Responsibility is the currency for growth,**
> **not something to be transferred when convenient.**

Reduce Responsibility to credit and blame, and you're not really living—you're just passing the buck. That mindset shrinks life into black-and-white sketches. When you own the moment without blame or credit, you finally see what is. You stop asking, "Why did this happen to me?" and start asking, "What did I do to get here—and what needs to change to move forward?" Responsibility matters because it reveals the causative cure—the solution is often hidden in the cause. Gary Gray, PT, teaches this in rehab: if a movement pattern caused an injury, you fix it by retraining that same pattern. In medicine, vaccines trigger immunity by introducing a trace of the illness itself. Same in life. If you built a business, a body, or a career, you can scale it by doubling down on what worked—add employees, add muscle, add education. If you're trapped in self-destructive habits, the same energy that created the problem can power the solution. Obsession doesn't disappear—it evolves. That's why so many ex-addicts become elite performers: they redirect the drive. You don't erase what got you here—you retrain it and aim it forward.

The Truth About Responsibility

Responsibility is the turning point where being stuck gives way to movement. It's not about pointing fingers—it's about stepping up. When you take full ownership of your situation, you reclaim the power to change it. No more waiting, no more hoping—just action.

- You are where you are because of your choices.
- You see what's broken, no matter the cause.
- You commit to fixing it, no matter the obstacles.

No excuses. If you refuse to take Responsibility, you stay trapped—stuck in a loop where outside forces dictate your life. It's not about what happened to you anymore—it's about what you do next. When I hear people complaining, blaming, or making excuses, I remind them:

"That's your old story. It doesn't serve you anymore."

How the Value of Accountability and the Virtue of Integrity Relate to this Step

The Value of Accountability and the Virtue of Integrity give Responsibility its backbone. Accountability keeps you honest about what happened, while Integrity ensures you follow through on what needs to happen next. Together, they turn ownership into consistent action.

Value: Accountability
Accepting Your Role

Where Responsibility is the Principle of owning your situation, Accountability is the mindset of accepting your role in that situation—without excuses. It eliminates blame, projection, and apathy. When you're accountable, you're not punishing yourself or being overly critical. You're simply observing the actions that brought you here. No judgment. No excuses. This is not a trial. No one's coming after you. No fear. No shame.

Most people who live in denial do so because they wrongly associate Accountability with failure, weakness, or shame. To avoid that uncomfortable mental state, they rationalize their situation or blame external factors. Of course, this only makes things worse and creates a cycle of unnecessary self-sabotage. The mindset becomes: "Since I didn't cause this, there's nothing I can do to change it." That's a dead end. No amount of excuses or finger-pointing will remove your Responsibility for your actions—or give you the power to change. If external factors played a role in your situation, fine. But the only thing you truly control is your decisions and actions. That's all you can be accountable for. Knowing the impact of your choices gives you a roadmap for positive change and forward progress.

Here's the irony: power is often sought by the weak—but they rarely want to pay for it with Accountability. They don't want the heat that comes with Responsibility and Accountability, so they rely on shortcuts and cheap tactics you can spot a mile away. How do you recognize a weak person chasing power? They're riddled with traits like envy, jealousy, and deceit—and they steal social valor. All that drama and deception just to avoid looking at a situation and honestly saying, "Here's what I could've done better." It seems crazy, but that's the way it is. Common sense isn't so common—and neither is Accountability.

Virtue: Integrity
Do What's Right, Not What's Convenient

Integrity is the action component of Responsibility and Accountability. This is where you commit to doing what's necessary to change your situation and move forward—without excuses, defensiveness, or half-effort. People with Integrity aren't guided by what's easy; they're driven by what's necessary. Once they identify the changes required for a breakthrough, they follow through. The best habit you can develop to embody Integrity? Do what's necessary, not what's convenient. When you trust yourself to follow through, taking Responsibility becomes second nature.

Here's one for you: "Don't abuse Integrity." I bet you haven't heard that before. What do I mean? Just because you'll finish what you start at all costs doesn't mean the road has to be the hardest one possible. Be smart when setting the path for change. Repetitions create habits, and constantly doing what's necessary becomes a trainable skill—it becomes part of who you are. When setting up the tasks, schedule, or plan, make sure it's progressive and gradual. Building the habit starts small and scales up. Taking Responsibility is hard enough without sabotaging yourself by setting unrealistic goals you can't sustain. Start small. Build the habit through easy-to-hard, two-week stages:

1. Pick something simple and doable.
2. Do it consistently for two weeks.
3. Build on that small success.

This method works because easy wins build momentum. Success compounds. Before you know it, what once felt impossible becomes part of who you are. At first, you're not even chasing change—you're building habitual momentum. Form the habit first, then gradually intensify it. It's harder to form a long-term habit than to achieve a short-term result, and the easiest way to build a lasting habit is to make it easy to start.

Why Some People Struggle with this Step

There are plenty of psychological theories explaining why people avoid Responsibility—but let's keep it simple: at the root, it's self-protection. Most people dodge Responsibility to protect their self-image and avoid uncomfortable emotions like shame, guilt, or fear of failure. That's it. That's the core. And the research backs it up.

Psychologists call this attribution—blaming outside factors when things go wrong to preserve your sense of competence. Another is cognitive dissonance—the mental friction that hits when your actions don't match who you believe you are. Instead of owning the truth, people twist the story.

Then come the ego-defense plays: denial, projection, rationalization. These moves might shield you for a moment, but long term, they blind you to the real issue. And nothing changes when you're blind. The one thread tying it all together? Fear.

Fear of failure.
Fear of being exposed.
Fear of not being enough.

Add low self-esteem, a belief that you're not in control, and a culture that hands out excuses like candy—and it's no wonder people run from Responsibility. But here's the kicker: Responsibility is the beginning of power.

If you won't own it, you can't change it.
No Responsibility, no control.
No control, no progress.
You stay stuck. Period.

Navigating this Step
Drop Your Story and Own Your Actions

- Stop justifying. Stop blaming. Stop explaining.

Just look at what happened—objectively. The moment you stop spinning the narrative and simply own the facts, you regain control. Facts don't care about feelings—they just show you where you are. If you don't like where you are, it's because of the choices you've made. That's the bad news. The good news? You're free to make better choices. Say, **"It's on me,"** and eliminate the victim mindset.

- Make that your default setting. Whether or not it was your fault doesn't matter—if it's your life, it's your Responsibility.

Say it out loud. Make it a habit. "It's on me" shifts your mindset from passive to active—it hands you the wheel. Life isn't happening to you; it's happening because of you. Take control of your narrative. Audit your actions, fix what you can control, and release the rest.

You're not here to fix the world. You're here to fix your part.

Focus on what you can do, what you can change, and what you need to learn. The rest? Accept it and move on. That's not weakness—that's wisdom.

Are you going to keep promises to yourself? That should be your first commitment. Are you going to do what you say you'll do? That should be your ultimate goal. If there's one piece of advice I'd give a young person, it's this:

Do what you say you are going to do.

Personal Reflections
**Self-Assessment (Demonstrating the Value of Accountability
and the Virtue of Integrity)**

- Is there a pattern in my life that keeps repeating, causing conflict or issues?
  - o These patterns can be one thing or a combination. You repeatedly end up in fights with your partner and it's never your fault. You constantly land jobs where your boss or co-workers can't stand you. You fall into the same drinking binges that leave you with no memory of the night before.
  - o The degree of the issue isn't the concern—the repetition is. More importantly, your refusal to acknowledge it.
- Do I rarely (or never) admit being in the wrong in conflicts or critical discussions?
  - o If you never initiate resolution or clean-up in a conflict—fault or not—your ego is in control.
- Do I accept my role in my current state?
  - o Do I understand I'm the common denominator in my recurring issues?
  - o Do I accept that Responsibility?
- Can I admit my position and role in it to others without apprehension?
  - o Can I participate in conflict resolution without shutting down or deflecting?
  - o Even if I struggle to verbalize it—do my actions reflect acknowledgment and Accountability?

**Application (Practicing the Principle of Responsibility,
the Value of Accountability, and the Virtue of Integrity)**

- **Fitness:** Am I truly owning my health and fitness—or am I blaming age, genetics, my schedule, or those around me?
- **Business:** Do I take full Responsibility for my results and failures—or do I blame my boss, my employees, my team, or company policies?

- **Family:** Am I accountable for how my actions affect my loved ones—or do I deflect Responsibility and blame others for every family challenge?

Final Thought

Nobody's coming to save you. That's not negative gloom and doom—it's just reality. If you want a different output, you've got to take control of the input. Excuses don't serve you. They don't move you forward. Blame doesn't absolve you of your Responsibility—much less change your circumstances. The only thing that shifts your trajectory is taking Responsibility—owning your role in how you got here and what happens next. That doesn't mean beating yourself up or wallowing in guilt. It means being honest about your actions and decisions—then doing something about it. Responsibility gives you the wheel. From there, it's simple: you can steer into your future or crash. You're free to stay stuck and circle the drain. You're also free to get unstuck, flush this situation into the past, and move forward. But you don't get both.

Be responsible. Be accountable.
Take ownership—and let's $#%! go.

STAGE 1, PRINCIPLE 3—Self-Reflection
What Did I Do to Get Here?

We continue in Stage 1 with the third Principle—Self-Reflection. Self-Reflection is about looking back with purpose. It's not about blame—it's about understanding the cause and effect of your actions. Below, we'll recap Stage 1 and then break down the Self-Reflection Chain, which turns Analysis into Clarity.

Stage 1 Recap—Principles 1–4: Own the Problem & Find the Way Out

- **Principle 1—Humility:** Admit you are in over your head, you don't know everything, and you are open to learning.
- **Principle 2—Responsibility:** Own your role in your current situation—no blaming or excuses.
- **Principle 3—Self-Reflection:** Understand how your actions created your situation—analyze cause and effect.

The PB² Alignment—The Self-Reflection Chain

- **Principle: Self-Reflection**—Understand what got you here.
- **Value: Analysis**—Analyze how your actions got you here.
- **Virtue: Clarity**—Objectively analyze how actions caused the outcome.

Principle 3—Self-Reflection—Understand How Your Actions Created Your Situation

Asking the right questions points you toward change. What patterns keep repeating? Are you creating them through action—or inaction? Is fear, procrastination, or lack of a plan holding you back? Have others pointed this out and you ignored it? These questions cut through denial and force you to face reality as it is, not as you wish it to be. The moment you start answering them honestly, you begin gathering the data you need to make better decisions. Honest answers won't fix everything overnight, but they shift your direction—and that shift is the start of change.

Why this Is the Third Step

Where Humility lets you say, "I'm over my head and need help," and Self-Reflection says, "I own it," Analysis figures out, "This is how I did it." Before you can fix anything, you must accept that you're not where you want to be, own the moment, and understand what you did to get there so you can correct it. Once you see the cause, you can address the effect. That's the only way to make change. Show me someone who's been divorced four or five times and still blames the opposite sex, and I'll show you the common denominator. The old saying holds true: if you don't understand your history, you're doomed to repeat it.

Self-Reflection isn't self-punishment. It's Clarity—seeing what actually happened, what your role was, and what patterns or decisions keep you stuck. With Clarity, small course corrections add up fast. As Jordan Peterson advises: "If you want to pray, I will give you a prayer. Sit on the edge of your bed and ask yourself: 'What is the one thing I can do, that I'm willing to do, that if I did it, my life would improve?' Sit there and wait for the answer. The answer will surely come. It may not be the answer you want, but it will be the answer you need."

You don't have to overthink the process. Gained weight? Maybe business dinners got out of hand. Relationship struggling? Maybe you've been more interested in being right than resolving things. The challenge is blind spots—things you can't see without perspective. That's why Humility and Responsibility come first. And if you can't figure it out on your own, get help:

- Have a real conversation with a friend who will tell you the truth.
- Watch a YouTube lecture from someone you trust.
- Read that book you bought but never opened.
- Hire a coach or therapist if needed.

Not everyone grows up with these tools, and that's okay. Self-Reflection can be developed with practice. Sometimes the fix is simple but hidden in a blind spot—something you'd never see without the right prompt. And sometimes all it takes is one sentence, one question, or one perspective to crack it wide open and show you the path forward.

The Truth About Self-Reflection

Self-Reflection is not self-blame. It's recognizing what's working, what's not, and what needs to change. The one thing you must avoid is skipping this step and projecting your flaws onto others. That's why Responsibility comes before Self-Reflection—it prevents you from externalizing blame.

- Understand how you got here—what happened.
- What you did that caused it—your role in it.
- How your actions created the situation—the 'cause and effect' of your behavior.

Sometimes you are where you are because of good decisions—or at least the best ones available at the time. Other times, you may be stuck because of bad choices. Regardless, if you want change, you must develop Self-Reflection: take an honest inventory of your situation and commit to the steps needed for transformation. Here's how Self-Reflection plays out in two very different areas:

Career Growth

You're working in a warehouse. After three years, you realize your earning potential is capped. You reflect on your skills, update your résumé, and start applying for better roles. Soon, you land a manager position with higher pay and mobility. Self-Reflection here isn't emotional—it's practical Analysis.

Now let's say you want to move up again—maybe become a regional director earning $100K+. You'd go through the process again:

- **Humility (Principle)**—realize you're not where you want to be.
- **Responsibility (Principle)**—own your current position.
- **Self-Reflection (Principle)**—identify which skills and behaviors need upgrading.

Marriage Pattern

Now shift from career to relationships. You're on your third marriage, and your spouse says you're emotionally distant and controlling—just like the last two did. Through Self-Reflection, you see the pattern came from your upbringing. You decide to seek therapy to break it. This isn't tweaking a résumé—it's deep work, but the formula is the same: Humility, Responsibility, and Self-Reflection.

As you can see, Self-Reflection isn't always emotional heavy lifting—sometimes it's just Analysis and Execution. Other times it's deep work. When your behavior is the real problem, reflection can feel like breaking an addiction. It takes Prioritization, honesty, and constant reinforcement—one step at a time. The decision to go down that path is yours. No matter how difficult the crisis, the formula doesn't change: be humble enough to know you're in trouble, take full Responsibility for where you are, and reflect honestly on how you got there.

How the Value of Analysis and the Virtue of Clarity Relate to this Step

Analysis is about understanding, not judgment. It's the step where ownership turns into insight. You trace the path of your actions to see how each decision shaped your current reality. This is where Clarity anchors Self-Reflection into measurable progress.

Value: Analysis—Analyze How Your Actions Got You Here

Analysis means breaking down how your choices created your present—tracing the chain of cause and effect that led you here, without judgment, just truth. If things are good, you study what worked so you can scale it—like a business owner who doubled revenue by improving recruiting, onboarding, and marketing, then examines why those systems worked to replicate them in a second location. Success leaves clues, and Analysis helps you identify and repeat them.

If things are bad, you confront the decisions that trapped you—like an athlete who keeps re-injuring the same knee because they skip the tedious rehabilitation work, or an addict asking hard questions about what pain they're numbing and whether they're truly ready to change. Maybe you've overextended your finances—new house, new car, luxury trips—and now you're drowning in debt. Analysis forces you to pause and ask: Where did I start living above my means? What emotion was I chasing with those purchases? It's not about guilt—it's about locating the exact point where momentum turned against you. Or maybe your business hit a plateau: leads dropped, team morale is low, clients are disengaging. Analysis here means reviewing your systems—are you measuring the right metrics, rewarding the right behaviors, or clinging to outdated methods because they once worked?

At this stage, you're not fixing everything—you're flushing out the main issues holding you back. You're identifying the leverage points—the 20% of factors causing 80% of your outcomes. Once those come into view, the next step—the Fixing Part—becomes simple. You can't fix what you won't face, and Analysis is how you face it.

Virtue: Clarity—Objectively Analyze How Actions Caused the Event

Clarity is where you connect actions to results. Newton's Third Law says that for every action, there is an equal and opposite reaction. That's not just physics—it's life. If something's pushing back, it's because you pushed first.

Analysis identifies the action; Clarity reveals the reaction. You don't control how the world responds—but you control what you put into it. Skip this step, and you'll stay stuck, repeating the same patterns and never knowing why. Connect the action to the reaction, and you gain insight—and insight gives you leverage that leads to the playbook for change.

What leverage really means here: once you see the real cause and effect, you can actually make a choice. Without that Clarity, you're blind—you're just guessing and repeating the same behavior. With Clarity, you have leverage because you finally see what's true, and that truth gives you control over your next move.

- Your choices become simple:
- Keep doing it.
- Stop doing it.
- Or, change it and do something better.

That's leverage—the power to choose based on truth, not excuses. Without it, you're stuck reacting. With it, you're steering your own direction.

A Live Example

As of this writing, I'm four weeks out from a total knee replacement. I've been through plenty of injuries and rehabs—but this one's the toughest. It's been four weeks of constant pain or high discomfort, 24/7. Progress feels very slow. Pain meds help the pain but wreck your insides. With a few exceptions, every rehab session hurts. I'm 100% responsible for my recovery—with help from my friend, and IHP resident PT, Dr. Joseph Sobucki, and Dr. Nick Cress, DC.

I'm doing 3–5 sessions a day: scar tissue work, ROM, strength, compression, ice, and e-stim. Fun? HELL NO. Could I lie and say I'm doing the work while I skip it? Sure. Could I lean on painkillers and avoid the grind? Sure. Would anyone know? Probably not. But life would. Action and reaction always win—that's a Principle. The truth always shows up in the results.

The Consequences of Not Doing What's Necessary

- My knee would heal in the comfortable position it likes—semi-flexed.
- In 2–3 months, the scar tissue buildup would prevent me from fully extending or flexing my knee.
- My gait and knee function would be altered, and I would limp for the rest of my life.

- Then, of course, I'd start lying and making excuses about what happened to my knee.

That's the power of Clarity. You can lie to others, you can lie to yourself, but you can't lie to life.

No matter what the outcome is, I can face it. Why? Because I was honest, diligent, and did my best. I did the research, followed my plan, and constantly updated and re-evaluated. With that Integrity and Clarity, I can face any outcome. If it ends up great, I'll rejoice. If it ends up unsatisfactory, I'll do the process all over again—with more wisdom. This is life—and it's how I choose to live it.

Why People Struggle with this Step

- A habit of internal lies and self-deception
- Emotional or chemical attachment to destructive habits and beliefs
- Ego and insecurity
- Lack of Humility and Responsibility
- Genuine lack of information

Many people are part of what I call the "I'm trying" gang. How many times do you hear:

- "I'm trying."
- "I'm doing the best I can."

Most of the time, they're not. They're doing just enough to claim they're trying—but deep down, they know they're not. Certainly not giving it their all. They're giving what they're willing to give—and that's rarely enough for excellence.

Take obesity, for example. Ask anyone which is better for losing weight: the same number of calories in pizza, or in veggies and lean chicken? Ninety-nine percent will answer correctly. Yet 40% are still overweight.

That's not an information issue—it's a Responsibility issue. And if your struggle is lack of information? There's no excuse. The Internet, AI, mentors, professionals—all are available to help you take positive steps forward. So—no excuses.

When you point fingers outward, your other three fingers point back at you. Self-Reflection forces you to accept and Analyze truths, even when they're uncomfortable.

Application (Practicing the Principle of Self-Reflection, the Value of Analysis, and the Virtue of Clarity)

- **Fitness:** Have I examined at why I go on great streaks of training and weight loss, only to quit for months and yo-yo back?
- **Business:** Do I keep avoiding real work and leadership, making excuses, and hiring more people to cover what only I can do as the leader?
- **Family:** Do I listen to my family's needs and suggestions, or do I rule my home like a dictator who assumes he knows everything?

Final Thought

Without Self-Reflection, you're flying blind. You can't move forward with precision if you don't first face what really happened. This isn't about shame—it's about truth. Truth is the ultimate leverage. With it, you see what's broken and what's not. Without it, you're just guessing—fixing what doesn't need fixing and ignoring what does. That's why Self-Reflection is freedom: once you know what happened, what you did, and how your actions shaped the outcome, you gain the Clarity to move forward with purpose—and power.

STAGE 1, PRINCIPLE 4—Self-Awareness
What Options Do I Have to Move Forward?

We've reached the final Principle of Stage 1—Self-Awareness. This is where reflection turns into direction. Self-Awareness is about identifying what needs to change and choosing the most practical way to start moving forward. Below, we'll recap Stage 1 and then break down the Self-Awareness Chain, which turns Recognition into Objectivity.

Stage 1 Recap—Principles 1–4: Own the Problem & Find the Way Out

- **Principle 1—Humility:** Admit you are in over your head, you don't know everything, and you are open to learning.
- **Principle 2—Responsibility:** Own your role in your current situation—no blaming or excuses.
- **Principle 3—Self-Reflection:** Understand how your actions created your situation—analyze cause and effect.
- **Principle 4—Self-Awareness:** Identify which of your actions have to change—identify your best choices.

The PB² Alignment—The Self-Awareness Chain

- **Principle: Self-Awareness**—Identifying changes needed to fix it.
- **Value: Recognition**—Recognizing your best options.
- **Virtue: Objectivity**—Taking the best course of action from your best options.

Principle 4—Self-Awareness—Identifying Changes Needed to Fix It

Self-Awareness isn't just about identifying great options—it's about choosing the best option you can actually execute. Sometimes, the perfect solution isn't realistic, and that's where people get stuck. They see progress as an all-or-nothing deal. If they can't achieve the perfect solution, they assume no solution exists. But that's not how progress works. A perfect solution is worthless if it's impossible to execute.

The real move? Once you have a general fix in sight, break it down into small, actionable steps that move you in the right direction—one step at a time. The one thing you must walk away with at this stage is a clear, actionable path forward that you can actually pull off. As we've mentioned before, at this stage it's better to focus on forming lasting habits than chasing fast results. Habits last—results fade if they're not built on good habits.

- You don't need all the answers—just the next right move.
- Form the habit first, the increase the intensity.
- The best solution is often slow moving and uncomfortable—but necessary.
- If you skip this step, you'll act on impulse or stay paralyzed in indecision.

This is where reality checks meet action. The path forward, not necessarily the solution, is there—you just have to recognize it and commit to it. At this initial stage of Self-Awareness, you're not dealing with details—you're looking at the macro level. The goal is to identify the major change needed to move forward in the right direction. Often, what needs to change is a single major thing. The fewer things that need to change, the easier it is to compartmentalize and take action. Singular focus is key at this stage—broad, scattered thinking leads to overwhelm and inaction. For example:

- I need to create a surplus of money each month.
- I need to drop weight.
- I need to be more patient.
- I need to listen better and stop interrupting.

Once you identify the big change needed, you can then look at what solutions are available to accomplish it. These should be smaller, doable steps.

Say you want to buy a house. Your Self-Awareness breakthrough is realizing you need a monthly surplus. The next step—Recognition—is finding practical ways to make that happen:

- Instead of going out each week, I'll go out only three times each month.
- Instead of ordering takeout five times a week, I'll cook at home.
- Instead of drinking alcohol six days a week, I'll cut my drinking in half.
- I'll use my talents or skills (DJ, web design, bookkeeping, or cleaning) to work once a month and earn extra money.

These are all doable steps that just about anyone can use to create a monthly surplus. You can tackle one at a time or multiple steps simultaneously, depending on your situation and what's most practical. Although this process seems logical, many people still struggle with it. Emotions cloud judgment, and sometimes pure laziness kicks in—causing distractions and a lack of action instead of addressing the core issue.

Why this is Is the Fourth Step

At this stage, you're ready to stop looking backward and start moving forward. Self-Awareness is where problem-solving begins—identifying what needs to change so you can move beyond your current situation. Knowing why something broke isn't enough—you also need to recognize how to fix it. This is the bridge between Analysis and action. Let's look at an example of how Self-Reflection and Self-Awareness work together.

Example: The MMA Fighter

Let's say you're a top MMA fighter on a four-fight losing streak that just ended in a knockout loss. You lose your contract with the promotion you fought for and now find yourself at a career crossroads.

- Self-Reflection helps you see that your training habits have been a major issue—you're constantly over-trained and never step into the cage at 100%.
- Because of this, you haven't been able to showcase your full skill set, leading to subpar performances.

Now comes Self-Awareness—your training and recovery approach must change. Next comes Recognition—identifying good options.

- Change MMA academy
- Fire all coaches
- Hire new technical coach who trains smarter.
- Hire a new conditioning coach to take over your schedule.
- Hire a nutritionist.
- Hire a sports psychologist.
- Utilize IV therapy for faster recovery.
- Limit hard sparring to once per week.
- Implement hot and cold for faster recovery.

You find the most effective and practical course of action is to:

- Optimize your training balance between technical work, strength and conditioning, nutrition, and—most importantly—recovery.
- Hire a new head coach who takes over your training, prioritizes skill work, and limits sparring.

See how naturally that can flow?

From there, your new coach might bring in a strength and conditioning expert to add another key component to the equation. Maybe a nutritionist is consulted once it's established that your diet was lacking. The key point: the fighter only made one major decision—to hire a new head coach—based on the awareness that the entire training system needed revamping. One decision. One move. And now more solutions emerge as a result of basic Awareness. Principles are rarely a mystery. Once you learn them, they just click—you think, "Yeah, I get it." They may not always be comfortable or easy, but they're clear and easy to understand.

Self-Awareness bridges the gap between what happened and what needs to happen next—what patterns to break, what habits to change, and what steps will actually lead to the outcome you want. You can't move forward if you don't know the way. Self-Awareness turns insight into direction.

The Truth About Self-Awareness

Self-Awareness is the shift from understanding the past to mapping the future. You're not just identifying what went wrong—you're determining what needs to happen next. Without it, you either stay stuck in reflection mode, overanalyzing every detail, or you react blindly without direction. This stage is about:

1. Figuring out what will get you out of your situation.
2. Identifying the best options for your specific circumstances.
3. Taking the best possible course of action available at the time.

Many people never reach this point because they either avoid the truth and blame external factors—or they analyze so much that they freeze. That's why the Principles of the PB² System build in sequence:

- If you're still blaming others, you stalled at Responsibility—you have to fix that before moving forward.
- If you're drowning in analysis and can't act, you stalled at Self-Reflection—you must regain focus before advancing to Self-Awareness.

How the Value of Recognition and Virtue of Objectivity Relate to this Step

This stage shifts you from information gathering to applying knowledge. Recognizing that not all great options are necessarily the best options is a crucial distinction. Objectivity is key here—if emotions take over, you'll make decisions based on comfort rather than effectiveness. At first, you'll have a list of possible actions. Objectivity helps narrow that list down to the best solutions that are actually doable. That doesn't mean they're the easiest or most comfortable solutions. The best doable solutions aren't always the easiest—but they are the ones that will actually move you forward.

Value: Recognition
Recognizing All of My Best Options

Once you identify the major thing that needs to change, the next step is figuring out what options are available to fix it. This is where Recognition kicks in—it's about seeing clearly, not perfectly. Your goal is to identify all the viable routes forward before judging or ranking them. Think of this as your strategic brainstorm. You're not throwing spaghetti at the wall—you're mapping possibilities with intention. Start by asking the following:

What are all the realistic ways I can address this problem?
Which of these are within my control right now?
Who or what resources could help accelerate progress?

As you build this list:

- Separate distractions from real solutions. Some ideas look productive but are really just mental busywork—ways to delay the hard stuff.
- Distinguish between efficient solutions and complicated ones. The best ideas usually simplify, not expand.
- Stay open to everything reasonable. Sometimes the right option isn't comfortable—it's just effective.

The key here is not to filter yet. You're exploring, not editing. Recognition is about awareness—seeing what's in front of you without bias or emotion. When you recognize your options, you take chaos and turn it into Clarity. You're now moving from reaction to Strategy. The next step—Objectivity—will help you refine this list, prioritize the lowest-hanging fruit, and start executing with confidence.

Virtue: Objectivity
Taking the Best Course of Action from My List of Options

At this point, you're narrowing down from possible solutions to the best solutions—the ones that aren't just theoretically effective, but practically doable. Continuing the funnel analogy, this is where the finest material emerges. You've filtered through what needs to change, explored available solutions, and now you're selecting the most effective and achievable path forward.

- This is where you move from "What could work?" to "What will work?"
- These solutions are typically the low-hanging fruit—the most logical, simplest, and easiest to execute.
- Not every option is a good option—and not every good option is a viable option.

At this stage, you've gone from "What needs to change?" to "What solutions do I have that I can actually pull off?" Early wins matter. This is where we want to create the habitual momentum we mentioned earlier in this book. The more you succeed, the more success reinforces itself—momentum is everything. Success breeds success. Setting yourself up for small, achievable wins creates momentum—and momentum fuels sustained action. Here's an interesting take on building a winning addiction. Candace Pert, in Molecules of Emotion, proposed a fascinating theory:

- When you do something that generates a specific feeling, your body releases chemical messengers called peptides.

- The more you experience that feeling, the more your body begins to crave those peptides.
- Over time, you can become chemically addicted the peptides associate with the behaviors that produce those emotions—whether positive or negative.

This means that building momentum through early wins isn't just psychological—it's biochemical. When you design small, consistent wins into your plan, your body starts associating action with reward. You're literally wiring yourself for progress. That's why choosing the right initial steps is so critical—your actions don't just shape your results; they rewire your brain and body to chemically crave success.

Why People Struggle with this Step
Over-Analyzing Every Option Until Paralysis Sets In

- Letting emotions cloud judgment and derail Objectivity
- Confusing 'hard' solutions with 'effective' solutions
- Picking the easy way out and wasting time on distractions
- Avoiding uncomfortable truths that require Humility and Responsibility

Most people get stuck here because they want perfect answers before moving forward—or they cling to comfortable answers that don't actually solve the problem. Progress is not about the perfect choice; it's about the best choice you can realistically execute. Self-Awareness is about Clarity in direction, not fantasy in perfection.

Now, what's left on the table are the things you can actually do—like cutting down on frivolous expenses, asking your boss for a raise, looking for a parallel move with slightly better pay, or picking up a side hustle to generate a few hundred bucks extra per month. Maybe you do all three. These are practical, effective, and achievable. And they're a hell of a lot easier than magically doubling your income or crashing at your parents' downsized two-bedroom condo.

This is where people go off track. Some let emotions take the wheel and lose clarity. Others skip the simple step-by-step process that keeps them grounded. Some waste time on easy fixes that don't produce real results, while others aim so high they flame out early. Then there are those who aim so low that even improvement still leaves them stuck in the gutter of despair. Objectivity helps you steer between those traps—toward action that actually moves you forward.

Navigating this Step

- **Don't Start Big and Hard**. Those options usually aren't doable—or the risk-to-reward ratio isn't in your favor. Failure becomes almost inevitable.
- **Don't Start Small and Easy.** Those options rarely create noticeable results and often end up being a waste of time.
- **Stay Simple.** Keep your changes general at first so they're easy to identify and adjust.
- **Lists Don't Suck.** Once you know what needs to change, write down every possible solution. Putting thoughts on paper has power—it brings order to chaos.
- **Big To Small.** Organize your list from hardest at the top to easiest at the bottom—just like your funnel.
- **Isolate 1–3 Small Actions** you can do immediately to improve your situation. Not necessarily fix it—just move it forward.
- **Commit Right Now** to 2–3 logical steps under each small action.

This is the early phase of planning that follows Self-Awareness. Success in this stage depends on your ability to get out of your own way and be honest about what truly needs to happen. Stay big in concept but simple in solutions. Break it down into doable steps—and then into smaller tasks. Stay Disciplined and remember:

BIG PICTURE → small actions
small wins → BIG WINS

Personal Reflections

- Do I let my emotions run away with the task at hand?
- Do I stay organized in my thinking—**BIG PICTURE** to **small actions?**
- Do I get distracted by "pie in the sky" solutions?
- Do I avoid work and chase easy fixes?
- Do I use lists to stay focused and on track?

The answers to these questions must be addressed before moving to the next stage. This is the whole point of sequencing principles—anytime you get stuck, you know exactly what to go back and work on.

Application (Practicing the Principle Self-Awareness, the Value of Recognition, and Virtue of Objectivity)

- **Fitness:** Are you being real about your health and fitness? Are you choosing the smartest training and nutrition plan you can sustain—or just the one that feels easiest? Are you chasing long-term success, or falling for shortcuts like appetite-killing drugs that strip away muscle mass? Real progress comes from right effort, not least effort.
- **Business:** Are you making the smartest move for growth—or just the one that feels safe? Are you showing up as the kind of person who elevates everyone within 15 feet? Or are you "working from home" and giving excuses for not showing up? Growth doesn't demand crazy-hard work—it demands smart, consistent work.
- **Family:** Are you facing conflicts head-on with real solutions—or just bitching, blaming, and doing nothing? Are you avoiding tough conversations? Avoidance doesn't fix relationships—honest discussion and a real plan for change do.

If you don't apply Self-Awareness to these areas, you'll keep repeating old patterns instead of making progress.

Final Thought

Self-Awareness isn't about having all the answers—it's about identifying what needs to change and creating a doable list of actions that move the needle in a positive direction. If you can recognize the smartest and easiest way forward—and commit to it—you've already won half the battle. From there, it's simple: right foot, left foot, repeat.

"Anyone can draw a map to success,
but few can walk the road less traveled."
~ JCS

11

CREATE
AND EXECUTE
THE PLAN
(PRINCIPLES 5–7)

Stage 2—Create & Execute the Plan

Where the first four Principles of Stage 1 focus on owning the problem and identifying the best next steps, this second phase—and the next three Principles—shift toward building and executing a plan based on the options uncovered in the Self-Awareness phase. This chapter covers the importance of creating a plan—and, more importantly, committing it to paper (or digital format). We'll also tackle the Principle of Sacrifice—the truth that anything worthwhile requires you to give something up. Everyone knows there are no freebies in life. High-value goals demand time, money, or emotional energy. Often all three.

This phase ends with the Principle of Facing Fear—"just do it." Sounds simple. But the reality is, taking action almost always requires confronting fear—and that's exactly what we'll dive into by the end of this chapter. Now let's get into Stage 2 and Principle Number Five: Strategizing.

STAGE 2, PRINCIPLE 5—Strategizing
The Plan to Move Forward—The Playbook

The Principle of Strategizing is understanding that a clear plan is necessary—and will always outperform winging it. Strategy connects all the insights you gained from Self-Awareness and channels them into a practical, executable format. Without Strategizing, you won't see the cause-and-effect relationships between your actions and your outcomes. Even if you get lucky and succeed, you won't fully understand what caused the win. And if you can't replicate it, no real learning is taking place.

Stage 1 Recap—Principles 1–4: Own the Problem & Find the Way Out

- **Principle 1—Humility:** Admit you are in over your head, you don't know everything, and you are open to learning.
- **Principle 2—**Responsibility: Own your role in your current situation—no blaming or excuses.
- **Principle 3—Self-Reflection:** Understand how your actions created your situation—analyze cause and effect.
- **Principle 4—Self-Awareness:** Identify which of your actions have to change—identify your best choices.

PB² Alignment—The Strategizing Chain

Principle—Strategizing (turn solutions into a plan)
Value—Prioritization (structure the plan using the best solutions)
Virtue—Execution (implement without hesitation)

Now we move into Stage 2, beginning with its first Principle—Strategizing: the need for a plan.

Principle 5— Strategizing—The Need for a Plan

After identifying the best and simplest solutions to break past your current limitations, the next logical step is to organize and structure them into a clear plan. Without a strategy, even great ideas become scattered and inefficient. Much of this groundwork was already done in the Self-Awareness Chain. You've listed your best options—from easiest to hardest, and from short-term to long-term. Now it's time to put them into motion. The Principle of Strategizing is your commitment to this process—the belief that order, not luck, drives results.

Many people think planning or note-taking is overkill. I'm here to tell you it's not. You don't need to write a diary, but you do need a system—some form of schedule, log, or tracker you can reference daily. It could be a

Google Calendar, Notes app, or an old-school notebook—whatever keeps your plan visible and actionable.

At IHP, I learned this through experience. Life gets crazy, and with so many clients, there's no way to remember every detail of every session. That's why we chart everything: sets, reps, weights, dates, and session numbers. If a trainer doesn't log a session, they don't get paid—because at IHP, if it isn't documented, it didn't happen. You get paid for a full job, not a partial one—and charting is part of the job. I credit IHP's global success to that discipline. Our planning and charting system has been the backbone of our continuous improvement. We don't guess—we track. We don't hope—we plan. That's the essence of Strategizing.

Why this Is the Fifth Step

Once you have the best possible solutions, then you need to strategize a plan, because order of execution is extremely important. The plan is exactly how something as simple as cooking works: you may have the perfect and best ingredients to create a masterpiece dish; however, the cooking instructions are essential to the final product, and if you overcook or over-spice one of the elements of the dish, the whole dish is ruined. Strategizing is the plan that will allow you to manage the best solutions isolated in the last stage. Writing a book is no different—you can have all of the information, but putting it in the right order of flow is what will clearly convey the information in the book. Effective Strategizing takes the understanding you've developed, honestly prioritizes the best path forward, and deliberately executes the plan step-by-step.

Having the great fortune of being considered a leader in the fitness industry for decades, I'm often asked who I learned from. My answer never changes: "I learned from practicing what I teach—and then sharing it clearly and consistently." Whether as a coach, author, or presenter, teaching has always been my ultimate form of Strategizing. I reflect on experiences—what worked and what didn't. I become aware of why those experiences unfolded as they did. Then I carefully Strategize to ensure my message comes across logically, sequentially, and in an impactful way. This strategic approach embodies real-world learning. Writing a book or crafting a presentation isn't just about sharing what you know—it's about turning:

$$Data \rightarrow Information$$
$$Information \rightarrow Knowledge$$
$$Knowledge \rightarrow Wisdom$$

...and then delivering it in a way people can actually understand and apply. If that isn't structured learning—if that isn't evolution—then nothing is.

The Truth about Strategizing

Strategizing is the moment when vision becomes direction. It's not about dreaming—it's about designing. When you build a plan, you turn ideas into an action roadmap that connects where you are to where you want to be. Without a plan, even the best intentions drift into chaos.

- You identify what matters most—and what doesn't.
- You organize your moves in the order that makes success inevitable.
- You act with purpose, not impulse.

No more guessing. No more "I'll figure it out later." If you refuse to Strategize, you stay reactive—spending energy on everything and progressing on nothing. It's not about how much you do—it's about doing the right things in the right order. When I hear people say, "I'm just going with the flow," I remind them: That's not flow—that's drift. **Drifting doesn't build mastery. Strategizing does.**

How the Value of Prioritization and Virtue of Execution Relate to this Step

The Value of Prioritization and the Virtue of Execution bring Strategizing to life. Prioritization gives your plan structure and direction—it focuses your energy on what matters most instead of what feels most urgent. Execution turns that structured plan into reality through consistent, disciplined action. Together, they transform strategy into progress. You stop reacting and start advancing with intention. That's how thinking becomes doing—and doing becomes mastery. That's how you turn planning into progress and progress into mastery.

Value: Prioritization—Structuring a Plan for Effectiveness

In today's world of social media, influencers constantly post themselves doing extreme stunts—running three marathons in a row, free climbing without safety lines, diving with sharks on zero experience.

They call it fearless.

But let's be real—that's not how you inspire the uninspired or teach people how to grow. The intention might be good, but the Execution is way off. Mastering anything, including fear, takes planning. And real planning demands Prioritization—doing the right thing, in the right order, for the right reasons. In sports, we call this pedagogy: the method and practice of teaching. Good pedagogy isn't random; it follows a sequence that gives the learner the highest chance of success:

- Simple before complex
- Easy before hard
- Slow before fast
- Skill before conditioning

Why? Because skill is fragile. Pressure breaks it if it hasn't been ingrained under control. Speed, intensity, or brute force without skill—that's how you burn out. Life's no different. You don't start with the hardest change first. You start with what's doable—small wins and early progress that build momentum and confidence. Once the basics are locked in, then you add load: more Responsibility, tighter Consistency, harder reps. That's how you build the habit of Execution—just like training strength or endurance. When you prioritize well, you stop wasting energy. You stop trying to do everything—and start doing what matters. You channel time, focus, and attention toward high-yield actions: planning, skill-building, and disciplined follow-through. The rest—recovery, hobbies, mental resets—still matters, but they support the main mission; they don't replace it. This is why strategy and Prioritization matter. They give you structure, flexibility, and the ability to adapt without losing momentum. When things get hectic, you don't panic—you go back to the plan.

Virtue: Execution—Implementing the Plan Without Hesitation

Once you have the right actions, in the right sequence, with clear priorities, there's only one thing left—the doing. Execution is what turns plans into reality. Your plan doesn't matter if it lives in a notebook and never hits your calendar. Execution is disciplined, deliberate action pointed at your goal—and it starts now. Not tomorrow. Not Monday. Not next month. Execution is the separator between dreamers and doers. Everyone intends to act—few actually do. Plans without Execution become regret. Movement, no matter how small, converts belief into evidence. That's why Execution isn't just a behavior—it's a mindset: a commitment to act before comfort sets in.

- **Diet?** Starts at dinner—salad, veggies, chicken.
- **Exercise?** Too late for the gym? Walk your dog for 15 minutes.
- **Sleep hygiene?** Phones out at 10:30, lights out at 11:00.
- **Business plan?** Open a doc and write the first line.
- **Résumé?** No TV—start after dinner, get it done.
- **Messy room?** Clean your desk now—clear space clears your head.
- **Behind on calls?** Make one call right now, or today—momentum starts with one.
- **Avoiding finances?** Open your banking app and face the numbers.

Sure—some things can't start this second. Fine. Then they start tomorrow morning—first thing. But something always can start now—whether it's adding tasks to your calendar or gathering info so nothing slows you down later. That's the signal to your brain that you're in motion. Action is symbolic power. One move forward breaks months of procrastination.

Why Some People Struggle with this Step

- **Laziness:** Many don't want to invest the time in preparatory work.
- **Lack of Clarity:** Without a clear plan, action feels aimless.
- **Lack of Focus:** Too much noise, too many distractions, zero follow-through.

We live in a world where you can get by without ever leaving your house—but don't confuse that with living. Is it any wonder people have gone soft?

Laziness evolves from practicing being lazy—from rehearsing 'doing less'.

When comfort is delivered on demand, Discipline erodes. You can work out, diet, even hold two jobs—and still be mentally weak where it matters. Physical toughness doesn't equal emotional resilience. Just because you can survive special-forces training doesn't mean you can win a 15-minute fight in the UFC. PB² work is internal work—Humility, Self-Reflection, Self-Awareness, and Strategizing. You can't out-train that.

Some people aren't lazy—they're lost. They have energy but no Clarity. They don't know where to start. That's where Strategizing comes in. It's your GPS. It shows you where you are and where you're going. Use Prioritization to pick the most efficient steps, and keep it flexible enough to adjust when life throws a curveball.

Start with what's doable. Don't chase the biggest fix first. If you're broke, cutting Uber Eats might be smarter than chasing a 30% raise tomorrow. Grab the easy wins, stack progress, and let momentum build.

Then there's focus—or the lack of it. In the age of Amazon Prime and dopamine loops, attention spans are shot. The average person's focus is like a squirrel on espresso. When a goal has no schedule, no supervision, and no consequences, most people drift. Here's the truth: if imagining a better life, a stronger family, or a powerful legacy doesn't light you up, nothing will. Like AA's twelve steps, this only works if you admit you need it and do the work. If your goal isn't bigger than your distractions, you have the wrong goal! If it is—but you're acting like it's not—then: **Stop being a bitch. Have some pride. Show some spine.**

Navigating this Step

Do you have the basics covered, or are you still skipping the obvious?

People love to bypass fundamentals because they think the basics are for beginners. Going back feels like failure, like admitting you missed something you should have mastered. So even when they're stuck, unhappy, or facing consequences, they resist returning to the essentials that actually move the needle. It's the boxer who refuses to practice his jab because he's won a hundred street fights. It's the executive who won't attend therapy or leadership training—even as his team collapses—because he believes he's 'past that'. That mindset kills progress. The truth is, mastery is built on relentless review of the fundamentals. The best don't outgrow the basics—they own them so completely that execution becomes second nature. If you want to master Strategizing, go back to the fundamentals: plan, organize, and execute—over and over—until it becomes automatic. That's how structured repetition creates freedom, and freedom becomes power.

Street Fights and Competitive Boxing Are Not the Same

Managing a three-man crew isn't the same as leading a full-scale project with engineers, architects, city officials, permit officers, and construction teams. Big, complex things need a foundation built on the basics—

repeated through deliberate practice until those basics become automatic inside a complex system. If you grew up rough and never learned core social skills—communication, conflict resolution, basic manners, compromise—you won't survive in a leadership setting. You'll have to go back and fill in what you missed. You'll need something like the PB² System just to level the playing field. It's okay to get help with the basics. Be honest. Be humble. Go back to the beginning and close the gaps that left you stuck. Are you willing to commit your basic strategy to paper? Create the list.

You Gonna Create that List—or Keep Winging It?

Sit your ass down and write while you're thinking and strategizing. Everyone thinks writing a plan is for beginners. Wrong. What do you think a calendar is? A to-do list? A hit list? Anyone who needs to remember multiple things and stay organized uses some form of list.

How many times have you gone shopping without a list and forgotten something—usually the very thing you went for? So let me get this straight: your simple groceries deserve a list, but your complicated life doesn't? Build your list using the steps from Self-Awareness and Strategizing. Line items up from easy to hard, short-term to long-term. Then go into sniper mode and take them out—one by one.

Stick to the List: Prioritize Based on Impact, Urgency, and Feasibility

Do you actually prioritize—or do you have Execution ADHD, chasing quick fixes that go nowhere? People who've never practiced structured focus get distracted fast. They love shortcuts and 'no-effort, all-results' promises. Look around—the market is built on that mindset: Ozempic, liposuction, pills, surgeries. If something helps people dodge the discomfort of Discipline, they'll throw money at it—no matter the cost. But the easy path is what got you here. You wanna stay stuck? Keep doing the same. If not—go the other way. Put your big-boy (or big-girl) pants on, make a simple plan, write it down, and start executing. *Period.*

Regularly Review and Adjust the Plan

Do you re-evaluate and readjust based on what's actually happening?

I love long, multi-month plans—but they're general. What matters are the short-term specifics: one to two weeks at a time. Depending on how your week goes, next week's list will change. And how this month unfolds might shift your timeline by a few months.

Plan for the future—but live in the NOW!
Strategize this month—execute today!

That's why I review my calendar every night. It takes minutes, but that check-in tells you whether you crushed it or coasted. That feedback becomes tomorrow's focus. Review your list daily—especially in the beginning, when habits are forming.

Personal Reflections
Self-Assessment

- Am I trying to wing it without a structured approach?
- Do I have a clear, written, actionable plan?
- Have I set real goals and clear priorities?
- Do I check in and adjust based on how I'm doing?

Application (Fitness/Business/Family)

- **Fitness:** Do I have—and follow—a real plan for training and nutrition?
- **Business:** Do I actually track what I'm doing and how it's moving me toward my career goals?
- **Family:** Have I written down how I want to lead, teach, and be present for my family? If so, do I even look at the list—much less follow it?

Final Thought

You don't accomplish anything worthwhile by winging it. Building a business, earning a degree, or training for a championship—all require a plan. When serious change is needed, don't drift into success; get there deliberately. You won't stumble into Consistency or hope the right sequence magically unfolds. Take deliberate steps—and write them down. Why? Because life gets loud. When it does, you need a GPS—that's what Strategizing is. At any given moment, you should be able to look at your plan and know:

- Where you've been.
- Where you are.
- Where you're going.
- Whether you're ahead, on time, or behind.

Structure gives Discipline a backbone. A strategic plan keeps you moving when your feelings don't want to. If you believe in universal or celestial energy, writing it down is the ultimate act of intention—aligning thoughts, words, and actions toward a clear outcome. It gives shape to what's been floating in your head and starts pulling it into reality. You either build a plan—or keep reacting to life like a rookie.

Create the list. Work the list. Adjust the list.

That's how you get out of where you are. That's how you become who you want to be.

STAGE 2, PRINCIPLE 6—Sacrifice
You Have to Be Willing to Pay

The Principle of Sacrifice is understanding that everything of value carries a cost—and you must be willing to pay it. Sacrifice connects your plan to your commitment. Without it, even the best strategy remains an idea with no engine. You can't move forward without exchange—time, comfort, ego, convenience, or control. Sacrifice is what converts intention into effort and effort into transformation. Without embracing it, you'll keep chasing results you're not willing to earn.

Stage 1 Recap—Principles 1–4: Own the Problem and Find the Way Out

- **Principle 1—Humility:** Admit you are in over your head, you don't know everything, and you are open to learning.
- **Principle 2—Responsibility:** Own your role in your current situation—no blaming or excuses.
- **Principle 3—Self-Reflection:** Understand how your actions created your situation—analyze cause and effect.
- **Principle 4—Self-Awareness:** Identify which of your actions have to change—identify your best choices.

Stage 2 Recap—Principles 5–7: Create & Execute the Plan

- **Principle 5—Strategizing:** Put those solutions into a plan—the creation of a PLAYBOOK.

You have to be willing to GIVE something of value to GET something of value.

The PB² alignment

- **Principle: Sacrifice**—Anything of value requires something of value.
- **Value: Commitment**—Investing time, energy, or resources for greater outcomes
- **Virtue: Selflessness**—Letting go of comfort or immediate rewards for long-term success.

Principle 6—Sacrifice—Anything of Value Requires Something of Value.

Real talk: If something truly matters, it will cost you something mean-ingful. But don't mistake Sacrifice for suffering. More pain doesn't guarantee better results. That's a trap. Let me give you two examples.

Example 1—Same Car, Different Price

Let's say you want to buy a car—Model X. You have two options:

Option 1: Luxury concierge dealer. Massage chairs in the lounge, organic buffet, no-wait appointments, salesmen in thousand-dollar suits, a private test track. Model X lists for $80,000.

Option 2: Local dealer that just opened. Free coffee and water, modest waiting area, courteous staff in polos, test drives on the street. Same exact car. Same exact features. Same exact warranty. Model X lists for $75,000.

Which one do you choose? The $75,000 one—of course. Here's the point: the luxury dealer demands a bigger Sacrifice—an extra $5,000—but you don't get any more car for it. More Sacrifice doesn't always mean better results. This is why Self-Reflection and Self-Awareness matter. You've got to know what you're sacrificing—and what you're getting in return. Let me give you another example—one that's close to my heart.

Example 2—MMA Culture

I've trained MMA fighters for over 30 years. No other sport—except bodybuilding—equates suffering with success like MMA. Fighters train harder than the fight requires, and I've seen brutal sparring sessions that go way past competition intensity—career-threatening injuries in practice, sabotaged performances, and shortened careers. Why? Because they believe more pain equals better results. That's a lie. History has proven it false, yet the culture refuses to change. For three decades I've pushed back—preaching technical skill, better conditioning, and less destructive sparring. I've tried to eliminate the unnecessary abuse. It hasn't fully changed the culture, and honestly, that's one reason I've lost some love for the sport. They've misunderstood Sacrifice completely.

When you use Self-Reflection and Self-Awareness, you start prioritizing efficiency. This is where smart Sacrifice comes in. I always tell my athletes: "Don't do the maximum you can do—do the minimum necessary for maximum results." In training, we call it *'optimal strength'*—the point where more strength doesn't add performance. If 200 pounds on the bench is enough for peak wrestling, chasing 220, 250, or 275 is pointless. More won't help. Same with life: more Sacrifice doesn't guarantee better results.

Rule: Do the minimum necessary for maximum results.

Sacrifice must be a strategic investment—planned, organized, precise. It's the shortest distance between two points. Not corner-cutting—unless the 'corners' you're cutting are the senseless, painful, and unnecessary ones.

Why this Is the Sixth Step

Sacrifice comes after Strategizing because once your plan is clear, you must willingly accept the price required to carry it out. This is not the phase where you do the Sacrifice; this is where you accept the concept of Sacrifice. Accepting Sacrifice means getting comfortable setting aside personal comfort or short-term convenience—selflessly committing to what matters more. Without embracing this Principle, you won't effectively confront Facing Fear, stay Consistent, or Persevere through the obstacles that inevitably arise.

The realization of this Principle is often brought on by pain—by hitting bottom. There's nothing like rock bottom to create the realization where you say, enough is enough, I'll do anything not to stay here. But that's a reactive adaptation to stress. Unless you understand the mechanics that got you to this point, there's very little learning in the experience.

If we go in knowing Sacrifices will be required—and that some of them will feel extremely uncomfortable—we have a better chance of sticking to them. It's like the jump-scare in a movie: you're constantly startled because you don't know what's coming or when. But if you were warned, you wouldn't be as scared because you'd be ready. Sacrifice is that jump-scare. If you know it's coming and you know its nature, it's much easier to accept.

When you live reactively, you keep reacting to the same things. There's no Analysis of what happens, when it happens, why it happens, and what to do to avoid the next crisis. This is where the value of the PB² system lies—it's a systematic flowchart for troubleshooting any crisis, any change you want, and any repetitive actions that keep delivering less-than-ideal results.

The Truth About Sacrifice

- Sacrifice isn't loss; it's an investment. If you're not willing to Sacrifice something lesser today, you'll never achieve greater rewards tomorrow.
- Success and Sacrifice always walk hand-in-hand—no shortcuts exist.
- Sacrifice is essential—meaningful achievement demands giving something up: comfort, time, convenience, or immediate gratification.

Just like failure is misunderstood (it's feedback, not final), Sacrifice is also misunderstood. Sacrifice isn't something lost—it's a resource invested for a later reward. When you plan well, the greater the Sacrifice, the greater the reward. The better you plan, the better your Sacrifice-to-reward ratio—you live easier because your thoughts and actions are more efficient. Again: living and organizing your life according to Principles is a cheat code.

Sacrifice is the currency of accomplishment.

You don't walk into a market without cash. The better the goods, the higher the price. Life is the ultimate marketplace—everything has a price. You can shop to your heart's content, but just like the store, you leave life with what you paid for. You cannot steal respect or good fortune because you cannot steal Principles.

Sacrifice—and the suffering often associated with it—sits at the root of the human spirit and of religious teachings. Beyond the exchange of effort for value, at a spiritual level it prepares you for life's challenges. Across major religious texts, there's a shared understanding that anything truly valuable requires Sacrifice, Perseverance, and struggle:

The Bible (Christianity)—Luke 14:27 (ESV): "Whoever does not bear his own cross and come after me cannot be my disciple."
Meaning: True Commitment requires Sacrifice and personal Responsibility. The "cross" symbolizes the burdens you must willingly bear in pursuit of a greater purpose.

The Quran (Islam)—Surah Al-Baqarah 2:286: "Allah does not burden a soul beyond that it can bear..."
Meaning: Struggles and challenges are part of life, within one's capacity to endure. Personal Accountability matters—work through hardship to achieve goodness.

The Torah (Judaism)—Genesis 22:1–2 (The Test of Abraham): God asks Abraham for the ultimate Sacrifice.
Meaning: Willingness to Sacrifice what you love most is a test of faith. Blessings often require profound Sacrifice.

Common theme: Sacrifice, Responsibility, and Perseverance are fundamental to meaningful achievement. Nothing truly great comes without a price—Sacrifice is the currency of life.

How the Value of Commitment and the Virtue of Selflessness Relate to this Step

The Value of Commitment and the Virtue of Selflessness bring Sacrifice to life. Commitment gives Sacrifice its backbone—it's the decision to stay the course when motivation fades and comfort calls. Selflessness gives that decision meaning—it shifts your focus from "What do I get?" to "What do I need to give?" It's not about what you want right now; it's about what's needed right now so you can have what you truly want down the line. Together, they transform Sacrifice from struggle into purpose. You stop chasing comfort and start choosing growth. That's how endurance becomes strength—and strength becomes legacy.

Value: Commitment: Investing time, energy, or resources for greater outcomes

Commitment is the upfront understanding of Sacrifice—the real price you choose to pay. This is where your Analysis, preparation, and Prioritization all come together. When everything is in order, Commitment drives the process as smoothly as possible. That doesn't mean it will be easy—Sacrifice is still required. But it's much easier to commit when you know the plan upfront. If you trust that serious preparation went into it, and believe it's the best available strategy, Commitment becomes easier to sustain.

Without Commitment, Sacrifice feels painful and meaningless—making it easy to quit. The biggest reason people give up on their goals? Confusion and short-term failures, often caused by a lack of a well-thought-out plan. A solid plan fuels Commitment. It gives Sacrifice purpose. It turns intentions into reality.

Virtue: Selflessness: Letting go of comfort or immediate rewards for long-term success

The hardest part of Sacrifice is Selflessness. And I'm not just talking about money. I mean the non-material aspects of who you are—your beliefs, your habits, your attachments. Giving up comfort-driven habits is far harder than giving up dollars. And while money is sometimes part of the Sacrifice, you can't just throw money at Selflessness.

Look around any gym and you'll see it. Someone wants to lose ten pounds, so they think the answer is simple: join a gym, hire a trainer, swipe the card. They Sacrifice a little money and expect the problem solved. But the truth is that the financial Sacrifice is the easy part. The real price is paid outside the gym. Success in weight loss comes from the 24/7 Discipline, determination, and Consistency it takes to stay in a calorie deficit over time.

People will gladly spend money on pills, meal plans, trainers, even surgery. They'll put it on a credit card without hesitation. But fewer than four percent of people are willing to pay the real price: giving up the comfort-driven habits that caused the weight gain in the first place. This is what people get wrong about Sacrifice. Just like you can't buy leadership, character, love, or Discipline—you can't buy Selflessness.

Selflessness means letting go of creature comforts, feel-good activities, and ingrained customs that have defined you. And that, my friend, is the hardest price to pay. But here's the truth: when Selflessness is practiced with purpose, it transforms Sacrifice from a painful loss into a powerful act of Clarity, growth, and Dynamic-mastery. That's the difference between wasting effort and investing effort.

Why Some People Struggle with this Step

There are plenty of reasons why people struggle with Sacrifice, Commitment, and Selflessness, but if I had to pick one, it would be this:

We value comfort more than meaning.

214

We're all guilty of wanting Prime Delivery on everything. Hell, I don't even like waiting one to three days for shipping. If I can find a similar product overnight, I'll switch. That works for Amazon—but not for life. If you struggle with this step, it's likely because:

- You feel overwhelmed by all the things you have to Sacrifice and aren't sure they'll even get you to your goal.
- You don't have a clear, sequential plan, making it easier to quit when challenges arise.
- Your choices are ego-driven, prioritizing self-interest in ways that sabotage real progress.

I get why we've become impatient, shortsighted, and hooked on instant gratification. We've been fed popularized beliefs like "I'm OK, you're OK," "Live in the moment," and "Seize the day." Those ideas carry deeper meaning, but society has twisted them into excuses for impulsive, shortsighted living.

Think about it: if today were your last day on Earth, would you plan for the future? No. Would you go to work and try to accomplish something? No. Would you go to school, train, or focus on your nutrition? No. That's why "Live every day like it's your last" isn't the best life advice—unless you add context. A better mindset?

Plan like you will live forever.
Work like your life depends on it.
Live like you will die tomorrow.

This approach balances investment and gratitude. It recognizes that Sacrifice, Discipline, and Selflessness are essential for achieving something meaningful. But it also allows you to appreciate the journey—even the challenges—because they often teach us the most.

Navigating this Step

Clearly define what Sacrifices are required—and why they're necessary.

- Once you identify the best possible options (Self-Awareness), figure out what Sacrifices you need to make to execute those options.
- Start with low-entry points that build early momentum—small wins matter. Success breeds success.

Embrace Selflessness—accept that short-term discomfort is necessary for long-term results.

- Brace for concentrated effort and discomfort—not necessarily pain—by working in short-term intervals.
- Commit to two-week blocks; that's the window where new habits start locking in and becoming easier to sustain.

Remind yourself regularly of your purpose to reinforce your Commitment to Sacrifice. Visualize the end goal—and imagine the satisfaction of achieving it.

- See yourself ten pounds lighter, licensed in your profession, leading your team, strengthening your marriage, or living debt-free.
- Visualization isn't wishful thinking—it's a proven performance tool used in sports psychology and rehabilitation to wire the brain for success.

Personal Reflections
Self-Assessment (Demonstrating the Value and Virtue)

- Am I prioritizing short-term comfort—or embracing Selflessness to reach my goals?

- Have I clearly identified the Sacrifices required, and am I truly Committed to paying the price?
- Do my daily actions reflect selfless Sacrifice toward my goals—or am I clinging to comfort and convenience?

Application (Practicing the Principle, Value, and Virtue)

- **Fitness:** Am I prepared to selflessly Sacrifice immediate comfort for lasting health and performance?
- **Business:** Am I willing to set aside personal convenience to consistently show up and lead my team at a higher level?
- **Family:** Do I prioritize my family's long-term well-being over short-term personal gratification?

Final Thought

Sacrifice is unavoidable—you either trade something of value for something greater, or you pay the cost of regret later. But Sacrifice should never be confused with pointless hard work. Just because you're grinding doesn't mean you're progressing. Self-Reflection and Self-Awareness are what separate efficiency from exhaustion.

You must create a logical, intelligent plan—identifying the right Sacrifices that actually move the needle. Anything else is guesswork and wasted energy. The difference between those who succeed and those who don't isn't talent or luck—it's preparation and the willingness to selflessly trade short-term conveniences for long-term rewards. The only question is this: **Will you prepare and Sacrifice by choice—or will your lack of preparation force life to teach you the hard way?**

STAGE 2, PRINCIPLE 7—Sacrifice
Fear Is Unavoidable but Must Be Faced

The Principle of Facing Fear is about confronting the obstacles that keep you from executing your plan. You've accepted Responsibility, reflected on your situation, gained Awareness, built your plan, and committed to the necessary Sacrifices. Now comes the test—fear. Whether it's fear of failure, rejection, change, or success itself, fear is the final gatekeeper between intention and transformation. Facing Fear doesn't mean you eliminate it—it means you move forward in spite of it. Fear loses its power the moment you act with Courage and Discipline.

Stage 1 Recap—Principles 1–4: Own the Problem and Find the Way Out

- **Principle 1—Humility:** Admit you are in over your head, you don't know everything, and you are open to learning.
- **Principle 2—Responsibility:** Own your role in your current situation—no blaming or excuses.
- **Principle 3—Self-Reflection:** Understand how your actions created your situation—analyze cause and effect.
- **Principle 4—Self-Awareness:** Identify which of your actions have to change—identify your best choices.

Stage 2 Recap—Principles 5–7: Create & Execute the Plan

- **Principle 5—Strategizing:** Put those solutions into a plan—the creation of a PLAYBOOK.
- **Principle 6—Sacrifice:** Be willing to pay the price.

PB² Alignment – The Facing Fear Chain

- **Principle—Facing Fear (confront what intimidates you)**
- **Value—Courage (choose action over avoidance)**
- **Virtue—Bravery (stand firm when tested)**

Principle 7—Facing Fear
Fear Is Unavoidable but Must Be Faced

We hear it all the time: "Conquer fear." "Get rid of fear." "Master fear." But that's the wrong mindset. The moment you try to conquer fear, you've already made it the enemy. Fear isn't the enemy—it's a necessary ingredient of the process. It's fuel, not fire. Facing Fear isn't about manipulation or avoidance—it's about acceptance. Fear will always show up in one form or another. When you're rooted in present-moment awareness, it loses its edge. You gain Clarity to respond deliberately, not react impulsively.

Facing Fear should never be reduced to an instinctive reaction; it should be elevated to a deliberate response.

If there's no fear, there's probably nothing at stake. And if nothing's at stake, there's nothing meaningful to gain. Pressure and fear make the moment matter—they give the moment weight.

After more than 30 years in this game—first as a combat athlete, now as a coach—I can tell you: no matter how prepared you are, fear always shows up before the fight. Why? Because in practice, nothing's really on the line. But in the arena—when family, friends, and critics are watching—the ego is exposed. That's when the fear of embarrassment and failure hits hardest. I've seen fighters so nervous they throw up before walking into the cage. That's the adrenaline dump—your body floods with energy, then crashes. You explode through round one, and by round two, you're toast. People think it's bad conditioning—but it's not. It's neurological. Hormonal. And it drains you fast.

Even veterans feel it. Step into a championship fight and that same surge can still wreck you. Because fear evolves with the stakes. The goal isn't to beat fear—it's to use it. Sit with it. Channel it.

Calm beats chaos—especially when fear is high.

The bigger the moment, the more energy fear brings. But staying calm in the storm lets you set the pace, see openings, and make the right moves. Take a soldier in close combat—his life is on the line. The calmer he stays, the better he performs. He recalls training, assesses threats, and executes under fire. Most of us will never face life-or-death fear, but the Principle is the same: stay grounded, and you stop reacting to imagined futures.

Facing Fear isn't about defeating it.
It's about neutralizing it—so it can fuel your forward movement.

Why this Is the Seventh Step

This isn't a deep dive into psychoanalysis or academic fear models. We're not here to wade through dense theory. We're here to give you universal Principles anyone can understand, relate to, and apply incrementally. By the time you've reached this point, you've already brushed up against fear—especially during Humility and Self-Reflection. But it's easy to miss that confrontation if you focused only on external problems instead of internal fears. So first, let's get clear on what we're really facing. Every one of us has a personality shaped by both nurture (life experience) and nature (genetic wiring). The ratio doesn't matter here; both influence how you perceive and respond to fear. Both are somewhat flexible—but both have limits:

- You can never nurture away your nature.
- You can't blame your nature for a lack of nurturing.

No matter how you were built or raised, everyone carries something they wish they could change or eliminate—something we'll call fear.

External Fear

External fear is the most visible form. It's tangible, measurable, and often easier to confront because it can be controlled, replicated, and practiced through repeated exposure. That's why exposure therapy works: gradual, consistent exposure builds familiarity, acceptance, and even confidence. Psychologists call this the mere exposure effect—what first scares you can eventually become something you accept—or even prefer.

Example: If you fear heights, start small. A low platform. Then a ladder. Then a balcony. Eventually, a skyscraper view feels normal. That's exposure. That's how capacity grows.

But not every fear can be practiced in a controlled setting. Some situations demand real-world experience:

- The fear of competition in sports.
- The fear of rejection when asking someone out.
- The fear of risking everything to start a business.

You can't fully rehearse those moments—they have to be lived. And that's why life experience is irreplaceable. You can't buy it or shortcut it. Exposure takes time, patience, and repetition.

Internal Fear

Internal fear runs deeper—and it's far more dangerous because it hides inside your head. These fears are self-generated, born from upbringing, trauma, learned behavior, or insecurities that seem to appear out of nowhere.

Example: One of the most common internal fears is the sense of not being enough. Sometimes you can trace it back to childhood or a specific failure; other times it feels like it's always been there. The problem is, internal fears don't just sit quietly. They embed themselves into your identity and influence every decision you make. You may fear rejection, abandonment, being unloved, or being powerless—and those fears can steer your life without you even realizing it. That's why some of the most accomplished people you'll ever meet are still deeply troubled inside.

You've heard the phrase, "Never meet your heroes." I can tell you—it's true. I've met some of mine and walked away thinking, Really? This is the guy I looked up to? Because success in one domain doesn't erase fear in another. External victories don't necessarily fix internal conflicts. That's the reality: conquering external obstacles is easy compared to confronting your internal ones. Until you face the fears inside you, fear will always have the upper hand.

The Truth About Facing Fear

- **Fear is energy.** Misdirected fear destroys—directed fear creates.
- **Fear can protect or paralyze.** It warns you of danger but can also stop you from moving forward.
- **Sacrifice and the unknown both generate fear**—but they're non-negotiable for growth.
- **Fear triggers three common reactions:** denial, withdrawal, or projection / over-compensation.
- **Acceptance neutralizes fear.** You don't love it or hate it—you face it for what it is—it's an emotion.

Fear isn't the enemy—it's raw power. Like fuel in a car, it can drive you forward or blow up in your face. The fuel isn't good or bad; everything depends on how you handle it.

Legendary boxing trainer Cus D'Amato, who coached Mike Tyson and Floyd Patterson, drilled this truth into every fighter he trained:

"The hero and the coward both feel the same thing, but the hero uses his fear and projects it onto his opponent, while the coward runs. It's the same thing—fear—but it's what you do with it that matters."
~Cus D'Amato, quoted in Mike Tyson's *Undisputed Truth*

D'Amato also compared fear to fire: **"Fear is like fire—it can burn your house down, or it can cook your food."** That perspective reshaped Tyson's mindset. Courage isn't the absence of fear—it's action in spite of it.

Fear isn't always bad. Sometimes it protects you. But when it blocks growth, it becomes your ceiling. Evolution demands two things—Sacrifice and facing the unknown—and both will always generate fear. For most, that fear alone stops progress cold.

Across every tradition—religion, philosophy, psychology—the message stays the same: fear is part of the process. The question is never whether you'll feel fear. The only question is—what will you do with it?

Being with Fear Dissipates Fear

One of the most universal strategies for dealing with fear is staying in the present moment. This idea shows up everywhere—from ancient religions to modern psychology—and the message is always the same: the present dissolves fear. Fear feeds on past regrets and future projections, but in the now, there's no room for it. The more present you become, the weaker fear grows. Across every major tradition—Buddhism, Stoicism, Vedanta, Psychoanalysis, and modern psychology—the message about fear is consistent: it lives in the past or the future. Fear feeds on memory and imagination, not on what's happening right now.

Buddhism calls it attachment.
Stoicism calls it anticipation.
Psychology calls it projection.

No matter the language, the antidote is the same—presence. The moment you return to the here and now, fear loses its grip, because the present moment holds no threat—only truth. Eckhart Tolle put it bluntly: "Fear cannot exist in the present moment. It is always of something that might happen, not of something happening now."

Dr. David Hawkins echoed the same truth: "Fear arises when we anticipate future pain or suffering, drawing on past experiences. In pure presence—the now—fear cannot exist."

Bottom line: fear thrives in psychological time—past and future. It disappears in presence. The antidote is simple: stay here. Drop the old story. Stop rehearsing worst-case futures. Root yourself in the now—and fear loses its grip.

How the Value of Courage and the Virtue of Bravery Relate to this Step

Fear isn't optional—it's everywhere, especially in the past and the future. It's part of being human. Yet growth demands that we face it head-on. Courage is the mindset that acknowledges fear but chooses to act anyway. Practicing that mindset consistently gives rise to Bravery—the behavior that proves you've truly faced your fear.

- **Principle:** Facing Fear — Fear is unavoidable but must be faced.
- **Value:** Courage — The mindset that acknowledges fear yet chooses to act anyway.
- **Virtue:** Bravery — The behavior that proves you acted—taking steps while fear is still in the room.

Here's how it flows: the Principle gives you the truth—fear is inevitable. The Value of Courage provides the mindset—"I'll move anyway." The Virtue of Bravery is the proof—visible action that shows you followed through.

That's the PB² chain at work:

Principle→Value→Virtue.
From knowing, to believing, to doing.

Value: Courage
Willingness to Act Despite Fear

Now that we know fear isn't going anywhere, the question becomes: how do we adopt the Value of Courage? Can we accept Fear isn't going anywhere? The real question is—can you act anyway? Can you accept the Responsibility and practice the Discipline of Facing Fear?

To live the Value of Courage, you must understand that fear is natural, necessary, and never a legitimate reason to back down. Courage doesn't deny fear—it walks alongside it. Avoid the mental traps: waiting for fear to vanish, over-analyzing every scenario, or confusing fear-based paralysis with caution. Courage helps you move forward when nothing feels certain.

Accept fear. Understand it can't hurt you—it can only scare you. Whether imagined or real, fear usually lives in your head. Even when the threat is real—like a bear charging you—staying calm and present gives you the best chance of survival. I'm not saying it's easy; I'm saying it's your best move. Fear is everywhere—and it visits us all. Learning to accept it is always the right call. It can warn you, protect you, and even fuel you—but only if you learn to listen without panic and use it with purpose.

Virtue: Bravery
Taking Action in the Presence of Fear

Bravery is Courage in motion—the 'do it anyway' moment when fear is loud, logic feels fuzzy, and action is the only move left. When you're brave, fear doesn't stop you—it fuels you. Mike Tyson has said he was terrified before every fight. He didn't know why, but his wiring made him jump into the chaos as soon as he felt fear. He believed that fear sharpened him; without it, he wouldn't have performed the way he did. Hearing that reframed my own pre-fight fear: if Tyson felt it and wasn't a coward, neither was I. That's what Bravery looks like—focused, deliberate action. Making the call. Having the conversation. Stepping into the moment even when your heart races and your voice shakes.

When I coach an athlete—or catch myself spiraling—I ask:

- Does this happen often?
- What's the usual outcome?
- Are my thoughts accurate?
- Is this real risk—or just distorted emotion?
- Who's in control—me or my triggers?
- How did we get here?
- What 1-2-3 combo are we committing to?

Here's a real sequence from my life:

- I get triggered—usually by money.
- Outcome? Nothing actually happens; it's all in my head.
- The account dips, but bills are paid—we're fine.
- We've been here before and made it through.
- Conclusion: it's a trigger, not a threat.
- Path: stay calm, reassess, refocus the systems.

Sometimes that means:

- Rechecking financials
- Tweaking recruitment or training processes
- Pulling the ripcord—reassigning sessions and trimming payroll

Simple. Not easy. But doable.

Bravery isn't mystical—it's the byproduct of every Principle before it. When fear shows up, you already know what to do. Your trigger may not be money—it might be rejection, failure, loneliness, stagnation, a breakup, being overlooked, or not liking who you see in the mirror. Whatever it is, ask the hard questions. Stick to facts. No drama. No head talk. Just truth. When you do that, the next step becomes clear—and Bravery becomes automatic.

The Reality Check

Facing Fear is never comfortable—but it's always required. People freeze at this stage because:

- They misunderstand fear and how to deal with it.
- They lack a roadmap built on facts, not feelings.
- Distraction and procrastination become the norm.
- They wait for fear to disappear—never realizing it fades only after action.
- They see fear as weakness instead of proof they're growing.

Here's the real problem: emotions take over, facts vanish, and nothing moves. Fear lives rent-free in your head until you evict it. When I get stuck, my son Rio says, "Dad—get out of your head." Best advice I've ever gotten. Lying to yourself during the hard questions only creates more lies in your actions. That's False Evidence Appearing Real—F.E.A.R. in motion. Discipline without honesty? Useless. Honesty without action? Still stuck.

Bravery requires both.

At the end of the day, Bravery is action. Reflection, planning, and preparation only matter if they lead to movement. Move—or stay stuck. It's that simple.

Why Some People Struggle with this Step

Most people struggle with Facing Fear because they treat it as an enemy instead of an advisor. They think courage means feeling nothing—and when fear shows up, they assume something's wrong. That misunderstanding keeps them stuck. The most common reasons?

- They wait for fear to disappear. They keep saying, "I'll start when I'm ready," not realizing fear fades only after action.
- They confuse fear with weakness. They misread adrenaline and uncertainty as failure instead of fuel.
- They avoid discomfort. Comfort is addictive—it disguises itself as safety while quietly killing progress.
- They lack exposure. Without repetition, fear always feels unfamiliar. Familiarity breeds control.
- They overthink. Instead of facing fear directly, they analyze, debate, and delay.

When fear hits, the brain shifts from logic to survival mode. Thoughts race, breathing shortens, and reason goes out the window. The fight-flight-freeze response takes over. Most people either fight everything, flee from everything, or freeze in indecision. That's why Facing Fear requires practice—deliberate exposure to the uncomfortable. The goal isn't to eliminate fear, but to stay calm in its presence. Fear isn't proof that you're weak; it's evidence that you're growing. Every breakthrough—whether in business, athletics, or personal healing—starts with discomfort. The only question is whether you'll let that discomfort define you or drive you.

Navigating this Step

Stop overthinking. Start moving. The fastest way through fear is immediate—but strategic—intentional action:

- **Be Humble**—accept fear without judgment.
- **Reflect**—use Self-Reflection to identify what you're actually afraid of.
- **Be Aware**—apply Self-Awareness to pinpoint your best options.
- **Strategize**—build a plan of action.
- **Face Fear**—and pull the trigger.
- **Rinse and repeat.**

Everything repeated becomes a habit—including Bravery.

At IHP, we teach something simple but profound: "Relax the Face." When reps get tough, we coach clients to accept the sensation, stay neutral, and breathe through it. Don't tighten your face—don't fight the feeling. It's just a feeling. We remind them:

- It's not hard.
- It's not easy.
- It doesn't feel good.
- It doesn't feel bad.
- It just is.

Then we tell them, "I've never given you a task you couldn't complete—neither will life."

Every rep at IHP is a practice in present-moment awareness. If you do a thousand reps a week without reacting to fear-based stories in your head, how can you not get better at staying grounded in life? That's why IHP has been a pillar of strength for over 25 years. That's why we call it 'The Church.'

"Relax the Face" is more than a cue—it's a reset. It helps you drop the old story, silence self-limiting beliefs, and release outdated value systems that no longer serve you. It embodies everything we've covered so far—presence, awareness, and mastery of the moment.

It's simple. Powerful. Lifelong.

The goal isn't to eliminate fear—it's to stand with it. Courage isn't fearlessness—it's choosing the right response while fear is still in the room. Avoiding fear gives it power. Facing fear makes it fuel. Repeat that long enough, and Bravery becomes your habit. Choose Bravery.

Personal Reflections
Self-Assessment

Make sure you're not one of the people I mentioned earlier—the ones who never ask themselves:

- Do I see fear as weakness and avoid it—or face it as an opportunity for growth?
- Can I tell the difference between real fear and FEAR (the one in my head)?
- Am I always waiting for a 'better' or 'perfect' time?
- Have I gone through the Principles and created a clear blueprint of action steps?
- Am I stuck in planning mode and never get to the action stage?
- Can I put distractions aside and stay Disciplined in executing that blueprint?

This sequential thought process—simple and logical as it may seem— is rarely taken. Why? Because, as I always say, "common sense ain't so common."

Application (Practicing the Principle, Value, and Virtue)

- **Fitness**
  - o Do you keep postponing the diet or workout plan—Monday, next week, next month, January 1st?
  - o Are you afraid to join a gym because you're ashamed of how you look or perform—afraid of being judged?

- **Business**
  - o Do you manage from home so your employees won't notice your leadership gaps?
  - o Or do you show up, stay vulnerable, and grow through action?
  - o Are you stuck in a secure but unfulfilling job—or ready to finally pull the trigger on that business plan you've dreamed about for years?

- **Family**
  - o Are you willing to have the hard conversation with your spouse— telling them you're not happy and something must change, like starting therapy?
  - o Or will you avoid it and let a great relationship slowly die?

Final Thought

Whether fear is real or just in your head, one thing's certain—staying present is your best move. I'm not saying it's easy; I'm saying it's the way out. When you're in the moment, you can build a clear, efficient blueprint for action. That blueprint might come together in a split second during crisis—or take days or weeks. It doesn't matter. What matters is having it. Once the plan is in hand, all that's left is the doing. Fear isn't the enemy— the refusal to face it is. Face it. Stay present in its presence. Act. Even if your legs are shaking, take the first step. Then another.

The lesson is in the action, not the feeling.
The doing is where you Finish Big—
because the plan only matters if you do.

"An instant push can start a race,
but only persistent focus wins it."

~ JCS

12

STAY THE COURSE AND FINISH BIG (PRINCIPLES 8–10)

Stage 3—Stay the Course and Finish Big

The final phase of the PB² system is about staying the course—and finishing what you started. You've admitted you were stuck, owned your role, reflected honestly, became aware of your options, created a plan, accepted the price, and acted. Now the challenge becomes Consistency, Perseverance, and Finish Big.

This chapter covers the final three Principles—the ones that separate short-term change from lasting transformation. It begins with Consistency: building the right habits. Then we move to Perseverance: pushing through resistance and setbacks. Finally, we land with Finish Big: the full integration of the entire experience. These Principles don't just get you to the goal—they lock in the mindset, behaviors, and deliberate reps needed to live this way long-term. If the first seven steps got you moving, these last three keep you growing.

STAGE 3, PRINCIPLE 8—Consistency Success Comes from Repeated Principle-Driven Actions

Consistency is where plans turn into habits and habits turn into transformation. You can have the best strategy in the world, but without Discipline and repetition, nothing sticks. Consistency is the bridge between intention and integration—it's what locks the previous Principles into permanent change. This is where effort stops feeling like effort because action becomes automatic. The goal isn't perfection; it's steady, repeatable execution under all conditions. Without Consistency, every gain fades. With it, progress compounds and growth becomes inevitable.

Stage 1 Recap—Principles 1–4: Own the Problem and Find the Way Out

- **Principle 1—Humility:** Admit you are in over your head, you don't know everything, and you are open to learning.
- **Principle 2—Responsibility:** Own your role in your current situation—no blaming or excuses.
- **Principle 3—Self-Reflection:** Understand how your actions created your situation—analyze cause and effect.
- **Principle 4—Self-Awareness:** Identify which of your actions have to change—identify your best choices.

Stage 2 Recap—Principles 5–7: Create & Execute the Plan

- **Principle 5—Strategizing:** Put those solutions into a plan—the creation of a PLAYBOOK.
- **Principle 6**—Sacrifice: Be willing to pay the price.
- **Principle 7—Facing Fear:** Just do it—Commitment.

PB² Alignment

- **Principle:** Consistency—Success comes from repeated right actions.
- **Value:** Discipline—Stay the course. Keep going.
- **Virtue:** Tenacity —Keep moving despite distractions.

Now, let's dive into the first Principle of the first chain of this Stage 3—Consistency.

Principle 8—Consistency: Keep Doing the Right Things, Over and Over

You don't need to be extraordinary every single day—that's unnecessary pressure. Instead, focus on your attitude and outlook. Your mission: show up and patiently master the fundamentals. Fundamentals are the low-hanging fruit—the actions that deliver maximum return on your effort and time. Yet most people chase the flashy, complicated stuff first. The irony? Shortcuts usually take the longest path to lasting success.

The truth is, mastery doesn't come from hacks or hustle—it comes from Consistency. Fundamentals practiced daily become the foundation for everything else. Consistency is the quiet force that transforms short-term wins into permanent results.

Take fitness, for example. Instead of starting with simple, achievable steps—like daily walks and balanced meals—people jump straight into the grind. They buy supplements, sign up for memberships, hire trainers, meal-prep obsessively, and dive into extreme diets. It looks impressive, but it rarely lasts. Two weeks later, they fold like a beach chair. Meanwhile, those who quietly master the basics build lasting success. They don't "embrace the grind" or suffer endlessly—they adopt sustainable habits. They become consistent, winning the classic tortoise-and-hare race: slow and steady wins the race.

A hidden gem of Consistency comes from psychologist John A. Nevin's theory of Behavioral Momentum: "consistently reinforced behaviors resist disruption." I've expanded this into something deeper—Habitual Momentum—the process where consistent reinforcement turns effort into identity. The more consistently you practice good habits, the easier and more natural they become—until they're part of who you are. But here's the kicker: Habitual Momentum doesn't just sustain itself—it compounds. And compounded momentum is the ultimate multiplier.

- One good action builds confidence.
- Confidence ignites deeper belief.
- Belief fuels more consistent action.

This multiplier doesn't just accelerate progress in one area—it creates lateral momentum that spills into others. Success in one domain sparks growth everywhere, fueling continuous expansion. Stay in that cycle long enough, and you won't just change what you do—you'll change who you are.

Small battles win big wars.

Why this Is the Eighth Step

Consistency doesn't get much love—but it quietly builds empires. It's the silent work that eventually screams success. You can't skip this step because without Consistency, life becomes transient—nothing sticks.

Without consistency, any success is coincidental.

Consistency isn't 'mindless grind.' It's deliberate repetition—done with focus, feedback, and purpose. It's how practice becomes habit, and habit becomes identity. Here's the twist: most people confuse habit with practice—a massive blind spot.

- Habits are automatic—triggered by cues and done without much thought. Sometimes good (brushing your teeth), sometimes bad (repetitive, unproductive routines).
- Deliberate practice is intentional—conscious repetition with feedback, focus, and refinement. It's the grind with purpose that creates the flow zone—where everything moves effortlessly in the right direction.

**The more you treat life as deliberate practice,
the more Consistent your habits become.**

How Does Practice Become a Habit?

Imagine moving to a new city. At first, everything takes effort—routes, addresses, routines. But repetition turns confusion into confidence. Eventually, it becomes second nature.

We all practice our way into habits, but we rarely see everyday repeats as practice. What you practice is what you become. Being on time, being honest, being disciplined—these are skills, just like a golf swing or a piano scale. Any skill can be mastered and made habitual through deliberate practice. Add purpose, planning, and execution—and transformation stops being a hope and becomes reality.

The Truth About Consistency

- Consistency isn't about intensity—it's about persistent, quality repetition.
- Repetition is the mother of mastery.
- High performers are consistent performers, not perfect performers.
- If it's not repeatable, it's not sustainable.
- Habits don't care how you feel—show up anyway.

True Consistency isn't blind effort—it's deliberate reps that polish and perfect.

**The popular thing isn't always the important thing—
but the important thing is always the right thing.**

Quality matters more than time or intensity. Can it be hard? Hell yes. Can it be exhausting? Absolutely. But the real grind isn't the work—it's the patience to slow down and execute with precision. Top performers show effortless execution. They're not straining—they're flowing, locked in, repeating flawlessly what they've perfected over time. Not everything can be practiced. Life throws curve balls that never repeat. But when you've mastered the basics, you can improvise. Like music solos—unrehearsed but born from mastery. That's spontaneous brilliance. If you don't practice consistently, your skills fade. If it's not repeated, it's not sustainable. And if your reps lack quality, your outcomes will too. Consistency is:

- Being deadly accurate with your intentions.
- Being precise with your reps.
- Being calculated with your time.

It's about smart work, not just hard work. In a world driven by feelings and opinions, people think they deserve success because they 'work hard'. No—you don't. Clint Eastwood's character, William Munny, said it best in Unforgiven:

"Deserve's got nothin' to do with it."

Hard work guarantees nothing. Smart, consistent, high-quality effort does. You don't get what you deserve—you get what you earn—through precision, patience, and performance.

How the Value Discipline and the Virtue of Tenacity Relate to this Step

Consistency isn't just about showing up—it's about showing up with purpose. It's not talent or luck; it's your Discipline when nobody's watching and nothing feels urgent. Talk is cheap—but the walk tells the truth. It reveals the truth in you. Discipline gives structure to your actions—it's the daily follow-through that protects your vision from chaos. Tenacity brings the staying power. It's how you keep pushing when comfort calls your name, when distractions multiply, and when progress feels invisible. Together, Discipline and Tenacity form the muscle and bone of Consistency—the inner framework that keeps you powered up when motivation fades.

Value: Discipline—Stay the Course.

Discipline is the daily vote you cast to stay committed, especially during long stretches of sacrifice. It silences the little voice whispering excuses—why today should be easier, more comfortable, or less demanding. Discipline is the confident voice that says, "We promised ourselves—we're doing this." It might look like self-control, but true Discipline isn't forced effort—it's effortless alignment with your principles. Discipline isn't punishment, just as Sacrifice isn't suffering. Sacrifice is simply trading time, money, or comfort for something greater—and Discipline ensures that trade happens.

"When you have a big enough why, you can withstand any how."

This captures the power of your WHY—your purpose. When your WHY aligns with your principles, Discipline stops being a struggle and becomes your natural state. It also neutralizes instant gratification. When you're disciplined, shortcuts don't exist—you're locked on the long game.

Time and disciplined sacrifice are the currency of accomplishment.

- You train intelligently instead of abusing your body or skipping workouts.
- You deliver what you promise rather than breaking your word.
- You stick to the plan even when there's no pressure.
- You push past "I don't feel like it" because your WHY transcends temporary comfort.

When you truly value discipline, you don't negotiate with fleeting emotions—you honor the promise you made to yourself when your vision was clear.

Virtue: Tenacity—Staying on Course Despite Distractions

Tenacity is the sustained ability to apply effort toward your goal—especially when things get tough. It means holding firm to your actions and principles without compromise, regardless of external pressure or internal doubt. People often mistake Tenacity for stubbornness or sheer grit—someone who just won't quit. But genuine Tenacity isn't about raw toughness; it's principled persistence. It's easy to stay consistent when things go your way, when motivation is high and results come fast. Tenacity begins when the honeymoon with "easy" is over:

- When you're weeks in with no applause, no visible progress, and endless distractions.

- When boredom or burnout begs you to stop.
- When shiny distractions tempt you off course.
- When shortcuts start to look attractive.
- When your pace slows and your WHY fades.

Tenacity fuels your resolve when you start questioning the value of sacrifice. It makes you non-negotiable in a world of endless distractions. While others flinch, scroll, or chase novelty—you stay locked in, steady and focused. That's Tenacity. Not louder. Not flashier. Just steady—right foot, left foot, repeat.

Why Some People Struggle with this Step

- **The Amazon Prime Model**—Instant gratification rules.
- **Romanticizing 'The Grind'**—Mistaking punishment for progress.
- **Start Hard, Quit Early**—Emotions drive unsustainable pace.
- **Chasing Gimmicks**—Impatience leads to shortcuts.
- **Grind Now Instead of Flow Forever**—Flashy starts overshadow steady progress.

You've heard it—society's gone soft. Comfort replaced challenge, and validation replaced value. We crave next-day delivery, remote ease, and online applause more than meaning and mastery. As the culture weakens, the noise gets louder. Social media overflows with ex-military hardos, business tycoons, and teenagers preaching "grind" and "warriorship."

"Follow me—I ran 200 marathons."
"Follow me—I'm ex–special forces."
"Follow me—I went from homeless to $30 million."

It's entertaining, even inspiring—but it conditions people for hype over habit. They start at full throttle, then burn out fast. Like sprinting the first lap of a mile race—you already know how that ends. They overtrain, overspend, and overcommit. The high fades, the novelty dies, and the project fizzles. Want to avoid that trap? Start slow. Set achievable goals. Stack small wins early. Like a smart runner, save your kick for the end—not the beginning. When you stack enough wins, winning becomes who you are.

Navigating this Step

The first move is obvious—avoid the traps we just covered. Next, shift your outlook: think principles, not obstacles. Do you force yourself to go to work, shower, or brush your teeth? Do you need extraordinary Discipline or Tenacity for that? Of course not. Why? Because repetition built momentum. Those tasks became habits—no grind, no drama, no negotiation. Start your journey the same way. Don't chase massive achievements out of the gate. Build Habitual Momentum through small, steady actions. Think high volume, low intensity—then stack wins.

- **Don't** wake up at 4 AM and run 5 miles starting today.
  Do walk your dog for 10 minutes after dinner.
- **Don't** start a professional bodybuilding routine five days a week.
  Do begin with three strength sessions and a short daily walk.
- **Don't** jump into a 17-credit semester after years off.
  Do start with two 3-credit courses to rebuild study habits.
- **Don't** psychoanalyze your partner to prove you're right (even if you are).
  Do sit still, listen fully, and don't interrupt—no matter what's said.
- **Don't** overhaul your office on day one as director.
  Do begin with 30-minute weekly team meetings to set procedures and build culture.

You don't have to suffer to succeed. Hard work alone doesn't guarantee anything—smart, consistent work does. Yes, there will be hard pushes, but those belong to key moments, not daily survival. If life feels like a constant grind, you're missing strategic consistency and discipline.

The More Consistency and Discipline You Live, the Less You'll Have to Grind.

Finally—stick to your plan. Adjust when necessary, but believe in it and execute it. Look at everything you've already done:

1. You've been Humble through Humility and realistic about your situation.
2. You've taken full Responsibility for being here.
3. You've reflected deeply through Self-Reflection on the causes.
4. You've become aware through Self-Awareness of actionable solutions.
5. You've created a workable plan through Strategizing.
6. You've accepted the price through Sacrifice and committed to paying it.
7. You've embodied Consistency in your process.
8. You've developed Tenacity to stay the course.

With all that in place, how could you go wrong?

Work your plan—don't let life work you.

Personal Reflections and Self-Assessment

- Do I act on emotion instead of following a clear plan?
- Do I pause and take internal inventory before committing to action?
- Do I focus more on how hard change feels now—or how great the outcome will be later?
- Am I easily distracted by "shiny objects"?
- Do I start fast and fade once the excitement wears off?
- Does my past show more attempts than achievements?

Application (Practicing the Principle, Value, and Virtue)

If you're struggling to stay consistent, it's rarely about desire—it's about planning and perspective.

- **Fitness:** Have I built a fitness and lifestyle plan I can sustain without turning every day into a grind?
- **Business:** Are my systems structured to consistently maintain—and elevate—a productive culture?
- **Family:** Am I making steady emotional deposits into my family's bank account through quality time and presence?

Final Thought

As I always told my daughters, "Every man has a one-hour rap." Any man can impress you for an evening—maybe even a weekend cruise. But move in with him, and you'll see the real man. You'll see him clearly when he's exhausted, fired, broke, or when his dreams have turned to dust. That's when truth shows up.

Will he bring you a single rose when he can't afford a dozen?

Will he plan a sunset picnic when the five-star dinner's out of reach?

Will he make you laugh when he secretly wants to cry?

And will he stay that man through every hard time—until he's back on top again?

That's a consistent man. Marry him.

And for my sons, the message was even simpler: BE THAT MAN!!

STAGE 3, PRINCIPLE 9—Perserverance
Growth Requires Enduring Hardship

Every journey hits resistance. Momentum slows. Progress stalls. Most people stop here—not because they can't continue, but because they expected it to be easier.

Perseverance isn't about powering through blindly; it's about staying engaged when progress feels heavy and results come slow. It's the commitment to keep showing up, adjusting, and advancing even when the excitement fades. This is where grit matures into growth—and where you prove that what you started wasn't a phase, but a transformation.

Stage 1 Recap—Principles 1–4: Own the Problem and Find the Way Out

- **Principle 1—Humility:** Admit you're in over your head, you don't know everything, and you're open to learning.
- **Principle 2—Responsibility:** Own your role in your current situation—no blaming, no excuses.
- **Principle 3—Self-Reflection:** Understand how your actions created your situation—analyze cause and effect.
- **Principle 4—Self-Awareness:** Identify which actions need to change—recognize your best choices.

Stage 2 Recap—Principles 5–7: Create and Execute the Plan

- **Principle 5—Strategizing:** Turn your solutions into a plan—the creation of your Playbook.
- **Principle 6—Sacrifice:** Be willing to pay the price.
- **Principle 7—Facing Fear:** Just do it—commit fully.

Stage 3—Principles 8–10: Stay the Course & Finish Big

- **Principle 8—Consistency:** Keep doing the right things, over and over.

PB² Alignment

- **Principle: Perseverance**—Growth requires enduring hardship.
- **Value: Fortitude**—Courageously working through difficulty
- **Virtue: Resilience**—Bouncing back from setbacks

Special Note

As life often reminds us, the lessons that shape us most come through hardship—whether in relationships, business, or health. Right before writing this section, I had a total knee replacement. Not exactly what I had planned for my life—this year, this month, or even this week. I had dates, events, and projects lined up that would've pushed surgery way down the 'To-Do List'. But life doesn't always give you what you want—it gives you what you need. Once I finally accepted that, after years of hoping technology would bail me out, I took the first surgery date available. So everything you're about to read is fresh off the grill. This isn't theory or hindsight—this is me living it, right now. I know what I'm feeling. I know what I'm facing. And as always, life feeds us both: I get to grow through this challenge, and you get to take the lessons that resonate. **Win-win.**

Principle 9—Perseverance: Growth Requires Enduring Hardship

The Principle is the ideal model—a self-evident truth everyone respects. Perseverance is one of those universal truths. It shows up in headlines, novels, movies, and the history of humanity. Like we've said before, no one argues with this: "What doesn't kill you makes you stronger." Consistency is steady work—showing up and repeating the process. Perseverance is what you need when things go wrong while you're already working hard.

Even steady work can become a grind when the volume stays high. A hobby turns into labor once it's your job. Doing something you love on weekends isn't the same as doing it every day—especially when you don't feel like it.

- Being a full-time musician isn't jamming with friends.
- Being a personal trainer isn't working out with your buddies.
- Being a lifeguard isn't just hanging at the beach.

Consistency keeps you in the game.
Perseverance keeps you there when everything goes sideways.

Why this Is the Ninth Step

Excitement starts the race.
Consistency drives the work 24/7.
Perseverance repairs what breaks mid journey.

From the outside, Perseverance can look like suffering—and yes, sometimes it feels that way. But perspective changes everything. When you see it as a Hollywood highlight reel or a self-help 'grind' montage, you miss the point. Perseverance isn't what you endure—it's how you endure it. This is where you breathe, "relax the face," and reconnect with your why—because now you're deep in the how. This stage tests purpose against resistance: bigger than comfort, bigger than convenience, and bigger than temporary feelings. Anyone can start strong, but few keep going when the finish line disappears in the fog. Perseverance isn't blind effort; it's purposeful endurance in the face of resistance.

Marathon vs. Sprint

The sprinter explodes—it's over in seconds. The marathoner trains for months to face hours of unpredictability: cramps, fatigue, weather, and pain. And still, they don't stop. They've trained not quitting until not quitting became who they are. That's why Perseverance follows Consistency and comes before Finish Big. Consistency gets you showing up; Perseverance keeps you showing up when it hurts. At this level, real obstacles appear—and that's not failure; that's growth calling your name. You're not just working smart anymore; you're braced for setbacks that test your why. If your why stays alive, it will always outweigh the how—and that's how you reach your what.

The Truth About Perseverance

Perseverance isn't just about endurance—it's about attitude and context. The right attitude changes everything. The very obstacles that make you want to quit—financial hits, illness, family chaos, acts of God—are often the same ones that expose weak links in your system and force evolution. Catching blind spots mid-execution can feel chaotic in the moment, but that's how you get sharper. Maybe you missed a detail, or maybe life threw a new kind of curveball. Either way, the message is the same: pausing, pivoting, or even canceling isn't failure—it's refinement. Sometimes cutting losses is the smartest move you can make. Other times—like my knee replacement—it's a detour that adds to your library of wisdom. And it's not just what you learn; it's how others watch you walk through it. That's leadership in motion. That's why IHP has lasted decades—because it's family, not just facility. It's built on principles, not hype. When life hits, you've got two options:

- **Victim mode:** "Why me?"
- **Growth mode:** "This is hard—but it's here to test and shape me."

Yeah, life piles it on—three artificial joints, prostate issues, bad genetics, you name it. Do I like it? Hell no. Do I whine about it? Not anymore. My mindset is simple:

- It is what it is.
- Bring it.
- Do what's required, as best as possible.
- Be grateful—because it could always be worse.

I tell people all the time: Be grateful—and don't let God hear you bitching. The moment you complain, He might remind you how good you actually had it. When I catch myself slipping into self-pity, I think of John Walsh. In 1981, his six-year-old son, Adam, was abducted and murdered. That kind of loss would destroy most people—but John turned pain into purpose. He built the National Center for Missing and Exploited Children, launched America's Most Wanted, and helped catch over a thousand fugitives. He didn't just survive—he rebuilt. That's perseverance: choosing strength when life gives you every reason to fold. So when the mountain shows up, don't curse it—thank it. It's the exact challenge you need for your next evolution. You'd never choose this lesson voluntarily, so life handed it to you. Maybe it's saying, "You're meant for more—and I'm not letting you stay where you are." Remember:

- Perseverance isn't stubbornness—strategic redirection is strength.
- Hardship isn't a stop sign—it's a growth signal.
- If your WHY isn't alive, you'll quit before the breakthrough.
- The discomfort of growth is temporary—the regret of quitting lasts forever.

How the Value of Fortitude and the Virtue of Resilience Relate to this Step

Perseverance isn't just about effort—it's about endurance with purpose. Fortitude gives that endurance structure. It's the quiet strength that holds your line when everything around you shakes—steadiness under stress, composure under fire. It's what keeps you rooted when life feels unstable and unpredictable. Resilience brings the rebound—the ability to absorb impact, reset, and rebuild without losing heart. It's not about being unbreakable; it's about being unshakable. Resilience turns recovery into forward motion, converting pain into progress. Together, Fortitude and Resilience form the core of Perseverance—the foundation that lets you endure hardship without losing hope, adapt without losing direction, and rebuild stronger every time.

Value: Fortitude
Courageously Working Through Difficulty

Strip it all away—no money, no safety net, no applause—and that's when real fortitude shows up...or doesn't. That's why I don't get starstruck by social media 'fortitude-selling' gurus. I respect the accomplishments, but let's be honest:

- Everyone has a one-hour rap.
- It's easy to play hero when you're winning.
- Easy to be generous when you're wealthy.
- Easy to be brave when you're protected.

Choosing suffering in a controlled environment isn't the same as facing it uninvited, with no end in sight. One is rehearsed and timed; the other just shows up and dares you to quit. You trained for months to pass the boards. You did special ops selection five times. You ran 30 marathons in a row, peed blood, soaked in ice, refused medical care—because that's your 'brand'.

Okay...cool. But now what?

Does that mean you've mastered fortitude—or just trained yourself to handle predictable pain? And what about what's under the hood? How's your marriage? Your friendships? Your peace of mind? What happens when the lights go out and it's just you and your thoughts? If you're good, great.

But don't confuse physical toughness with the internal work most people avoid. Real fortitude isn't about bleeding for applause; it's forged in isolation, despair, and hopelessness—when the only thing left is your spirit, choosing to keep going. Let's be real: I don't even think fortitude plays a major role in my knee rehab. It's not because I'm a beast—it's because I've lived enough to stay grounded. To me, it's just:

- Handle today.
- Tomorrow will come.
- Rinse. Repeat.

No magic. No superhuman feats. Just gratitude, perspective, and a steady walk—right foot, left foot, repeat.

Virtue: Resilience
Bouncing Back from Setbacks

As a strength and conditioning coach, I live by the principle of training specificity. It's simple: you get good at what you train.

- Train isolated muscles—you get good-looking muscles.
- Train coordinated movement—you get beautiful movement.
- Train for endurance—you won't gain max strength.
- Train distance—you'll struggle with sprints.

That's the Specificity Principle, also known as the SAID Principle—Specific Adaptations to Imposed Demands. What you train for is what your body becomes good at. Training mirrors life. The Ten Principles in this book were built on that truth. Outside of genetics and luck, everything else is training—and even training responds to genetics.

If you've ever played sports, you already know what Resilience looks like. It's not enough to show up, work hard, and stay consistent—you'll still get hurt, lose games, and have days when you're exhausted, doubting, and done. That's when Consistency and Perseverance reveal their action hero: Resilience. Being consistent is great—until life smacks you with the unexpected. That's when you don't just push through—you bounce back. Here's what most people forget about training: time off—whether by choice or by force—happens. And when it does, the skill fades. Life works the same way.

- Stop showing up with integrity—and your worth gets questioned.
- Get used to being late—and your presence stops mattering.
- Cut corners—and competence never completes its transformation.
- Normalize quitting—and nobody, not even you, will count on you when it matters.

That's not who you want to be—and it's not who you're meant to be. Resilience is what you lean on when the plan goes sideways. It's who you become when Consistency and Perseverance run out of gas. Talent is great, but when the pressure's on, Resilience beats talent every day of the week—and twice on Sunday.

Why Some People Struggle with this Step

Let's get real. Most people collapse under hardship not because they're weak—but because they've never practiced being resilient. They don't treat righteous living as practice, and that's the disconnect. What you practice becomes habit—and what becomes habit becomes who you are. But training consistency isn't the same as training resilience. Staying on a hard routine is one thing; bouncing back after getting smashed sideways is another. The physiological and emotional demands of crisis are nothing like the steady grind of routine. Think of two fighters—equally skilled, going the distance. Brutal already. Now imagine one of them:

- Takes a deep cut—blood pouring into his eye.
- Gets dropped—twice in a round.
- Eats a liver shot and fights crippled for two rounds.

Who keeps fighting? The one who lives Perseverance and embodies Resilience.

It's in Our Genes

Let's get real. We're not built for hardship—we're built to conserve energy, stay safe, and avoid pain. That's not laziness; it's biology. The Principle of Economy says: "All biological systems achieve their goals using the least amount of energy possible." Translation: we're wired to want less, do less, and keep it easy. Unless we override that programming with awareness, we default to this—settle for less, just to do less. But there's a right and wrong way to apply economy. One builds life; the other destroys it.

- **Productive economy:** simplifying life by eliminating the unnecessary—big car, big house, expensive clothes, exotic vacations. Living with less to gain peace, freedom, and joy.
- **Destructive economy:** simplifying life by eliminating the essentials—work, responsibility, discipline, respect—and ending up directionless or homeless.

Here's the line you need to draw: doing less is smart only when it still leads to meaningful gains in quality of life. Want less stress? Live with less, and you'll have more time to enjoy life. Some people thrive on more time and less stress, choosing simpler lifestyles that are easier to maintain. But you can't apply that same thinking to Principles. Why? Because Principles are absolute. You can't choose less honesty, less respect, or less love and still expect a high quality of life. You can drive across town in a Toyota coupe just as effectively as in a Mercedes Maybach S-Class—but you can't say, "Let me cut back on being responsible, accountable, and respectful so I can save stress and time." If I save 50% on living expenses through simplicity, I'll thrive. If I take 50% responsibility for my obligations to save energy, my life collapses. That's not practicing economy—that's moral bankruptcy.

They Mistake a Crisis as Failure

Many people can handle a hard schedule—but introduce a crisis, and they crumble. Why? Because they never trained beyond the edge of their routine. They think showing up every day is enough, but that's not the same as being battle-tested. Consistency gets you to the edge; crisis tests what's beyond it. That's why consistency must come first—without it, you've got nothing to fall back on.

They Lack a Compelling 'WHY'

You can't take the hard road without a solid WHY pushing you forward. And when things get brutal, you need a WHY so big that quitting feels like betrayal. Let me make it personal:

- I started pre-med for my parents. I didn't want to be a doctor. When it got hard—I quit.
- I built a touring band for the fun and the fame. I loved the music but not the business. When it got hard—I quit.
- I opened a bar for fun, not the business. When it got hard—I quit.

No shame. Just truth.

In each case, the WHY wasn't strong enough to survive the price the project required. Now flip it:

- Every sport I played—I loved.
- Going back to school as an adult—I chose it, and I loved my major and the academic environment.
- Opening IHP—I knew it would be my church.

Result? I did very well in all those endeavors—and I didn't quit. Why? Because the WHY was always bigger than the HOW. My journey was fun, exciting, and full of purpose. I believed in what I was doing. I did it for me, not for anyone else. That's the takeaway: your WHY has to prop up your will when it's tested by hopelessness. When life pushes you to the edge, your reason to keep going must stay crystal clear. Train your WHY. Revisit it. Reinforce it. Let it evolve as the journey evolves.

And don't be surprised when you realize—your WHY is your journey.

Navigating this Step

- **Redefine success.** Sometimes the real prize isn't winning—it's surviving what once felt impossible. Think of the first Rocky movie. Rocky loses the fight but wins by going the distance. Nobody expected him to last a few rounds, yet he finishes the bout—cut, battered, but unbroken. He earned everyone's respect because he refused to fold.
- **Practice a winning mindset.** Anything repeated becomes a practice. So practice a winning mindset—not fake positivity or cheerleader energy, but quiet resolve. You don't panic over what might happen; you deal with what's happening. No excuses. No victimhood. You do the best with what you've got—and you don't let up.
- **Crisis is the best teacher.** Rewire your response so crisis puts you in execution mode, not complaint mode. It's never pleasant, but it sharpens your process and builds depth. The payoff? More wisdom, more skill, more respect, more love.

Personal Reflections

- When have I pushed through a tough situation, and what happened?
- When did I quit too early—and what was the result?
- When did I persevere in a relationship, and what changed?
- When did I give up too soon, and how did it affect me?
- When did I push through a health challenge?
- When did I fail to push through—and what did I learn?

Self-Assessment

- After frustration or anger hits, what's the first thing I say or do in a crisis?
- Do I revisit my WHY during challenges—or only when things go wrong?
- Do I view crisis as a chance to learn—or as a reason to quit?
- Do I interpret struggle as disaster—or as opportunity?
- Is my first instinct denial—or decisive action?

Application (Practicing Perseverance, Fortitude, and Resilience)

- **Fitness:** When my schedule collapses, do I still move? If I miss the gym, do I walk instead? If I blow my diet Saturday, do I fix it Sunday—or wait for Monday?
- **Business:** When growth slows or the economy dips, do I adapt and find ways to thrive—or sit back and take the hit?
- **Family:** When relationships need repair, am I patient and present—or do I disappear when things get uncomfortable?

Final Thought

I want to close this section with a story of Perseverance. My dear friend, Ruben Payan Jr., successfully summited Mount Everest—the highest point on Earth—in May 2013. His training was insane, driven by Consistency, Discipline, and Tenacity. For months he endured:

- 30–40 hours of training per week
- 4–5 practice climbs on major peaks
- Weight training 4–5 days weekly
- Cardio sessions on the VersaClimber wearing a weighted vest
- Technical hikes with 60–80 pounds on his back

He dropped from 220 pounds to a lean 185—pure functional power. Most people couldn't survive a single day of his regimen, let alone months of it. But because he trained intelligently and consistently, his body adapted. Then came the final ascent.

Everything had gone about as smoothly as a Death Zone climb could—until disaster struck. Ruben realized he had accidentally left his protective eye drops behind. At high altitude, that oversight became life-threatening. With oxygen thinning and wind howling, his eyes began to burn. Within minutes, snow blindness set in. Total darkness. Most climbers would've turned back. Honestly, that would have been the smart move. But Ruben, guided by his Sherpa Lhakpa Gelu, made the call to continue. Step by step, completely blind, he climbed on—driven only by trust, focus, and sheer will. Hours later, he stood blind at the summit of Mount Everest.

Then came the descent—the harder half. Still blind, still trusting every word from Lhakpa, Ruben descended the mountain inch by inch until he reached base camp to a standing ovation. When he finally applied the recovered eye drops, his sight returned—and for the first time, he could see the mountain he had just conquered.

That's Perseverance.

That's Fortitude.

That's Resilience.

It's not about avoiding pain—it's about finding meaning through it. It's not about seeing clearly—it's about believing when you can't see at all.

STAGE 3, PRINCIPLE 10—Finish Big
It's About the Close, Not the Finish

This is it—the summit. Finish Big isn't about crossing the line exhausted; it's about crossing with purpose. You've built awareness, discipline, and resilience through every stage. Now it's time to integrate it all and close strong. *Finishing Big* means finishing right—anchored in mastery, gratitude, and legacy. Because in PB², the goal isn't just to reach the end—it's to elevate how you end.

Stage 1 Recap—Principles 1–4: Own the Problem and Find the Way Out

- **Principle 1—Humility:** Admit you are in over your head, you don't know everything, and you are open to learning.
- **Principle 2—Responsibility:** Own your role in your current situation—no blaming or excuses.
- **Principle 3—Self-Reflection:** Understand how your actions created your situation—analyze cause and effect.
- **Principle 4—Self-Awareness:** Identify which of your actions have to change—identify your best choices.

Stage 2 Recap—Principles 5–7: Create & Execute the Plan

- **Principle 5—Strategizing:** Put those solutions into a plan—the creation of a PLAYBOOK.
- **Principle 6—Sacrifice:** Be willing to pay the price.
- **Principle 7—Facing Fear:** Just do it—Commitment.

Stage 3—Principles 8–10: Stay the Course and Finish Big

- **Principle 8—Consistency:** Keep doing the right things, over and over.

- **Principle 9—Perseverance:** Push through when it gets hard.

PB² Alignment

- **Principle:** Finish Big—It's not about finishing, it's about closing. Be the closer.
- **Value:** Dynamic Mastery—Where wisdom is synthesized. You integrate knowledge into its highest level—wisdom.
- **Virtue:** Integrated Repetitions—Each rep integrates new-found wisdom into life experience.

Principle 10—Finish Big: It's About the Close, Not the Finish

The concept of finishing big is usually saved for movies and novels—but it's not rare, and it's definitely not unreachable. We see it all the time in real life.

Take a top band getting ready for a massive concert. They've spent weeks—maybe months—rehearsing, refining, and syncing their rhythm. Most people think the hard part is over—that they just show up, rock out, and enjoy the moment. Not true. Yes, the groundwork is done. Yes, they'll have fun. But even while crushing solos and riding the crowd's energy, they're still making micro-adjustments, integrating everything they've practiced into this performance—and already thinking about what they'll tweak for the next one.

Finishing Big isn't the end—it's practice for future finishes. Every close is a chance to refine how you'll close next time. That's why I always say: Attitude, context, and framing can take a flat concept and set it free. Few Principles show this truth better than Finish Big.

Traditionally, finishing is seen as coasting across the line or collecting the ceremonial diploma—no effort left, no thought required. It's like the last few days of school when you're there but not really learning. Or the end of a workweek—who's really pushing hard after lunch on Friday?

Culturally, we've been trained to miss the most valuable part of finishing: the active integration of a long journey into a single moment of awareness. That's where growth happens. We confuse closure with completion—as if finishing means you're done. But finishing simply means one stage is over, and the next is about to begin.

Until you die, no finish is meaningless.
All finishes should be big—
because they set the standard for the next one.

Why this Step Is the Last Stage

Some people cross the finish line just to say they finished. That's not us. In PB², the final step isn't about coasting—it's about closing with intention, presence, and power. You've earned it through the grind; now it's time to land it in a way that honors the journey. This isn't the time to zone out or relax—this is the moment where everything comes together. By the time you get here, you've dotted every 'i' and crossed every 't'. You've built a bridge of Principles that can carry you through any transformation. Each Principle, Value, and Virtue is already in motion. That doesn't mean perfection—it means presence, intention, and effort. Wherever you started, you're a stronger, wiser version of yourself now. Finishing Big is what the 10th Principle demands. It's not just about finishing—it's about how you finish. Think of it like finally catching the giant wave you've been training for. You studied the tides, checked your gear, watched the weather—and now the moment's here. The skill is built. The preparation is done. Now it's time to ride.

This is the most important phase of the PB² process because this is where your moral DNA gets tested—and upgraded. No matter the outcome, this moment locks in your next-level identity. The end matters for the same reason the end of a great movie matters—it pulls everything together. It's where you finally understand the why behind it all.

Wisdom crystallizes here.
That's the real win—not the medal, not the money, not the applause.
The win is becoming the person who made it all happen.

The Truth About Finishing Big

Here's the truth: if you're not finishing big, you're not really finishing. Coasting across the line is quitting on your evolution, authenticity, and integrity. You don't honor the process when you cruise through the close. I've seen it too many times in the fight game—a fighter thinks he's got it won and starts coasting through the final round to avoid risk. It backfires more often than not. Why? Because there's no such thing as "The fight is mine." Judges blow calls all the time. That's why we say: Don't leave it in the hands of the judges. You finish the fight like you're losing. That doesn't mean reckless—it means aggressively conservative. Keep attacking from defensive positions. Stay in control, but keep working. If you coast while the other guy is hunting you, he's getting free offense with zero risk. That's a losing formula. When the fight's close and you start running, showing your back, and acting like you've already won—the judges will turn on you. They'll give it to the fighter who came to Finish Big.

So be smart. Be sharp. Finish big.

You can't maximize growth or impact if you coast. The finish is where transformation happens. It's never been about the trophy, the title, or the check—those are just symbols of something deeper. What you're really chasing is proof of growth—the evidence that you faced resistance and didn't back down. That you stayed aware, planned well, and followed through. It was never the medal you were after—it was what the medal represented: the moment you became something more. That's what Finishing Big does. You strip the ego. You get honest about your role. You build a real plan—not a theatrical one. You show up with Discipline, Consistency, and Perseverance until execution becomes instinct. You enter the close fully present, making both small and large adjustments to deliver something you've never delivered before. Because here's the truth: if you finish on cruise control, you miss the best part—the transformation. The behavioral change. The spiritual growth. The mindset shift.

Wisdom is what happens when you pay attention to what you've just been through. If you don't recognize that evolution, there's no wisdom to take with you. That's the real loss—not missing the trophy, but missing the meaning behind the journey. The finish should never be easier than expected. It should be more significant than you ever imagined.

How the Value of Dynamic Mastery and the Virtue of Integrated Reps Relate to this Step

At this stage, it's not about learning something new—it's about integrating everything you've lived. Dynamic Mastery is the synthesis of knowledge into wisdom—the point where experience, discipline, and insight fuse into instinct. You don't have to think about it anymore; it just is. That's mastery—fluid, adaptive, alive. Dynamic Mastery doesn't mean perfection—it means integration. You can read, train, and study all day, but if the lessons don't merge into your behavior, they're just data. Mastery is when doing becomes being—when reflection and action operate as one. You speak truth naturally. You lead instinctively. You recover quickly. You adapt faster. You finish strong—not because you're forcing it, but because that's now your nature. That's where the Virtue of Integrated Reps comes in. Every repetition up to this point—every lesson, failure, and adjustment—has been a rep. Each one builds internal circuitry that links your past to your present performance. You've moved beyond practicing skills—you're now embodying them. Every rep has folded into the next, creating a continuous thread of growth.

Integrated Reps lock Dynamic Mastery into reality. They prove that repetition with awareness creates evolution. You're not just stronger—you're synthesized. Your past experiences are now tools, not trauma. Your scars are maps, not memories. You're living proof that consistency plus reflection equals transformation. This is the power of closing strong: every finish is a rep that prepares you for the next climb. When you Finish Big, you set the standard for what comes next—and that's how you live in a state of perpetual evolution.

Value: Dynamic Mastery
Where Wisdom Is Synthesized

How do you master something? Simple—you practice it. But not just any kind of practice. You already know this from earlier in the PB² process: the only kind of practice worth doing is deliberate practice. If repetition is the mother of mastery, and mastery is the mother of invention, then mastery itself must be a dynamic process—one that adjusts, evolves, and responds. It's not static—and it's never automatic—until it is.

Mastery at this stage means you've lived through every previous Principle. You've done the work, reflected deeply, built a strategy, sacrificed, stayed consistent, and leaned into fear. You've created space to think, analyze, and integrate. Now you're not grinding blindly—you're refining. You're operating at a higher level of clarity and control. Your actions are cleaner. Your adjustments are smaller. But their impact? Far bigger.

In the early stages of change, your corrections were large and slow—and that's normal. Now they're micro-level, but the internal integration is massive. These adjustments aren't just functional—they're transformational. You understand why the change is needed, what must be done, how to do it, and what it means to the bigger picture. That's the difference. You're no longer reacting—you're aligning. You're not just learning—you're absorbing. This is where Dynamic Mastery turns your reps into identity. It's not what you do—it's who you've become.

Virtue: Integrated Repetitions
Each Rep Integrates New-Found Wisdom into Life Experience.

As mentioned earlier, the reps you perform in this final stretch aren't the same ones you did when building Habitual Momentum. That phase was about learning new skills and repeating the full process—analysis, planning, execution, consistency, and perseverance. Those wins stacked up exponentially. Most reps in the first half of PB² happened at the macro level—obvious, repetitive, foundational. But that's not what happens when you're finishing big.

***Extraordinary performances don't come
from rehearsing ordinary conditions.***

At this stage, your skills are ingrained. You're on autopilot. You're not thinking about form—you've already mastered it. Most people stop here and coast. But high performers? This is where they start. This is where they rehearse extraordinary conditions. Integrated repetition doesn't try to perfect the rep—that work's already done. It tests the perfect rep under unpredictable conditions and turns that experience into behavior. It becomes the way you move, think, and decide. You shift from asking, "How did that rep look?" to "What did that rep impact?" and "How might it interact with everything else?" You're no longer performing the rep—you're executing the strategy the rep belongs to. Once you understand that level of complexity, you take it beyond the training environment and apply it everywhere. That's when knowledge becomes wisdom. That's when you start playing chess while everyone else is playing checkers.

**When you are guided by opinions, you are playing checkers.
When you are guided by Principles, you are playing chess.**

That's why we don't coast at the end of something meaningful. If it's just a game—fine, relax. But if the experience matters and you want it to change you forever—if you want it to become part of you—then finish big. You finish with Integrated Reps so the experience becomes woven into your reality, your behavior, and your identity.

Make your rep with a perfect rep.

That's the sophisticated side of showing up. People admire the daily grind—the consistency, the discipline, the effort—and they should. That takes character. But the finish? That's different. That's where elite-level processing shows up. To the outside world, your decisions look light-ning-fast, complex, even risky. But to you, it's not chaos—it's clarity.

You've rehearsed this level of execution countless times in less intense settings. This is deliberate practice in its purest form—not improvisation, not mindless repetition.

Picture this: a family walks out of a restaurant after dinner. A group of guys outside gets loud; one throws a comment at the daughter, another grabs her arm. Before anyone can react, the older son moves—clean, controlled, and efficient. A low leg kick drops the first guy. A single strike folds the second. The third—neutralized. It's over in five seconds. Security rushes in, statements are taken—and then they find out who the kid is: a former state wrestling champ, an MMA fighter about to go pro. He wasn't a brawler—he was trained, disciplined, ready. This was just another live rep for him. No one saw the years of training, the tournaments, the early mornings—but in that moment, his execution made the invisible visible. His finish became his reputation—and his rep became the town's pride. Everything is on the line at the end. And when people see someone perform at that level, it commands respect. It draws admiration. It moves the human spirit. That's what leadership looks like in action.

Why Some People Struggle with this Step

- It's not laziness—it's lack of awareness.
- They see the work as "done before the finish."
- They don't understand "practicing the finish."
- They don't think about the social consequence of finishing.
- They don't rehearse finishing through small things.

Much in life is about awareness—and awareness takes Humility, the ability to admit you don't know everything. Not because you're dumb, but because you simply can't see certain things without shifting your perspective. You've got to be willing to turn the beach ball and realize there are colors you've never seen. That's what Finishing Big is: a new color, a new rep. Most people don't finish deliberately because they've never been taught to look for it. They think the work is done before the finish. They check out once the main push is over. But finishing isn't the tail—it's the head of your reputation. If you don't train for it, you won't show up for it.

Finishing has its own reps. These aren't about learning a skill—they're about applying the consequences of the skill under pressure. The mechanics are already there. Now it's about subtle corrections, subconscious timing, and fluid decisions inside the chaos of the finish. You don't get that early on—you earn the right to train it later through lived experience. That's why it's rare. That's why it's hard. Not all reps are the same. That's like saying all cardio is the same. The Principle of Specificity applies here too. Running clean routes around cones is one rep. Running that same route against defenders with the clock ticking—that's a finishing rep. And you don't get many of them. How many championships, title fights, or boardroom closings will you see? Not many. That's why Finishing Big isn't something you just 'pick up'. Finishing Big has to become a habit. Habits come from repetition—but not just any reps. You need awareness first, then deliberate reps in the small things. Finish the small things with excellence until it becomes who you are. That way, when the rare big moment shows up, you don't rise to the occasion—you meet it with the habits you've built.

Small things are all things.

Finishing Big also raises your social stock. People remember the closer. They follow the finisher—the one who executes under pressure. They might respect the one who simply makes it to the line, but they reward the one who smashes expectations. A consistent finisher rises within the tribe, and the tribe rewards that with trust, credibility, and leadership. Power isn't bought—you pay for it with big finishes. And never forget—Finishing Big isn't only about championship games or boardroom deals. It's built in the reps of life: opening a door with presence, wrapping up a meeting with clarity, or giving full attention all the way to the last second of a workout. It's an attitude before it's a habit—and eventually, it becomes a way of life. Do the right thing in the small things, and when the big things show up, so will the real you.

Navigating this Step
Understand that Finishing Big Is a Skill in Itself.

- Most people coast at the end—so they never practice finishing-big reps. You won't. Treat them as unique, with their own variables.
- Don't assume the finish happens automatically—Finishing Big is an active process, not a passive sequence. The payoff lives inside the micro-adjustments you make in the moment.
- Big moments don't happen every day—so practice finishing big in the small things: training sessions, work duties, family moments, school projects. Those lower-level finishes forge the attitude that delivers at the highest level.

Shift from Reacting with Skills to Anticipation with Strategies

- By now, mechanics should be second nature—the reps are about micro-adjusting to flow.
- You're no longer reacting move by move—you're not playing checkers. You're anticipating three moves ahead—you're playing chess.
- At this stage, there's nothing left to see or think about—the future's already handled. This is flow—hard to achieve, but always the goal.

Build the Finish Big Attitude with Integrative Reps

- Attitude is like posture—repeated enough, it becomes automatic. Finishing Big works the same way.
- The mindset is about obsessive detail and competent execution—do it until it's who you are.
- It could be making your bed without leaving the last wrinkle, drilling fight prep three weeks out, or adding 30 minutes to a meeting to ensure the team's ready. These small reps forge the finishing habit.

- The wrinkle doesn't matter—the awareness does. What matters is training yourself to see details in everything. Enough practice, and the habit takes over. Thinking disappears.

Visualize Finishing Big as a Process—Not an Outcome

- If the process isn't right, the result never will be.
- The wisdom you acquire finishing big outlasts any trophy, belt, or title.
- Titles and records get attention—a finishing-big attitude earns lifelong respect.
- Character is defined in the process, not the result. Your tribe remembers the closer—not necessarily the winner.
- Your team watches how you land the deal—not how much it's worth.

Power isn't claimed or assigned.
It's granted to those with a finish big attitude.

Personal Reflections
Self-Assessment (Demonstrating Dynamic Mastery and Integrated Repetition)

- Do I let things slide when they're 'good enough', instead of finished right?
- Do I perform better when people are watching, or do I hold a high internal standard no matter what?
- Am I seen as 'nice', or as the go-to when crisis shows up?

Application (Fitness/Business/Family)

- **Fitness:** Do I train and eat right but quit a few pounds short of the goal?
- **Business:** Am I missing small, consistent details that could elevate my leadership and culture?
- **Family:** Do I promise time with family but fail to follow through—or worse, show up half-present?

Final Thought

I see it all the time in the UFC—fighters think the fight is locked up and start coasting in the last round. Big mistake. There's no such thing as 'in the bag'. Judges blow calls. Momentum flips in a heartbeat. Cruise, and you hand the other corner free offense while looking like you've already given up. Even if you're ahead, the image of running can cost you everything. That's why the fighters who finish like they're losing are the ones who win respect—and usually the fight. The lesson? Finishing Big isn't about the scoreboard. It's an attitude. A habit. You don't just cross the line—you close with intention.

Be smart. Be sharp. Be the closer.

> "Competent leaders build functional cultures. Principled leaders inspire people who build legendary cultures."
>
> ~ JCS

13

AUTHENTIC LEADERSHIP THROUGH PB²

What Is a Leader?

There's no doubt that the highest level of authority in any social hierarchy is that of the leader. Leaders come in many forms and flavors. A person can lead in one area of life while struggling in others. For example, an executive might lead their industry yet have a social or family life in crisis and completely unmanageable. But what it takes to be a leader—whether in one domain or across all of them—remains constant. The PB² System is built on a universal sequence of Principles that shape your character and guide you through any crisis.

Most leaders in any domain combine authenticity with true compe-tence. They're natural problem-solvers with a direct, no-BS communication style. It may not always be pretty, but it's effective. They also have a high capacity for pressure, workload, and consistency—visible character traits that earn respect and admiration from those around them.

The number one quality of a leader is competence—not necessarily being the most skilled in any one area, but knowing how to apply the right skills to solve the problem. Great leaders have no problem delegating to the person with the highest expertise. Most aren't specialists, but they know enough about each area to understand how it fits into the bigger picture. That global awareness—and the ability to pull it all together—is the hallmark of real leadership.

A leader is also authentic in both intent and communication. And by authentic, I don't mean friendly or social. I mean people always know what's on their mind—because they say what's on their mind. Some deliver that with polish, others don't. But either way, not having to guess where a leader stands is a real asset.

What a Leader Is Not

The competency and authenticity required for real leadership can't be faked. There's nothing more repugnant than someone who's been handed a title—or worse, promoted themselves—without earning it. A pretender to the throne. It doesn't matter what the structure is—family, team, or company—incompetent leadership screams disorganization and low morale. People feel it. The whole system suffers. Some of the typical signs of ineffective leaders are:

- **Delegation irregularities**
  - o Can't do the job, but doesn't want to relinquish control
  - o Hires people to do a job, but micromanages and takes credit for results
  - o Hires or throws money at leadership responsibilities—but hands them to non-leadership personnel
- **Absenteeism**
  - o Has every excuse in the world for not showing up—claims nonstop meetings or urgent calls. They're not.
  - o Relies on unnecessary surveillance—cameras, keystroke trackers, and message monitoring—to make up for their lack of presence
- **Lazy approach and lack of interest**
  - o Even when present, they're distracted and unproductive
  - o Long lunches and long conversations—none of it work-related
  - o Not involved in intake interviews or vetting new hires—leading to high turnover
- **Inappropriate presentation and attire**
  - o Dresses in a way that doesn't reflect a high professional standard
  - o Shows up to important meetings with influential people (like investors) without business attire
- **Lack of consistency and follow-up**
  - o Promises are made but never kept
  - o Projects or policies are started but rarely followed through
- **Lack of policies and organization**
  - o No clearly written policies or procedures
  - o Chain of command is absent—or ignored
- **Grandiose accommodations and perks**
  - o Big office, big desk, big perks...to make up for little character
  - o Status over substance

Now, don't get this twisted. Just because a leader shows one or more of these behaviors doesn't automatically make them ineffective. What matters is the pattern—and the effect it has on the people around them. If you want to know whether someone is a real leader, just ask the people they lead. If the first reaction is a smile, and the first word out of their mouth is something like "Fantastic," "Awesome," or "The best"—you've got yourself a leader. If the first response is a roll of the eyes, don't even wait for the explanation. Whatever praise comes next will be qualified, filtered, or filled with a disclaimer.

I especially respect leaders who have their lives in order outside their domain of expertise. Some people are geniuses in one area but lack the interpersonal skills you'd hope to see in a leader. That creates a high-pressure, hostile environment—one that may hit deadlines and drive results, but usually won't last. Yes, those teams can accomplish big things. But they're almost always short bursts—not something built to last for years. When I speak of leadership, I'm not talking about a big accomplishment followed by a crash and burn. There's a place for that in the world—but not in the context we're dealing with here. When I talk about a leader, I mean someone people want to see in the top position for years—even decades.

A real leader creates a lasting culture—one that often outlives them.

You see this in families and companies shaped by a beloved leader who showed character in all areas of life. That character didn't just inspire others—it permeated the entire culture and, in some cases, has lasted for generations.

Leadership Requires Living by Principles

Leaders have an inherent personality that allows them to be both competent and authentic. They live measured, responsible lives. It's not uncommon to see leaders express their talents outside their domain of expertise. Many politicians and high-ranking executives are also skilled musicians, artists, or even near-professional golfers. The reason is simple: leaders know how to apply principles across different domains—that's the essence of wisdom.

There's an energy about people who have their stuff together that naturally attracts others. It's a beacon of hope—and often, a desire to learn from them in hopes of adopting their way of life. Everyone admires when something is done right, and we gravitate toward it. First we admire it, then we analyze it, and finally we adapt what works into our own lives. We are attracted to greatness because we all aspire to be greater than we are. Witnessing greatness allows us to learn how to become greater. It's that simple—and that organic. If you want to be better, surround yourself with people who've accomplished more and are operating at a higher level.

The Leadership Culture and Circle of Influence

The culture set by most leaders is palpable—you can feel it in the room, sense it in the air, yet can't quite put your finger on what it is. It just feels good. I'm not saying everything is perfect or that crises never arise. They do—constantly. And that's a good thing. Challenging moments are necessary. Dealing with crises keeps leaders and their culture sharp—they're the resistance training of leadership.

As previously stated, competency is one of the key characteristics of a leader. So what does that really mean? That the leader is perfect, never makes mistakes, or that the group never fails? Of course not. All of those things happen. Competency comes from proactive behavior that prevents problems before they arise—and from corrective action and problem-solving in the moment of crisis. As they say, an ounce of prevention is worth a pound of cure. But prevention often goes unnoticed because it's invisible when everything runs smoothly.

What truly makes a leader—and a leadership culture—stand out is how they solve problems, not how they avoid them. More importantly, the strategies used to overcome challenges become part of the operational DNA of the group. That's how leaders Finish Big: they integrate the lessons learned from every experience into the fabric of their being—and into the culture of the teams they lead.

The Leadership Circle is Multi-layered

The makeup of a group is usually very predictable. Even in unorganized groups that lack strong leadership, hierarchy naturally emerges. Leaders may inspire and serve as role models to many, but they spend one-on-one time with only a small circle that works directly beneath them—usually one or two hyper-competent individuals. From this circle, a select few are promoted to positions of greater authority to guide others. This pattern repeats itself, and upward mobility is almost always dictated by competency and authenticity. Here's a simple example using a family, laid out like a military chain of command:

- Private = Youngest kid
- Sergeant = Second-oldest kid
- Lieutenant = Oldest kid
- Colonel = Older cousin
- General = Parents

In this example, the parents are the generals who enforce the rules. The cousin—staying in the house while finishing college—acts as the colonel, reinforcing the parents' rules while mentoring the oldest child. If the parents leave for a short trip, the cousin takes command. He works with the oldest sibling—the lieutenant—to ensure he understands his responsibility toward the younger ones. The second-oldest, the sergeant, is responsible for the youngest. His job is to keep the youngest safe and begin teaching basic responsibility. The youngest—the private—observes everything happening in the household but is closest to his older sibling, who carries most of the responsibility for him. Interestingly, the youngest often matures the fastest because he has no one beneath him and can focus entirely on observing and learning. Most groups and teams operate in a similar fashion. Some are more complex, but hierarchy always exists.

All of my children have worked at IHP. When they sit in team meetings or watch me interact with trainers and clients, they always say, "Dad, this is just like being at the house. These conversations are the same as what we have over dinner." And I always answer the same way: "Why wouldn't it be? Principles apply to the universe because they're self-evident truths. Why wouldn't I apply them at home and at IHP the same way?"

I'm grateful my kids were able to witness firsthand how principles lead the way. Every time they call me with a crisis, we find a way out by returning to principles. I didn't design it that way—it just turned out that way. And for that, I'm thankful. That's the point: leadership is always layered, and it always comes back to principles.

Why PB² makes a powerful Leadership Roadmap

As I've said before, PB² isn't the only game in town—it's a free-moving system. But when I did my homework on principles—how they've been written about and how they might be organized into a true problem-solving sequence—I couldn't find anything close. Sure, brilliant minds have written volumes on principles and problem-solving methods. But not like this—and honestly, that shocked me. Why wouldn't principles be laid out in a logical sequence, like a computer program? Computers don't 'think' like we do. They use true-or-false logic to reach a conclusion and issue a command. That's called Boolean Logic. Now, allow me to digress into my computer science and engineering geekiness—because this is exactly why PB² hits so hard. It's not just philosophy. It's a powerhouse program you can actually run your life on.

Boolean Logic and the PV²-PB² Connection

In the world of computers, there's no such thing as 'kind of.' Things are either on or off. True or false. Yes or no. That's Boolean Logic—the foundation for how machines process information and make decisions. Strict. Binary. Brutally clear.

Computers don't think like humans. They follow a sequence of steps—an algorithm. If the input is clear, the output is predictable. No drama. No excuses. Just execution. Humans are obviously more complex, but when it comes to living by principles, we can use the same approach. Here's the PB² sequence when applied to PV²—Principles, Values, and Virtues:

- **IF** a principle is clearly defined
- **AND** the corresponding value is genuinely adopted
- **AND** the situation is measured against that principle and value
- **THEN** the correct course of action—the virtue—becomes self-evident.

That's not philosophy—that's an algorithm. A decision tree you can run your life on. It's not emotional. It doesn't depend on mood, peer pressure, or convenience. It's a clean path that always leads back to integrity. When you live this way—when every action runs through a principle-based sequence—you become dangerous in all the right ways: calm under pressure, clear in conflict, anchored in something unshakable. And that's where PB²—Principle-Based Breakthrough—comes in. It's not just a system. It's the sequence that drives the breakthrough.

- **Principles give you the logic.**
- **Values give you the alignment.**
- **Virtues give you the behavior.**
- **PB² gives you the sequence breakthrough.**

Leading Through the PB² System

Now, let's provide a quick summary of how the PB² system works:

Step 1: Humility

- Admit you don't have all the answers—invite input from others.

- Humility is one of the most authentic forms of strength.
- People feel it—and are drawn to it.
- Once they're watching, you get the chance to show competency.
- If you're competent, people want to be led by you.

Step 2: Responsibility

- Own the outcomes—good or bad.
- No blame-shifting.
- If someone under you fails, it's on you—you co-signed their authority.
  o Just like co-signing a credit line: they fail, the creditor comes after you.

Step 3: Self-Reflection

- Put every decision through an honesty filter.
- What actions got us here?
- Make a TO-DO (TTD) list of errors and weak spots.

Step 4: Self-Awareness

- Identify what needs to change—systems, habits, attitudes.
- Take your TTD list and organize by:
  o Easy → Hard
  o Short-term → Long-term

Step 5: Strategizing

- Create a team playbook: clear roles, goals, and timelines.
- Start with simple things you can change immediately.
  o Get small wins → build habitual momentum.
- Slowly introduce more complex changes that require more time.
- We are NOT looking for MACRO perfection—we are looking for MICRO corrections.

Step 6: Sacrifice

- Something has to give to reach the goal—usually time and/or money.
- The leader must model sacrifice:
  o You make the final call—you carry the full weight.
- Responsibility and sacrifice roll downhill.
- Everyone on the team shares some of the pressure—the more authority one has, the greater the burden.

Step 7: Confronting Fear

- Courage is NOT the absence of fear—it's acting properly in the presence of it.
- Call out excuses. Push the group to act through discomfort.
- The leader must model courage.
- The culture must support this structure:
  o Everyone becomes a mini-leader.

Step 8: Consistency

- Be the most reliable person in the room.
- Stay on task—one micro correction after another.
- Create a culture that does the same.
  o Keep your eye on the prize.
  o Reinforce wins to build habitual momentum and consistency.

Step 9: Perseverance

- Rally the team during setbacks—perpetual forward motion is the goal.
- The strength of a group is measured by what it can overcome.
- This is when you turn up the volume—lead by amplifying positive accomplishments.
  o Remind everyone of their inherent greatness and potential for more.

Step 10: Finish Big

- Execute. Integrate. Celebrate. Debrief. Lock it in. Rinse and repeat.
- Every forward step is a win.
- o Adopting each Principle = a win.
- Be fully present—notice everything.
  - o Document as much as possible—that becomes your procedures manual and content for future .
- Integrate winning moments:
  - o Just like trauma changes you by searing emotion into your being, success should too.
  - o Celebrate key efforts and wins with the same intensity as trauma debilitates.
    - Reverse-engineer the emotional power trauma holds—use it for good.
- Debrief—lock in lessons before moving on.
  - o Lessons become future behavior.

Apply It: Fitness. Business. Family. Same Blueprint—Live the Life

Fitness
- Lead by practicing the life.
  - o Inspire family and friends.
    - Role model responsibility.
    - It has nothing to do with developing a six-pack.
    - It has everything to do with responsibility and consistency.
  - o Lead and inspire clients through example and competence.

Business
- Every employee is a potential leader.
  - o First: show you can lead yourself.
  - o Then: lead others through practiced Principles.
    - Inspire. Motivate. Train.

Family

- Show what principled living looks like.
  - o Don't preach it—live it.
  - o Kids follow what you model, not what you say.

Final Word: How Leadership Emerges

- If you don't believe it—start by doing it.
  - o "Fake it till you make it" is real: just do the next right thing, even before you're convinced.
  - o When habits take root, belief grows with success.
- Practice it when nobody's watching.
  - o Learn to self-regulate and do the right thing.
  - o Pick up the paper on the floor when nobody's watching.
    - That piece of paper is your life.
  - o Every small act matters.
- You will attract others who value Principles.
  - o A leadership position will organically emerge.
  - o You won't be perfect, but:
    - You'll own the issues.
    - You'll correct them.
    - You'll become better.

That alone defines you as a leader.

Closing

I hope you've enjoyed reading this book as much as I've enjoyed writing it. Truth is, writing it may have helped me more than anyone else. Looking back at the good, the bad, and the ugly—and then trying to make sense of it—has been one of the most powerful exercises of my life.

I've taken my swings at being rich and hyper-talented, but my journey was never about elite talent or extraordinary wealth. I chased both—and came up short on both. For those efforts, I'll proudly accept the "jack of some trades, master of none" award. And you know what? That's fine. Because everything I've built—physically, mentally, spiritually—has come through trial, error, failure, and a mountain of hard work.

Whatever wisdom I have has come more from falling on my face than from standing on a podium. And for that, I'm grateful. Grateful for the life I've been given. Grateful for the wonderful people I've met. Grateful that some of you might read this and see something in me I don't always see in myself. If there's one thing that has carried me through, it's PB². I didn't invent it in a lab—it's how I've had to live. And every time I lost my way, Principles got me back on track. Not motivation. Not emotion. Not hype. Principles.

So here's my final ask of you:

Adopt Principles.
Use the PB² system to live by them.
Fail. Get back up. Repeat.

You will fall. You will doubt. But in your darkest moments, return to Principles. They won't save you instantly—but they will save you eventually. Life isn't fast. It isn't easy. And success isn't measured by where you end up—but by how you take the trip. Character isn't forged in winning—it's revealed in how you play the game, especially when you're losing.

I wish you love.
I wish you health.
I wish you real happiness.

And above all, I trust you'll earn every bit of it—because you're stronger and wiser now than when you started this book.

DEDICATION

This book is dedicated to my two teachers of Principles—my parents: the late **Arnaldo Santana** and my mom, **Celerina Santana** (92 years old). One hundred percent of everything in this book comes from them.

My kids—**Rio, Caila, Dante,** and **Mia**—have been blessings I can't describe. They are also the Petri dish that allowed me to practice and test what my parents taught me. They have taught me more than I will ever teach them.

My sister **Belkis**, being my senior, always protected me "per my mother's instructions." That too taught me a lot about establishing a family culture. My niece **Moni**, nephew and Godchild **Eric**, cousins, aunts and uncles are also a great source of pride and a reflection of our crazy family culture. **This is our tribe!** Abu, Alberto, Alfonsito, Alex, Amelita, Ana, Annie, Angelina, Belkis, Caila, Cathy, Christie, Chuchi, Daniel, Daniela, Dante, Debbie, Diego, Eric, Giedre, Isabelle, Jesus, Karla, Madison, Maria, Maria Fernanda, Lee, Marisol, Mercedita, Michelle, Miguelito, Miguelito Jr, Mike, Moni, Nachi, Nancy, Nenin, Pedro, Rick G, Rick O, Rigoberto, Riguito, Rio, Sander, Scarlette, Sebastian, Stephanie, Yaime, and many others that we inadvertently left out.

My Miami friends from **Callahan Plaza** and **Miami High**, along with the **FAU crew**—who still get together yearly, forty years later—provide a sense of reference and illustrate the importance of brotherhood and connection.

All of my friends and members of **IHP** (the 'church')—you are too many to mention, and that speaks volumes about my blessings. You have served as beacons of hope, fountains of wisdom, and currents of inspiration. I can only hope to have impacted you even half as much as you have impacted me.

And finally, my beautiful wife, **Giedre**—for almost a decade, she has been a world of mystery and wonder. She has inspired me to evolve into a better version of the man she met ten years ago.

Collectively, this large energy—my spirits dancing in the flesh—has embraced me during times of sorrow, cheered me on when I felt I could go no further, and rejoiced in my successes. It is they who gave this book form and function, and I will use its contents in an effort to better serve all of them. I love you all, and I wrote this book for me—so I may serve you all as you have served me.

TO MY IHP FAMILY—PAST, PRESENT, AND FUTURE

You are the soul of this place. Every rep, every class, every conversation has shaped the energy that built this book. You are the living, breathing proof that Principles, Values, and Virtues are not just words on a page—they're actions, culture, and daily practice.

IHP isn't a gym; it's a church built on sweat, humility, and shared purpose. You've turned iron into art and training into transformation. You've carried our culture through storms, rebuilt when others would've quit, and stood shoulder to shoulder when life hit hard. That's why I call you family. This book may have my name on it—but its heartbeat is yours. Every page echoes your voices, your laughter, your struggles, and your wins. You've taught me as much as I've ever taught you. Thank you for making IHP the greatest experiment in human performance—and in humanity.

This is our blueprint. This is our legacy. This is us.

Isabela Abad-Ramirez
Azam Ali
Nurullo Aliev
Teresa Alliaj
Max Alperovich
José Antonio
Angelina Aponte
Anne Aponte
Fred Assini
Rob Autor
Alan Bank
Kenneth Barnett
Marc-Andre Barriault
Renheda Barros
August Batson
James Batson
Tiffany Benvenuto
Steven Benvenuto
Jorge Briceno
Jerome Bradley
Wyatt Brands
Danny Braid
Matthew Brill
Gilbert Burns
Gena Bussani
Massino Bussani
Piero Bussani
Joe Cannavale
Steve Cannavale
Caleb Caponera
Rinaldo Caponera

Candida Carrillo
Eamir Carpenter
Rosanna Castle
Lonnie Chenkin
Faust Checho
Fabio Cherant
Sam Cicogna
Jessica Cohn
Jay Cohen
Mike Coner
Hugo Contreras
John Courtney
David Corrado
Andres Corzo
Austin Dabiere
Andreas Da Silva
David Dipierro
Joseph Drake
Ardit Dullovi
Richard Estime
Erickson Family
Hayden Ferdinand
Rhett Fisher
Jose Flores
Michael Frank
Valery Forbes
George Foussianes
Alexandra Florez
Katina Garcia
Omar Garcia
Angelo Garavito

Allan Gittman
Dave Gottschalk
Fernando Goulart
Estelle Goulart
Robert Graham
Devin Grandis
Kathy Grandis
Ryan Grandis
Ian Heinisch
David Haycock
Jeff Harpster
Kathleen Herne
Brian Hirschberg
Matt Hodge
Nancy Hodge
Steven Hodosh
Joi Honer
Patrick Hurley
Jacob Israel
Thad Jean
Mike Jennette
Jonathan Kaufman
Saachi Kaur
Jim Kemish
Andrea Kennedy
Ariele Kennedy
Michelle Kirkendall
Scott Kirkendall
Brandon Large
Pedro Leon
Maria Lutz

Jack Lynch
Judy Lynch
Matt Lynch
Marcos Machado
Mark Malis
Daniel Marcos
Peter Mascaro
Dayna McLeod
Mary Ellen McGranahan
Peter McNeil
Lauren Meyer
Caren Neile
Ruth Nemire
Austin Novak
Emma O'Day
Colton Outcalt
Fotis Papamichael
Pelleya Family
Edcleuson Penha
Alex Phillips
Kelly Phillips
Dylan Piccolo
Juan Plotnicoff
Rob Post
Ross Pugatch
Maria Paredes
Harrison Queen
Daniel Radu
Matthew Reali
Emma Roeck
Sam Schell

Chloe Schmier
Cortlandt Schuyler
Scott Senft
Alex Senft
Mario Singer
Joe Sobucki
Gregg Smith
Pat Soares
Boukay Sung
Peter Theodore
Elsie Throckmorton
Peter Tierney
Angelica Toczko
Sidney Toman
Francisco Torres
Kevin Vance
Richard Vargas
Chris Vassel
Vanessa Villegas
Allen Vulakh
Catherine Warren
Tevvy Washington
Bill Watson
Ross Weisman
Stuart Wilkins
Eric Wolfe
Sammy Wroblewski